W9-ADK-150

WITHDRAWN

GENDER
AND AMERICAN POLITICS

GENDER
AND AMERICAN POLITICS

WOMEN, MEN, AND THE
POLITICAL PROCESS

Edited by
Sue Tolleson-Rinehart
and Jyl J. Josephson

M.E. Sharpe
Armonk, New York
London, England

147139

Coyright © 2000 by M. E. Sharpe, Inc.

All rights reserved. No part of this book may be reproduced in any from
without written permission from the publisher, M. E. Sharpe, Inc.,
80 Business Park Drive, Armonk, New York 10504

Library of Congress Cataloging-in-Publication Data

Gender and American politics : women, men, and the political process / edited by
Sue Tolleson-Rinehart and Jyl J. Josephson.
   p. cm.
Includes bibliographical references and index.
ISBN 0-7656-0408-6 (cloth) ISBN 0-7656-0409-4
1. Sex role—Political aspects—United States. 2. United States—Politics and
government. I. Tolleson-Rinehart, Sue, 1952– II. Josephson, Jyl J., 1960–

HQ1075.5.U6 G454 2000
305.3'0973—dc21   99–462069

Printed in the United States of America

The paper used in this publication meets the minumum requirements of
American National Standard for Information Sciences
Permanence of Paper for Printed Library Materials,
ANSI Z 39.48-1984

∞

BM (c) 10 9 8 7 6 5 4 3 2
BM (p) 10 9 8 7 6 5 4 3 2

Contents

About the Authors

R. Michael Alvarez is associate professor of political science at the California Institute of Technology. He is the author of *Information and Elections* and has written extensively on public opinion and elections. He has just completed a book with John Brehm called *Hard Choices, Easy Answers* and is now beginning a manuscript with Edward McCaffery called *Making Women Pay: How Politics Plays on the Gender Gap, and Why it Matters.*

MaryAnne Borrelli is an associate professor of government at Connecticut College. Her research interests center on the connections between gender, leadership, and organizational culture in the institutions of the presidency. She has published on the gender dynamics of senate confirmation hearings for cabinet secretaries and on cabinet appointments during the Clinton administration. She is the co-editor of *The Other Elites: Women, Politics, and Power in the Executive Branch* and is currently preparing a book manuscript entitled *Patterns of Opportunity, Patterns of Constraint: The Nomination and Confirmation of Women Cabinet Members in the United States.*

M. Margaret Conway is distinguished professor of political science at the University of Florida. She is the author of numerous articles and the book, *Political Participation in the United States,* 3rd edition. She is the co-author of *Women and Political Participation.* Her research focuses on political participation, political socialization, and women and politics.

Michael X. Delli Carpini is director of the public policy program of the Pew Charitable Trusts and professor of political science at Barnard College, Columbia University. He is the author of books and numerous articles on public opinion, the mass media, and political participation, and the co-author of *What Americans Know About Politics and Why It Matters.*

Richard L. Fox is assistant professor of political science at Union College, Schenectady, New York. He is the author of *Gender Dynamics in Congressional Elections* and has published articles in *Women and Politics, Social Science Quarterly, Political Psychology, Public Administration Review,* and *PS.* His primary teaching interests are women and politics, congressional politics, and media and politics.

Jyl Josephson is assistant professor of political science at Illinois State University, where she teaches public policy and state and local government. She is the author of *Gender, Families, and the State: Child Support Policy in the United States*, and of several journal articles on gender and public policy.

Scott Keeter is professor of government and politics and chair of the department of public and international affairs at George Mason University. He is co-author of three books, including the forthcoming *The Diminishing Divide: Religion's Changing Role in American Politics*, *What Americans Know About Politics and Why It Matters*, and *Uninformed Choice: The Failure of the New Presidential Nominating System*. Since 1980 he has been an election night analyst of exit polls for NBC News and is a consultant for the Pew Research Center for the People and the Press (formerly the Times Mirror Center).

Edward J. McCaffery is the Maurice Jones Jr. professor of law at the University of Southern California Law School and visiting professor of law and economics at the California Institute of Technology. He is the author of *Taxing Women* and is presently at work on a book length project with co-author R. Michael Alvarez titled, *Making Women Pay: How Politics Plays on the Gender Gap and Why It Matters.*

Susan Gluck Mezey, Ph.D., J.D., is a professor in the political science department at Loyola University Chicago. She is the author of *No Longer Disabled: The Federal Courts and the Politics of Social Security Disability*; *In Pursuit of Equality: Women, Public Policy, and the Federal Courts*; *Children in Court: Public Policymaking and Federal Court Decisions*; and *Pitiful Plaintiffs: Child Welfare Litigation* *and the Federal Courts* (in press). She has written numerous journal articles and book chapters on women and politics and law and courts. She teaches courses in constitutional law, judicial process, the federal courts, women and law, and children and law.

Eric Plutzer is associate professor of political science and sociology at Penn State University where he teaches courses on political opinion and ideology, political culture, and electoral behavior. He has authored or co-authored many articles focusing on the social basis of politics, with special attention to the roles of gender, family, and social class.

Dorothy McBride Stetson is professor of political science at Florida Atlantic University where she is a member of the women's studies faculty. She is the author of *Women's Rights in the U.S.A.: Policy Conflicts and Gender Roles* and co-editor of *Comparative State Feminism*. She is co-director of the research network on gender politics and the state.

Sue Tolleson-Rinehart is the program administrator of the UNC Program on Health Outcomes and the director of administration and dissemination of the Center for Education and Research in Therapeutics at the University of North Carolina at Chapel Hill. She is a former professor of political science at Texas Tech University. She is the author of articles on the political psychology of gender, *Gender Consciousness and Politics*; *Claytie and the Lady: Ann Richards, Gender and Politics in Texas* (with Jeanie R. Stanley), and a coauthor of health services research monographs such as *Evidence Report on the Pharmacotherapy of Alcohol Dependence*.

GENDER
AND AMERICAN POLITICS

Introduction. Gender, Sex, and American Political Life

Jyl J. Josephson and Sue Tolleson-Rinehart

"Gender" is a term that describes both men and women, yet texts on gender and American political life often address women only. In this volume, we consider the roles and behaviors of both men and women in political decision making, political institutions, and public policy. The essays in this book provide an overview of current empirical research on the contours of what is popularly known as the "gender gap": the difference between men and women in voting behavior, political leadership, and political beliefs and commitments. We also look at the role that gender plays in American political institutions by examining gender, men, and women in the executive, legislative, and judicial branches. And we examine the importance of gendered institutions and assumptions in the making of public policy. Overall, then, the essays in this volume look at gender comparatively—that is, comparing men and women—and focus on the differences in men's and women's roles in various aspects of political life, and in the way that gender affects both women and men.

The book thus intentionally takes the view that women are not "deviant" in political behavior, but rather that empirically observed differences and similarities between men and women provide fruitful ground for analyzing the nature of American political life and the functioning of American political institutions. The focus is on empirical evidence. Much of this evidence shows that men and women come to political life with different kinds of information, experiences, and priorities. Thus, the differences between the political behavior of men and women are not surprising, and the essays in this book will provide the reader with information regarding the contours of those differences.

Before we can discuss the effects of gender on politics, however, we must clarify what is meant by the term "gender."

What Is Gender?

While the term "gender" has come into common usage in public and academic discussion during the past decade, the term is often used interchangeably with "women." Thus, it is important at the outset to outline what is meant here by gender, to distinguish between "sex" and "gender," and to distinguish those aspects of gender that will be covered in this volume.

The entry of the term "gender" into academic study and usage, and later into common public discourse, originated from women's studies, and from the women's movement. As more scholars began to pay attention to the differences that the study of women might bring to the subject matter and to methodological approaches in their own disciplines, the study of women began to emerge as a distinct but important arena of academic inquiry. In turn, scholars began to note that the exclusion of women from consideration had both distorted and denied many significant arenas of knowledge, in disciplines ranging from the study of literature to the study of politics.

Was the problem simply that women and men are inherently different creatures, destined to live entirely different lives, in relation to politics as well as all else? Social scientists observed many ways in which the differences between men and women were influenced by social factors, ranging from the ways that adults treat infants—including everything from dressing them differently to providing them with different toys—to the different social roles played by adult men and women. As a result, social scientists began to distinguish between "sex" and "gender." According to this distinction, sex is the characteristic of the biological being; gender is the socially constructed aspect of the self. While one might describe sex as "nature" and gender as "nurture," the matter is a bit more complicated than this. For example, most people think of "sex" as coming in only two forms: male or female. Yet at least one percent of humans are born as intersexuals: neither male nor female, but with characteristics of both. Sex is thus not as dichotomous as commonly perceived. Similarly, seeing gender as simply "nurture" might fail to recognize the interaction between the biological and the social, and the complexity of the many social institutions that construct gender.

While the above discussion is intended to indicate the complicated nature of "sex" and "gender," for the purposes of the empirical studies in this book, we will utilize the standard distinction between the two: sex is biological; gender is socially constructed. Thus, for example, as Richard Fox shows in his chapter in this volume, it is one thing to note sex differences—or, in the instant case, growing similarities—between men and women who are running in congressional election campaigns. We can determine that female candidates who are running for Congress in open seat elections now tend to have, on average, the same chance of winning as male candidates. A candidate's sex, therefore, no longer seems to make a difference in electoral outcomes, at least in open seat elections for the House of Representatives. However, this does not mean that male and female candidates have similar *experiences* as candidates in their election campaigns—and these differences are about gender. As Fox shows, women candidates and their campaign managers cite many ways in which gender matters in election campaigns: men and women have different experiences as candidates.

To cite another example, political scientists have long observed sex differences in political knowledge between men and women. Men, on average, tend to know more about politics than do women, on average. These sex differences have narrowed somewhat as women's roles have changed, but they still persist. What Michael Delli Carpini and Scott Keeter examine in their chapter on political knowledge, are the sources of these sex differences in political knowledge in the different gender experiences and roles of men and women. In other words, the more interesting question is not the *fact* that men and women have different levels, and different kinds, of political knowledge, but rather the *reason* that they do. The reasons, Delli Carpini and Keeter argue, have to do with continuing structural inequalities in gender roles. Further, they examine how political knowledge might translate into political opinions—and find that the "gender gap" in opinions actually increases with increased political knowledge.

Thus, gender affects political life in multiple ways, and at multiple levels. Historically, it has shaped the structure and functioning of political institutions. Thus, as women come to be more included in political life and in positions of political power, the gendered aspects of the institutions will be reshaped. Much of this depends upon the nature of the decision-making structures of the institutions, as the chapters by MaryAnne Borrelli and Susan Gluck Mezey, on the Cabinet and the federal judiciary respectively, demonstrate. Borrelli shows that the first two women appointed to the "inner cabinet," U.S. Attorney General Janet Reno and Secretary of State Madeleine Albright, followed very different paths to political power and as a consequence have rather different leadership styles. Mezey shows that, though women have significantly increased their numbers on the federal bench, the evidence as to whether women bring a "different voice" to judicial decision making is mixed. Mezey's chapter suggests that the structure of legal decision making and the career paths of federal judges may limit the ways in which a judge's gender might influence decision making.

Gender affects political life in multiple ways and at many different levels of analysis. The chapters in this book examine gender at the level of the symbolic, the institutional, and the individual. Some chapters address the way that gender has structured the institutions of government and the means of delivering services to citizens. Others address the way that men and women as individuals become aware of and active in political life. Still others seek to explain the way that gender shapes the decision-making processes of public leaders. Gender has both profound and subtle affects on the way that politics is done in the United States. This book offers an introduction to the empirical evidence regarding the effects of gender on political life.

It is important to note that these essays do not necessarily agree regarding the source of observed differences between men's and women's political behavior. Given that gender roles, assumptions, and socialization affect both men and women in terms of their views of the world, the point is to look to the impact that gender has on the behavior of men and women in political life and political institutions. The book looks at the role that gender and gendered assumptions play in the operation of governmental institutions and the making of public policy. Since gender in American life is also inflected by considerations of race, the authors include analysis of the intersection of race and gender when appropriate.

The book is divided into three sections: political behavior, political institutions, and public policy. These three sections reflect three major areas of empirical study of American politics. While each arena is very broad, we believe the essays in this volume provide something of an overview of the state of research and empirical evidence regarding gender in each of these areas.

Political Behavior

The first section of the book addresses political behavior. The chapters explore numerous aspects of men and women's political behavior, including political knowledge and the factors that affect political knowledge, as well as the participation of men and women in political life, primarily through elections.

The first chapter, by Michael Delli Carpini and Scott Keeter, discusses empirical evidence regarding the differences between the political knowledge of men and women. The authors argue that political action is premised upon knowledge about politics. They note that many studies have found a difference between women and men in terms of knowledge about national politics, a difference that has persisted over the last half-century despite changes in men's and women's roles. Their chapter explores the dimensions of this gender gap in political knowledge. In particular, they seek to explain how structural inequities between men and women, that is, women's historic exclusion from national politics, and situational inequities, or the continuing differences between men's and women's lives with respect to working for wages, education, and so on, translate into differences in political knowledge. They utilize data from the National Election Study, from their own national survey, and from Gallup polls to examine changes in men's and women's comparative political knowledge from the 1940s through the 1990s.

Interestingly, the authors find that, although women tend to have less political knowledge on national issues, such as those having to do with foreign policy, there was little or no gender gap in political knowledge regarding issues that might be considered of special relevance to women, such as health care policy or candidate positions on abortion. Further, in survey questions about local politics, the authors found that women were as knowledgeable as men were in terms of identifying local elected officials, and were actually more knowledgeable regarding local school officials.

Finally, the authors examine the effects that political knowledge has on political opinions and interests. They find that, among men and

women with low levels of political knowledge, the gender gap in opinion is modest. However, as political knowledge increases, the gender
gap in opinion increases as well, with more informed men becoming
more conservative, and more informed women becoming more liberal
in their political opinions. Extrapolating from these data, they argue
that a fully informed citizenry would vote differently and hold different
opinions than at present. They conclude by arguing that, if democracy
is to be truly democratic, that is, representative of citizens' interests, a
more fully informed citizenry, with no gender gap in political knowledge, is required.

Eric Plutzer's chapter looks at the discussion regarding gender and
moral decision making that was stimulated by Carol Gilligan's book,
In a Different Voice. He links this decision making to the pessimism
about citizen competence in democratic decision making articulated by
the framers of the U.S. Constitution, such as James Madison. Plutzer
argues that debate about public policy in the United States is often
motivated by an underlying discussion about the capacity of citizens
to make their own choices regarding matters that may be of public
import or concern. Concern about women's capacity to make informed
moral judgments has motivated many public policy debates, including
debates over abortion policy.

To study this arena, Plutzer utilizes data from a study he and Barbara
Ryan conducted in the 1980s which examined the decision-making
process of women who had chosen to have an abortion. In this case,
the decision examined is whether to tell the co-conceiver about the
pregnancy and their decision to abort. Women were asked a series of
questions in the context of the counseling sessions that all patients
underwent prior to receiving services. The sample discussed in this
essay consists of about equal numbers of women who chose to tell,
and who chose not to tell, the co-conceiver.

Plutzer is interested in the reasons given by women for telling, and
for not telling, and especially in the decision-making process that
women go through. In terms of Gilligan's arguments regarding moral
reasoning based on an ethic of care versus moral reasoning based on
an ethic of rights, which type of reasoning predominates in women's
decision making regarding whether to tell? What he finds is that both
those who chose to tell, and those who chose not to tell, utilized both
modes of reasoning in their decision making. In addition, the context
of the relationship between the woman and her co-conceiver was a

crucial aspect of the decision-making process. He concludes that both men and women use both modes of reasoning, and thus scholars should be skeptical of efforts to essentialize decision making according to gender. Further, he notes that women who chose not to tell often were more concerned with rights and principles, and with their own autonomy, given the context of the relationship. However, Plutzer argues that this study shows that ethical reasoning is very much contextual, and affected by power and by the nature of the relationships involved— especially the relative power of the persons involved in the decision. Thus, what is perhaps most important in examining moral or ethical decisions as they relate to public life is to pay careful attention to the context in which decisions are made, and gender is an important part of this context.

M. Margaret Conway's chapter addresses differences and similarities between men and women in political participation. After briefly summarizing the historic exclusion of women from the right to participate in political life, Conway turns to an examination of three different types of election-related political activity: voting, making campaign contributions, and participating in campaign activities. Examining women's and men's participation in each of these activities, she finds that although women were less likely to vote than men were during the first six decades after they gained the franchise, since 1980 women have been about as likely to vote as have men. However, women remain less likely than men to participate in making campaign contributions and in campaign activities.

Conway then examines possible explanations for women's lower levels of political participation. Among explanations that have been offered by scholars are differences in gender role socialization, in available resources, and in social contexts. Conway explores another approach: generational differences in patterns of participation. Dividing voters into four different birth cohorts, she notes that men are slightly more likely to vote than are women in each cohort, but that the differences are not statistically significant. However, in each cohort there are significant differences in campaign contributions and activities. Conway examines the possibility that gender role orientations among women create differences between women with respect to political participation. However, the measure that she uses—orientation to feminism—yields results that are not statistically significant. Conway does not conclude, however, that gender role orientation makes no difference in political participation; rather, she concludes that more precise measures of gender role orientation are required to understand the role that gender consciousness plays in influencing men's and women's political participation.

Public Policy

Given some of the observed differences as well as the similarities in political behavior of men and women, what difference does gender make in the arena of public policy? How is gender reflected in the institutions created by public policy, and in the policymaking process? The chapters in this section address various aspects of the role that gender plays in policymaking and implementation.

Working at the intersection between political behavior and public policy, the chapter by Michael Alvarez and Edward McCaffery examines men's and women's attitudes regarding taxation, and the salience of tax policy for men and women when they cast their ballots. In particular, they look at two issues: First, are there differences between men and women's attitudes regarding redistributive taxation? Although it is a long-standing assumption and finding in studies of the gender gap that there are such differences, more recent studies indicate little difference between men and women on these issues. The second issue that they address is the question of tax policy: tax policy in the United States continues to provide substantial penalties to two-earner families. The authors examine attitudes and voter behavior of men and women with respect to this substantive feature of tax policy.

Alvarez and McCaffery argue that, while men and women may have similar first-order preferences with respect to taxation, their second-order preferences seem to be different. More specifically, when men and women are asked general questions about taxes, they answer similarly. However, when questions are asked that require a choice, for example, between tax reduction for working families or for deficit reduction, men are more likely to choose deficit reduction, while women are more likely to prefer tax reduction for families. To determine how these differences might be reflected in voting behavior, the authors analyze data from the 1996 national election. The authors find that tax is a significant issue in motivating how people vote, and that the salience of different issues with respect to taxation varied by gender. Men generally see taxes as a more important issue, and are thus more likely to vote on the basis of their views on taxes—which means that they are more likely to vote for Republican candidates. For women, taxes are less important, and so they tend to vote on other issues that have more salience for them. Interestingly, those women for whom taxes are the most salient issue actually are even more likely to vote for Republican candidates than are men with similar views on taxes.

Because taxes are more salient for men, McCaffery and Alvarez argue, tax policy tends to be made in ways that are more in keeping with men's tax policy preferences. The authors analyze the issue of marriage tax reform, noting that, although it would serve the interests of working women to reduce the secondary earner bias in marriage tax law, the fact that this issue is not as salient as social spending for this group meant that the Democrats for whom these women tend to vote did not support initial efforts to reform this policy in 1997. The authors conclude that, because tax policy is more salient for social conservatives—both men and women—policymaking in this area is driven more by their interests than by the general interests and preferences of voters on the issue of taxation. Thus, they argue, tax policymaking continues to be inflected by gender, and in ways that are often to women's disadvantage.

Dorothy McBride Stetson addresses the role of gender in the policymaking process by looking at public policy debates in two areas: job training and abortion. Examining the impact of feminist policy advocates, Stetson seeks to address the substantive representation of feminist ideas in the policymaking process. Viewing policymaking as a process in which there are regular patterns in the conflicting ideas regarding how a policy should be formulated and implemented, Stetson is especially interested in the framing of policy debates. She argues that feminist advocates seek both to place their policy concerns higher on the government's agenda, and to influence the way that policy debates are framed on issues related to gender.

To examine the role that feminist advocates play in policy debates where gender is a significant issue, Stetson analyzes policy debates in two different policy domains: job training, which is a distributive policy arena, and abortion, which is what Stetson terms an "emotive-symbolic" policy issue. The job training policy debates are addressed with respect to two job training initiatives: the Comprehensive Employment and Training Act (CETA) of 1978, and the Job Training Partnership Act of 1982. The abortion debates analyzed are the Freedom of Choice Act in the early 1990s, and the Partial-Birth Abortion Ban Act of 1995.

Stetson concludes that the job training debates show modest success on the part of feminist advocates, in that they were able to place a specific group of women—displaced homemakers—on the agenda in job training policymaking. On the other hand, in the abortion debates, feminists have become less successful in the 1990s than they were in the 1970s in influencing the agenda-setting and policymaking process. Stetson concludes that these policy arenas show both the complexity of the interaction of feminist advocates with government officials in the policymaking process, and the significance of language and ideas in the agenda-setting process.

The chapter by Jyl Josephson addresses the role that gender plays in the area of social policy, especially with respect to policy termination and the justifications provided for ending policies targeted toward specific groups. Drawing on a model developed by Anne Schneider and Helen Ingram, which argues that the political power and positive or negative perceptions of populations targeted by public policies play an important role in policy formation and implementation, Josephson applies their model to social policy. Specifically, she addresses two policy terminations of the 1990s: the termination of the General Assistance (GA) program in Michigan in 1991, which was a program perceived to be targeted primarily toward able-bodied men, and the termination of the federal Aid to Families with Dependent Children (AFDC) program in 1996, a program perceived to be targeted primarily toward poor women.

Josephson notes that gender played an important role in the formation of social policy in the United States: several of the social programs of the New Deal can be characterized as being targeted either toward men in their role as workers or toward women in their role as mothers. She then traces the history of the termination of each program, arguing that, although it was budget shortfalls and political ideology that placed program termination on the agenda in the case of both GA and AFDC, other programs were also proposed for budget cutbacks or for termination, but were not terminated. One reason that GA and AFDC were targeted for actual termination was the ability of policymakers to depict the recipients of each program as deviant. The deviant status of each target population had to do in part with its failure to comply with gender roles perceived as appropriate for that population. In the case of GA, recipients were depicted as able-bodied minority men who were simply unwilling to work; in the case of AFDC, recipients were depicted both as able-bodied women unwilling to work and as bad mothers who were not providing proper care for their children. Josephson shows that, in both cases, the empirical evidence regarding the population is decidedly different from the depictions of the population by policymakers.

Sue Tolleson-Rinehart's chapter addresses gender and health policy, looking at the difficulty of treading the line between similarity and difference in health care for men and for women. Tolleson-Rinehart notes that the adage among health care providers used to be that "women get sicker, men die quicker," but that this statement is both true and false. She documents the history of medical research that excluded women from most clinical trials but then utilized research on men to develop treatments for both men and women.

She then turns to some of the complications that arise when women come to be included in clinical research. After documenting the process by which this came about, she notes the high political saliency of issues related to women's health, as opposed to the lack of political saliency of addressing men's health as men's. That is, the universal indicator of the term "health" still applies to men, but women's health is seen as separate and requiring particular attention.

Nevertheless, the fact that much more attention is now being paid by political actors to women's health does not mean that addressing concerns with respect to women's health is a clearcut matter. As evidence, Tolleson-Rinehart discusses the controversy that erupted over the adoption of new standards regarding the frequency with which women in their forties should be screened for breast cancer. She also discusses the example of controversies among women's health groups over the treatment of early labor in pregnant women. She concludes that health policymakers need to carefully examine "when sex matters to health, when gender matters, and when *neither* might matter" in order to make health policy that provides for better outcomes for both men and women.

Institutions

The section on political institutions addresses the comparative roles of men and women in each branch of government. The chapters address the role that gender plays in the selection of public officials and in the role that public officials play once they are in office. They especially address questions of representation: does it matter, and if so, in what way does it matter, whether women and men are equally represented in public office? Because women historically have been excluded from most top government positions, what difference does it make, if any, that more women hold positions in the federal judiciary, in Congress, and in the cabinet, than has been true in the past? In what ways do men and women bring gender into the public arena in decision making, and what can an analysis of gender contribute to our understanding of public officials in American political life?

The chapter by MaryAnne Borrelli looks at the role of gender in the cabinet. Noting that gender has largely been neglected in analysis of the presidency and the president's cabinet, Borrelli seeks to examine the implications of the fact that men historically have held most cabinet posts, especially in the "inner cabinet," and the role that gender plays as women increasingly assume these roles. To do so, she analyzes the appointment and tenure of Janet Reno as attorney general, and Madeleine Korbel Albright as secretary of state. Her analysis focuses especially on what she terms "descriptive" and "symbolic" representation in the cabinet.

Albright and Reno provide useful subjects for study, Borrelli argues, because they are the first women to serve in the "inner cabinet," which forms the core of presidential decision making. Borrelli notes that, historically, women appointees have been generalists and members of the outer cabinet. The appointment of Albright constitutes a shift from this tradition in two ways. First, Albright was appointed to the prestigious position of secretary of state. Second, Albright is a "liaison" secretary, according to Borrelli: she has more expertise in foreign policy than the president who appointed her, making him more dependent on her than presidents have traditionally been on women appointees. Borrelli argues that Albright's career, with long experience in foreign policy but in circles outside of the State Department, where secretaries have traditionally gained their experience, constitutes a new way for women's entry into cabinet posts.

Reno's career path is rather different from Albright's, and Borrelli points out that it was both predictable and surprising that the post of attorney general was the first inner cabinet post held by a woman. Presidents have traditionally appointed a close ally as attorney general, so appointing a female attorney general, and one who came directly from a state-level office, was unusual. Yet it was not surprising that the office of attorney general was the first inner cabinet post held by a woman, given that women have made more significant inroads in the profession of law than in the other arenas represented in the inner cabinet. Borrelli argues that, in her tenure as attorney general, Reno has demonstrated a firm commitment to rights as well as a commitment to care and to social programs that will help to prevent crime. Thus, Borrelli suggests, Reno's career in the office of attorney general has helped to bring issues of gender more visibly into the public arena.

The chapter by Susan Gluck Mezey examines gender in the federal judiciary, both in terms of the number of men and women appointed to the bench and in terms of the role that gender plays in judicial decision making. The chapter distinguishes between descriptive representation, when public officials have characteristics similar to the characteristics of the population, and substantive representation, which occurs when public officials seek to accomplish the goals of the group that they represent. Mezey is primarily concerned with the extent to which women judges act as substantive representatives for women as a group.

Mezey examines claims by some legal scholars, based on Carol Gilligan's work in moral theory, that female judges might speak, and make decisions, in a "different voice." The empirical tests of these claims have yielded decidedly mixed results, finding that women sometimes speak in Gilligan's different voice of care and connection rather than rules and legalism, but that men judges also speak in this different voice at times. Thus, the literature on whether women utilize different or distinctly female approaches to decision making is mixed.

Mezey then traces the history of appointments of women judges to the federal bench. She notes that the first presidential administration that appointed substantial numbers of women to federal judgeships was the Carter administration, which appointed a total of 93 women to the bench. Given the increased number of women on the bench, the question of whether gender makes a difference in how judges make decisions becomes especially significant. Mezey reviews the studies that have addressed this question, noting that most have found little difference between women and men, or between racial minority and racial majority judges, in terms of their degree of activism on the bench. Mezey concludes the chapter by discussing the careers of the two most prominent women federal judges, Sandra Day O'Connor and Ruth Bader Ginsburg.

The chapter by Richard Fox focuses on gender in congressional elections. Fox notes that although women have been more successful in achieving election to Congress in the 1990s than in previous decades, both the House and the Senate remain overwhelmingly male-dominated institutions. After briefly discussing the history of women in Congress, Fox turns to a discussion of the role that gender plays in the process of congressional elections.

The chapter is in three sections. First, Fox compares the relative success of male and female candidates, and notes that the literature shows that women and men have similar vote totals, indicating that there is no "widespread voter bias" toward women candidates. In addition, recent studies indicate that there is little difference between men and women candidates in terms of fund raising. Thus, the incumbent advantage seems to explain much of the persistence of male domination of Congress. However, Fox notes that this does not tell the whole story. The second section of the chapter turns to regional variations in male and female success rates in congressional campaigns. Although political scientists have documented significant differences in women's electoral success from state to state, the reasons for these differences are not clear. Fox notes that more research is needed in this area to explain how political culture and other factors interact to cause these differences.

The heart of the chapter is the third section, which provides a more nuanced understanding of women's and men's experiences as candidates for House seats. The analysis is based on interviews with campaign managers for House races in California in 1992 and 1994. Examining men and women's experiences with respect to fund raising, media coverage, and party support, Fox finds that there are gender differences in managers' perceptions of each of these aspects of campaigning. For example, managers reported that women candidates had to work harder to raise the same amount of money, that party support was not always as forthcoming for women candidates as it was for male candidates, and that the way that a candidate was presented and perceived by the media varied for men and women. Fox also examines the way that male candidates react to running against female candidates. He provides evidence that male candidates alter their campaign strategies when facing a female opponent by attempting to appeal to women voters, and by hesitating to engage in negative campaigning. Thus, Fox concludes, despite the significant progress that women have made as candidates and as members of Congress, gender still plays an important, if more subtle, role in the process of congressional elections.

Conclusion

This book is intended to provide the reader with an overview and analysis of the role of gender in American politics. The chapters that follow provide an understanding of the significant role that gender plays in governmental decision making and the political process, as well as in parties, elections, and political behavior. They illustrate the importance of the context in which political decisions are made, and the role of both sex and gender in the American political process.

Part One
Political Behavior

1

Gender and Political Knowledge

Michael X. Delli Carpini and Scott Keeter

According to many indicators, the integration of women into the U.S. political system proceeds apace. Voting turnout among women now exceeds that of men, and the trend is for this gap to increase (Leighley and Nagler 1991). The number of female candidates for political office at all levels of government continues to rise, and women's chances for success at the polls appear greater as well (Delli Carpini and Fuchs 1993). The increasing presence of women in the work force, and in politically relevant professions such as the law, portends greater participation as candidates and activists in the future (Darcy, Welch, and Clark 1987; Taeuber 1991).

At the same time, women are becoming increasingly differentiated from men in their political views and preferences. The "gender gap" in partisanship and vote choice, rarely seen prior to the late 1970s, is larger than ever. Gender differences in attitudes on a variety of issues show no sign of diminishing (Shapiro and Mahajan 1986; Erikson and Tedin 1995, 209–212). The combination of greater participation and a distinctive agenda suggests the potential for women to exert a powerful influence in contemporary politics.

However, there remain important differences between women and men in the resources that fuel effective political action. Men still earn more than women, even in jobs requiring comparable training and skills. Child care responsibilities often restrict career progress for women, especially those who are single. Women are still less likely than men to engage in a variety of modes of political participation beyond voting, though the definition of "political" in this context is controversial (Verba 1990; Bourque and Grossholtz 1984). And there is growing evidence that even when women are granted nominal access to power, their effectiveness is undermined by gendered expectations and practices (Kathlene 1994; Mattei 1998).

21

This chapter focuses on a fundamental resource for political action: knowledge about politics. While several studies of political knowledge have found that men are better informed than women about national politics (Glenn 1972; Sigelman and Yanarella 1986; Bennett 1988), none have explored the size, significance, and sources of this "gender gap" in any detail. In the present study, we draw on a number of recent surveys, including several specifically designed to tap factual knowledge about politics, to document the nature and extent of the current gender gap in political knowledge. We also examine whether or not this gender gap has increased or decreased over the past thirty to forty years. We then test several explanations for the knowledge gap between men and women. Finally, we assess the political implications of gender differences in political knowledge.[1]

The Importance of Political Knowledge

The value of political knowledge has been attested to by numerous studies. First, knowledge stimulates and facilitates political participation. Both Neuman (1986, 84–89, 99–103) and Palfrey and Poole (1987, 524–529) found knowledge of politics, controlling for socioeconomic status, to be highly predictive of voting turnout. And Junn found a reciprocal relationship between knowledge and participation, with knowledge eclipsing most other predictors of a variety of forms of participation (1991, 203–209).

Second, political knowledge has a powerful impact on the formation of political opinions and the processing of new information. Elaborating on Converse's (1962) classic work on the role of stored information in mediating the effects of political communication, Zaller has developed a general model of the effects of knowledge on attitude change in a variety of settings (1991; 1992). Of specific relevance to our interests, he noted that gender differences in attitudes about the Vietnam War—with women less supportive than men—were manifested chiefly among individuals with high levels of knowledge, and concluded that high information levels were "necessary for the effective translation of political predispositions into appropriate policy preferences" (Zaller 1991, 1229). Several studies have also documented differences in how better and lesser informed individuals reason about political issues and decisions, demonstrating that political knowledge improves the speed and efficiency of information processing, and renders citizens less vulnerable to priming and other media effects (Fiske, Lau, and Smith 1990; Lodge, McGraw, and Stroh 1989; McGraw and Pinney 1990; Sniderman, Brody, and Tetlock 1991, esp. chap. 3, 4, and 7; Lanoue 1992).[2]

Third (and perhaps as a specific application of the previous point), the process of voter decision making among the well informed is very different from that of the less informed. Compared with uninformed voters, informed voters are likely to use a broader range of considerations in reaching a candidate choice, and are much more likely to use issues as a criterion (Moon 1990; Sniderman, Brody, and Tetlock 1991; Brady and Ansolabehere 1989).

Thus, political knowledge facilitates more effective citizenship in several ways. It promotes participation and engagement in politics. It enables citizens to comprehend the political world and to develop attitudes about politics that are consistent with one's basic values and orientations. And it is critical to an effective linkage between attitudes and political behavior.

Measuring Political Knowledge

The analyses in this chapter utilize a variety of data, nearly all of which were gathered by telephone or in-person surveys of random samples of the public. Three major national surveys are at the center of much of the analysis: one is a telephone survey of 610 adults, designed by the authors and conducted in 1989 by a university-based survey research center; the other two are the 1992 and 1996 National Election Studies (NES), conducted through in-person interviews by the Center for Political Studies at the University of Michigan (Miller and the National Election Studies 1992; 1996).

Our national survey included 51 knowledge questions covering a broad range of political topics, as well as an extensive set of attitudinal, behavioral, and demographic items. Our approach was to include questions of varying format and difficulty, covering several different topic areas. Following James David Barber's notion that citizens "need to know what the government *is* and *does*" (1973, 44, emphasis added), a large part of the questionnaire covered "the rules of the game" and "the substance of politics." A third important area, linked to the citizen's responsibility in a representative democracy, is the set of "people and players" in politics.[3] The specific topics covered by our survey, along with the percentage of men and women correctly answering each question, are provided in Table 1.1 (discussed below).[4] In addition to using the questions individually we also created a knowledge index by summing the number of correct answers to the questions (and assigning partial credit on some topics where appropriate). This index varied from 3 to 43 in the sample (with a theoretical range of 0 to 51), with a mean of 23.7 and a median of 24.[5]

The NES surveys typically devote relatively few direct questions to the measurement of political knowledge. However, because of the relative unidimensionality of the concept (see note 5), a good knowledge index can be constructed by combining the available direct knowledge items with other questions that also tap awareness and understanding of political phenomena (Delli Carpini and Keeter 1992; 1993; 1996; Zaller 1986). Using the 1996 NES we constructed a 16-item knowledge index, to which we added the two interviewer ratings of respondent's information level (preelection and postelection waves).[6] The resulting index varies from 0 to 24 in the sample, with a mean of 14.3 and a median of 15. The content is narrower than in our national survey, with no questions focusing on "civics knowledge," but this data set has the advantage of a large sample size and an extensive set of attitudinal and behavioral questions.[7] Table 1.2 shows the percentage of men and women correctly answering each of the items.

Past and Present Gender Differences in Knowledge of National Politics

In both of the national surveys, men as a group were more knowledgeable than women on nearly all of the factual political questions.[8] In our 1989 survey (Table 1.1), the average difference across all items in the percentage correct for men and women was 9.8. On only four items did a higher percentage of women correctly answer the question. The differences between women and men were similar in the 1996 National Election Study (NES) (Table 1.2). The average percentage difference was 9.5, with the gap ranging from less than 1 percentage point (on knowledge of the candidates' relative positions on abortion) to nearly 18 points (on knowledge of the candidates' relative positions on defense spending). In both surveys, the median score for men was approximately equal to the seventy-fifth percentile for

Table 1.1

Gender Differences in Knowledge of National Politics
1989 National Survey
(percent correct)

	Men	Women	Difference	Odds ratio
What is the superfund?	18	4	14	5.3
Percent unemployed	41	14	27	4.3
Percent vote required for veto override	50	21	29	3.8
Does U.S. have a trade deficit?	91	73	18	3.7
Percent black in U.S.	19	7	12	3.1
Contras are rebels	69	42	27	3.1
Sandinistas control Nicaraguan government	58	32	26	2.9
What is a veto?	94	85	9	2.8
Can veto be overridden?	89	75	14	2.7
Did U.S. support Contras?	80	60	20	2.7
Name governor	81	66	15	2.2
Describe recent arms agreement	57	39	18	2.1
Can Communist run for president?	59	41	18	2.1
Define the New Deal	20	11	9	2.0
Federal budget: percent for education	24	14	10	1.9
Name both U.S. Senators	31	19	12	1.9
Rehnquist's ideology	37	24	13	1.9
Define recession	65	50	15	1.9
What are first ten amendments called?	53	39	14	1.8
Size of federal budget	56	42	14	1.8
Federal budget: percent for defense	10	6	4	1.7
Who reviews constitutionality of laws?	72	60	12	1.7
U.S. supports El Salvadoran government	50	37	13	1.7
Percent poor in U.S.	23	15	8	1.7
Name vice president	79	69	10	1.7
Percent with health insurance	11	7	4	1.6
Who declares war?	40	29	11	1.6
Describe one First Amendment right	43	32	11	1.6
Does U.S. have a budget deficit?	82	74	8	1.6
Party control of House	73	64	9	1.5
Name one of your U.S. Senators	60	50	10	1.5
Describe one Fifth Amendment Right	56	46	10	1.5
Prior to *Roe*, was abortion illegal in all states?	63	54	9	1.5
Truman's party	63	54	9	1.5

Table 1.1

(continued)

	Men	Women	Difference	Odds ratio
FDR's party	67	59	8	1.4
Describe two First Amendment rights	21	16	5	1.4
Define effects of a tariff	56	48	8	1.4
Describe three First Amendment rights	9	7	2	1.3
Party control of Senate	58	52	6	1.3
Length of presidential term	96	95	1	1.3
Must students say pledge of allegiance?	78	74	4	1.2
Can states prohibit abortion?	75	71	4	1.2
Name U.S. Representative	31	27	4	1.2
Who appoints judges?	60	56	4	1.2
Date of women's suffrage	10	9	1	1.1
Nixon's party	76	76	0	1.0
Describe two Fifth Amendment rights	5	5	0	1.0
Did women always have suffrage?	89	90	−1	0.9
Date of New Deal	11	13	−2	0.8
Is there a right to counsel?	90	92	−2	0.8
Federal budget: percent for Social Security	4	6	−2	0.7

women, meaning that about three-fourths of women scored at or below the average for men.[9]

Many legal, social, and cultural changes during the past fifty years in the United States have resulted in greater political integration of women. It is thus reasonable to expect that the gender gap in knowledge about politics has declined during that period as well. Available data suggest that the knowledge gap narrowed very little over the period from the 1940s to the 1980s, but there is some evidence of greater parity between women and men in the 1990s.

We have two bases for making comparisons over time. Part of our 1989 national survey was devoted to the replication of several questions asked by the Gallup Organization during the 1940s and 1950s.[10] The other data source is the set of NES surveys, which date back to 1952. While there are only a few knowledge items in the time series, the study methodology for each of the surveys was nearly identical, providing some reassurance that differences (or lack thereof) reflect

Table 1.2

**Gender Differences in Knowledge of National Politics
1996 National Election Study**
(percent correct)

	Men	Women	Difference	Odds ratio
Identify William Rehnquist	15.2	5.2	9.9	3.2
Candidates' positions on defense	60.3	42.7	17.6	2.0
Interviewer rated respondent above average in knowledge	51.6	35.6	16.0	1.9
Party control of Senate	79.0	67.0	12.0	1.9
Parties' positions on defense	57.8	42.8	14.9	1.8
Party control of House	81.4	71.0	10.3	1.8
Identify Boris Yeltsin	72.1	60.0	12.1	1.7
Knows deficit declined in past 4 years	35.4	25.1	10.3	1.6
Candidates' positions on spending	75.0	66.1	9.0	1.5
Identify Al Gore	90.6	86.4	4.2	1.5
Parties' ideological placement	73.1	64.7	8.3	1.5
Parties' positions on spending	69.5	60.6	8.8	1.5
Identify Newt Gingrich	64.0	54.9	9.1	1.5
Candidates' position on health insurance	71.3	63.5	7.8	1.4
Candidates' positions on jobs	68.5	63.0	5.5	1.3
Candidates' ideological placement	72.6	67.7	4.9	1.3
Candidates' positions on abortion	60.2	59.6	0.6	1.0
Mean percentage correct	64.6	55.1	9.5	

the underlying phenomenon rather than differences in measurement or measurement error itself. Table 1.3 shows comparisons between men and women for the Gallup and 1989 political knowledge surveys, while Figure 1.1 displays trends from the NES data.

Across eight Gallup questions for which comparisons can be made with the 1989 survey, the gender gap in knowledge was smaller in five and larger in three. For questions with a smaller gap in 1989, the decline varied from two to nine percentage points, with a mean change of 4.5 percent. The other three questions showed increases of five to eight percentage points in the knowledge gap. The median change across all eight items was a modest decline of between two and three percentage points in the gender gap.

Table 1.3

Gender Differences Over Time
Gallup Surveys and 1989 Political Knowledge Survey
(percent correct)

	Gallup surveys		Difference (men minus women)		1989 Political knowledge survey	
	Men	Women			Men	Women
Name your U.S. Representative (1947)	49 (1,479)	36 (1,497)	13	4	31 (279)	27 (331)
Named both U.S. Senators (1954)	37 (653)	20 (712)	17	12	31 (279)	19 (331)
What does Fifth Amendment mean to you? (1957)	50 (792)	35 (851)	15	10	56 (279)	46 (331)
What is a presidential veto? (1947)	86 (1,455)	74 (1,498)	12	9	94 (279)	85 (331)
Length of president's term (1952)	94 (666)	91 (652)	3	1	96 (279)	95 (331)
Name the vice president (1952)	71 (666)	66 (652)	5	10	79 (279)	69 (331)
First ten amendments are called "Bill of Rights" (1954)	34 (653)	27 (711)	7	14	53 (279)	39 (331)
Two-thirds vote required to override presidential veto (1947)	54 (1,455)	33 (1,498)	21	29	50 (279)	21 (331)

Figure 1.1. Over-time Trends in the Knowledge Gap.

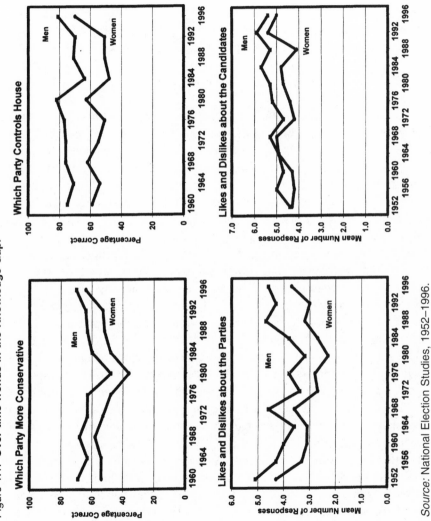

Source: National Election Studies, 1952–1996.

The NES data also suggest that there was little narrowing of the gap during this period. All four of the items depicted in Figure 1.1, however, show greater parity in 1996 than in 1992. And a more comprehensive comparison of indexes in 1988, 1992, and 1996 reveals a steady decline in the knowledge gap over this period.[11]

Explaining the Gender Gap in Knowledge

The existence of *some* gender differences in political knowledge is not surprising, given the history of women's exclusion from national politics in the United States, and the continuing inequality between women and men in many of the resources that contribute to political integration. However, its size and persistence over a period during which other indicators showed increased political engagement by women, raise questions about the genesis of the gap and the factors that contribute to its maintenance.

Most theories regarding gender differences in political orientations are rooted in structural and situational explanations: females know less about politics than males do because of differences in how the sexes are socialized and because of the different opportunities afforded them to engage the political world. But how, specifically, do structural and situational inequities translate into differences in political knowledge? The simplest argument is that they act as a barrier, preventing women who have the motivation to learn about politics from having the opportunity or ability to do so. Except among the youngest cohort of citizens, women have less formal education than men (and education is related to political knowledge). A smaller percentage of women than men are in the labor force (and employment outside the home provides politically relevant experiences). Women in the labor force are also likely to work in less "politically impinged" jobs than men (Luskin 1990). Unmarried women have lower incomes than unmarried men (and income is associated with political knowledge). Because of child care responsibilities, women have much less time for political activity, and spend less of their time in contact with adults, who are more likely than children to talk about politics (Sapiro 1983; Jennings and Niemi 1981). According to this argument, if women had the same incomes, educational attainment, types of employment, free time, and social and work-related contacts as men, their levels of political knowledge would be similar to men's. Yet even if these factors do not constitute barriers in the strict sense of the word, they may nevertheless act as negative reinforcement, discouraging women who have the ability and opportunity to learn about politics from doing so. Socioeconomic disadvantages simply make it more difficult for women to be politically engaged.

We designed a multivariate model to examine the ways in which structural-situational and attitudinal factors mediate gender's effect on knowledge.[12] The full model (for the NES data) includes 21 such variables, selected on the basis of theoretical considerations, the findings of other researchers in this area (Bennett and Bennett 1989; Luskin 1990), and extensive testing of the model with several different sets of data.[13] The simple correlation between gender and political knowledge (using the 18-item index in the 1996 NES) was −0.20, but controlling for theoretically relevant variables reduces this to −0.04 (standardized beta), indicating that most of the relationship between gender and knowledge can be explained by demographic, structural-situational, and attitudinal differences between men and women.

In order to test the specific relationships between structural-situational factors and attitudinal ones, we prepared a simplified version of the model. Latent variables representing the structural and attitudinal elements of the model were created and then included in a path analysis along with gender, race, age, and region, which are treated as intercorrelated, but causally exogenous. The model performed well, explaining an estimated 62 percent of the variance in the political knowledge scale. Figure 1.2 shows the path coefficients for the simplified model.

The path model allows us to decompose the simple bivariate relationship between gender and knowledge into four specific pathways. Consistent with the notion of structural barriers, about one-third of the original relationship is explained by the path from gender through structure to knowledge. A somewhat smaller portion (about one-fifth) is explained by the negative reinforcement argument, defined here as the path from gender through structure and attitudes to knowledge. Taken together, the two structure-based arguments account for about half of the original relationship.

The path model also provides some insight into what is missed by the structural arguments. More than one-fourth of the original relationship is accounted for by the path from gender through attitudes to knowledge, suggesting that even while in nominally equal socioeco-

Figure 1.2. **A Simplified Path Model of Knowledge.**

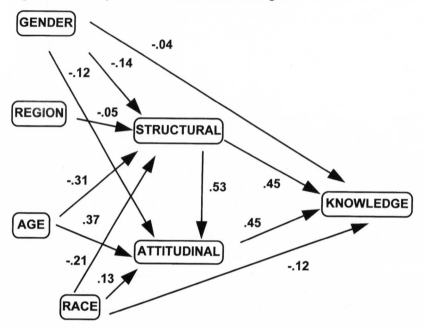

Source: 1996 National Election Study.

nomic circumstances, women are less psychologically engaged in politics, and thus less likely to be politically informed. And the direct path from gender to knowledge remains statistically significant, accounting for about one-fifth of the original relationship.

Socialization and Motivation

Undoubtedly some of the strength of these last two pathways results from measurement error and a failure to account for all of the relevant structural and situational factors that depress women's knowledge of politics.[14] However, it also seems likely that some is due to more deep-seated differences in socialization that are not erased by adult circumstances and a more nominally equal playing field. Most obviously relevant here is explicitly *political* socialization, which may be different for many females as a result of the legacy of de jure gender discrimination and attendant societal views of the "proper" (i.e., nonpolitical) role of women. Although few women alive today were ever prohibited by law from voting or taking part in politics, many were socialized to politics by mothers who were (and by fathers who directly experienced the pre-suffrage period). Traditional views of the "appropriate" role for women in politics have not vanished. While only a small minority of survey respondents express such views, they are found in younger as well as older cohorts (Bennett and Bennett 1989; 1992). Even when conservative norms were not explicitly transmitted to the next generation, the example of nonparticipation by mothers would still have a significant impact on daughters (and, in a different way, on sons).[15] Evidence to support a socialization theory of the gender gap in knowledge can be found in the civics knowledge and attitudes of school students. Niemi and Junn's (1993) analysis of data from the National Assessment of Educational Progress (a large national survey of school-age children) found that males were more likely than females "to say that government is their favorite subject, or that they enjoy civics classes more than their other classes" (p. 6). Male students were significantly more politically knowledgeable than females, even after controlling for a number of background and curriculum variables.

Theories of *gender role socialization* that are not explicitly political in nature may also have significant political implications. The nature of—even the very existence of—many of these differences is controversial. As summarized by scholars such as Gilligan (1982) and Tannen (1990), girls from an early age are less interested in the "rules of the game" and notions of "abstract justice" than are boys. Their games tend to be less conflictual than boys' games, and more likely to founder if disputes arise (Lever 1976, 483; Lever 1978, 476). In addition, girls (and women) are more interested in and more likely to talk about personal, immediate, consensual issues in their conversations, while boys and men turn to more conflictual, abstract, and less personal topics. To the extent that these generalizations apply to the political world, we would expect women to be less knowledgeable and concerned than men about much of mainstream national politics, given its conflictual, rules-driven, abstract, and physically and psychologically distant nature.

These socialization explanations are difficult to assess directly with the data we have available, though the path in Figure 1.2 from gender through attitudes to knowledge provides some circumstantial support for the political socialization argument, and the direct path from gender to knowledge is consistent with a gender socialization explanation. Beyond this, testing the socialization explanations necessarily consists of deriving plausible propositions that follow from them, and then looking for data that support or contradict these propositions.

One such proposition is that socialization away from mainstream politics would affect the motivation to learn about politics, rather than the ability or opportunity to do so. If this is the case, then we would expect women to exhibit greater levels of knowledge on issues of national politics that are perceived as more relevant to them. This was precisely the pattern we observed in a range of different surveys: topics of potentially special relevance to women showed smaller or nonexistent gender gaps. For example, a 1994 *Times Mirror* national survey found women to be 22 percentage points less able than men to name Boris Yeltsin as the president of Russia, and 18 points less able to name the Serbs as the group besieging Sarajevo; however on the issue of health care, which is a central concern in the "private sphere," women in the same survey were only 4 points less likely than men to know that President Clinton's proposed reform program mandated employers to provide coverage to their workers. There were also trivial or nonexistent gender gaps in knowledge of presidential candidate positions on abortion in the 1992 and 1996 National Election Studies (see Table 1.2), as well as in knowledge of gubernatorial candidate positions in two 1989 Virginia election surveys we conducted.[16]

As a somewhat more systematic test of this hypothesis, we placed five potentially gender-relevant knowledge items on a 1991 statewide Virginia survey ($N = 804$), along with five questions that measured knowledge of national politics more broadly. The gender-relevant items included two questions about the Supreme Court decision in the case of *Rust v. Sullivan*, one on Clarence Thomas's stand on quotas, one on the position of the political parties regarding abortion, and one asking if there were a woman on the U.S. Supreme Court (and if so, to name her). Table 1.4 presents the percentage correct for men and women on these ten items. As with other data we have reviewed, men were generally more informed than women. However, gender differences were much less substantial for the "gender-relevant" questions: five of the six smallest differences were on these items. And while the correlation between gender and knowledge was significant for both scales, it was smaller for the "gender-relevant" (−0.11) than the "gender-neutral" (−0.21) one. Finally, in a multivariate model controlling for structural variables, the beta for gender's direct effect on "gender-neutral"

Table 1.4

Gender-Relevant Items Compared with Others (Virginia Survey)

Subject	Males (% Correct)	Females (% Correct)	% Difference	Odds ratio
Percent needed to override a veto	48	25	−23	2.8
Government benefits are not guaranteed in Bill of Rights	71	57	−14	1.8
Consumer protection not guaranteed in Bill of Rights	54	42	−12	1.6
Length of Senator's term	30	22	−8	1.5
Free speech guaranteed in Bill of Rights	95	93	−2	1.4
Clarence Thomas opposes quotas	38	30	−8	1.4
Which party more opposed to abortion?	59	51	−8	1.4
Can Congress do anything about *Rust* decision?	62	55	−7	1.3
What was *Rust* v. *Sullivan* about?	21	17	−4	1.3
Name woman on Supreme Court	38	33	−5	1.2
Median difference: gender-neutral			−12	
Median difference: gender-relevant			−7	
Gender-neutral scale (0–5) (mean score)	2.98	2.39	−.59	
Gender-relevant scale (0–5) (mean score)	2.37	2.05	−.32	

knowledge was 0.17, compared with 0.07 for "gender-relevant" knowledge.

Equalizing Opportunity, Ability, and Motivation: The Case of Local Politics

An important implication of both the structural and socialization arguments is that women "opt out" of national politics because of some combination of their exclusion from it and its perceived irrelevance to them, relative to the costs of engagement. Thus, within more hospitable arenas for women's political activities, gender differences in knowledge should be smaller or nonexistent. Local politics may provide one such setting. Local government is the arena where issues that directly affect family, schooling, and community are most often and most tangibly debated. Given this physical and symbolic closeness to the "private sphere" of women, their participation in local politics has always been viewed as more acceptable, and so this arena has been more accessible than state or national politics. This access is reflected in the relatively high percentage of female representation in city and county leadership positions as compared with state and national legislative or executive positions (Darcy, Welch, and Clark 1987). If historical exclusion and a sense of issue-irrelevance are partly responsible for women's relatively lower levels of knowledge about national politics, then gender differences in knowledge should be muted at the local level.

Several surveys confirmed this expectation. Women in the Richmond, Virginia, metropolitan area were at least as knowledgeable as men on such topics as how the mayor and city council are selected, which party controlled the county board of supervisors, and the names of elected and appointed officials. Women were quite a bit *more* likely than men to know the name of the head of the local school system, a finding confirmed nationally by the General Social Survey. Table 1.5 shows the gender differences for all of these items.[17]

Two of our local surveys also included questions on national politics, providing a basis of comparison. As can be seen, the gender differences were much more pronounced for national than local politics. For all of the questions examined, the median gender difference on local politics items was –3 percentage points; for national (and state) items it was –11 points. Taking account of structural and situational differences between the women and the men in the local surveys (via multiple regression analyses), the gender gap in knowledge of local politics actually shows a small, though statistically nonsignificant, *female* advantage.

Our exploration of the sources of the gender gap in political knowledge highlights the complex, interactive effects of structural, attitudinal, and environmental factors, as well as the difficulty in capturing these processes with standard measures of political engagement and structural opportunity. The absence of legal barriers to participation in politics for women is no guarantee that the opportunities are, in fact, the same as for men.[18]

Table 1.5

Knowledge of Local Politics

Survey and Subject	Males (% correct)	Females (% correct)	% Difference	Odds ratio
Richmond City Survey (1991)				
N = 800				
Who is Boris Yeltsin?	43	23	−20	2.5
Percent needed to override a veto	45	26	−19	2.3
Party control of U.S. House	60	41	−19	2.2
Who reviews constitutionality of laws?	72	61	−11	1.6
How is city council elected?	60	53	−7	1.3
How is mayor selected?	62	59	−3	1.1
Name the city manager	60	60	0	1.0
Name the school superintendent	11	18	+7	0.6
Richmond City Survey (1990)				
N = 409				
Who is the current mayor?	31	28	−3	1.2
How is mayor selected?	62	59	−3	1.1
Heard or read about historic designation controversy	81	84	+3	0.8
Chesterfield County Survey (1991)				
N = 329				
National unemployment rate	55	31	−24	2.7
Does U.S. have a trade deficit?	92	81	−11	2.7
First ten amendments are the "Bill of Rights"	74	63	−11	1.7
Is there a county impact fee?	34	26	−8	1.5
Harry Truman's party affiliation	65	60	−5	1.2
Name the local U.S. Representative	35	31	−4	1.2
Which party has most seats on county Board of Supervisors?	33	32	−1	1.1
Name the school superintendent	30	40	+10	0.6
General Social Survey (1987)				
N = 1819				
Name Governor	82	71	−11	1.9
Name U.S. Representative	38	31	−7	1.4
Name head of local school system	28	33	+5	0.8

Source: Richmond and Chesterfield county surveys conducted by the authors. General Social Survey conducted by the National Opinion Research Center at the University of Chicago.

Note: Shaded rows contain national or state knowledge items for comparison.

The lack of a gender gap on gender-relevant issues and matters of local politics also provides a vivid example of the situational nature of political knowledge, and reinforces our earlier caveat regarding the dimensionality of knowledge (note 5). Political knowledge is mostly, but not entirely, unidimensional. Some types of issues are of special relevance to certain groups, and some arenas of politics are more accessible than others to them. Where this is true, the groups will be more motivated to learn and better able to do so.

The Consequences of the Gender Gap in Political Knowledge

The significance of the gender gap in knowledge ultimately depends upon the impact of political information on the formation and expression of citizens' individual and collective opinions. Elsewhere we have shown that more-informed citizens are more supportive of democratic norms, more likely to participate in politics, more likely to hold opinions, and more likely to hold opinions that are consistent with each other and that are stable over time (Delli Carpini and Keeter 1996, 220–238). Here we focus on two additional effects of political knowledge: enlightened self-interest and issue-consistent voting.

Political Knowledge and Enlightened Self-Interest

A healthy democracy requires a citizenry capable of knowing and expressing its interests, and doing so in the context of the broader public interest. Philosophers and theorists have long wrestled with the question of what is a citizen's political interest. Rightly enough, there is great reluctance to impute interests to individuals. At the same time, citizens clearly differ in the accuracy of their perceptions about the political world and about the likely impact of current or proposed government policies on them, on important groups to which they belong, and on the polity more generally. Where perceptions on these matters are incomplete or inaccurate, we would question whether a citizen had fully comprehended his or her interest. The lack of sufficient information is one barrier to knowing one's interest. Another is incorrect information. While political observers may debate the extent of "false consciousness" among the public, and few will offer an operational definition of it, most would agree that some citizens, on some issues, do not know their own interest because they have been manipulated by others who, in Hamilton's words, "flatter their prejudices to betray their interests . . ." (Hamilton, Madison, and Jay [1787–88] 1961, no. 71).

A common theoretical approach to the identification of interests is through the notion of "enlightened preferences." In this context, "enlightened" refers not to some absolute standard of what is right or just but rather to the conditions under which the individual chooses among alternatives available to him or her. For example, Dahl (1989, 180–181) writes, "A person's interest or good is whatever that person would choose with fullest attainable understanding of the experiences resulting from that choice and its most relevant alternatives." Similarly, Bartels's (1990) work on interests draws on three theorists across the political spectrum, whose common theme is information: what would an individual choose if she or he had perfect information and could experience the results of choosing each alternative (Mansbridge 1983; Connolly 1972), or "saw clearly, thought rationally, [and] acted disinterestedly and benevolently" (Lippmann 1955)?

Of course, greater information does not assure that citizens will reach a consensus on important issues of the day. Ultimately, each individual brings a unique mix of personal experiences to his or her political calculus. Nonetheless, values, attitudes, and opinions do not develop in a vacuum, but rather are *socially* constructed out of material conditions and cultural norms. While some of these conditions and norms are likely to be similar for all members of a polity, many vary depending on one's particular socioeconomic location. Thus, for some issues at least, greater information is likely to lead to clearer and more consistent expressions of group interests.

The combined concepts of "enlightened preferences" and "socially constructed opinions" permit an empirical study of interests. If more informed citizens are better able to discern their interests, and if material interests differ across groups in the population, it should be possible to detect the influence of information by comparing the opinions of better and lesser informed members of different groups. We should reiterate that we do not see information or knowledge as the *only* determinant of a citizen's interest. One's view of "the good life" is based on norms and values that are rooted in belief systems only partially connected to the empirical world. In addition, the foundational issues of politics and society are inherently contestable (Connolly 1983), and so cannot be "solved" through the technical appraisal of facts. Nonetheless, as with the other aspects of opinion formation examined in this chapter, factual knowledge can help facilitate the process by which values, attitudes, and beliefs are combined into the expression of political interests. These interests may be defined narrowly (What is in *my* best interest?) or more broadly (What is in the best interest of people like me? Of the polity more broadly?), but to be meaningful, they must be based, at least partially, on an accurate understanding of the processes, people, and substance of politics.

Political Knowledge and the Expression of Gender-Based Interests

Numerous studies have documented the emergence of a gender gap in public opinion over the past fifteen years. Much of this gap is attributable to the divergent financial and social situations of men and women and the way in which the parties have responded to issues affecting women.[19] Overlaid upon emerging gender differences in opinion are differences by marital status, which often reinforce the gender schism (Weisberg 1987). To the extent that political interests do in fact differ by gender and marital status, we would expect to see these differences reflected in the expressed opinions of married men, married women, single men, and single women. And to the extent that knowledge facilitates the connection between political interests and public opinion, we would also expect differences in the opinions between less and more informed members within each group. Whether the net effect of knowledge is to create greater polarization or greater consensus, however, depends on the specific way in which informed men and women define their group interests and/or the public interest more generally.

We used data from the 1992 NES to examine how gender differences in opinion were affected by variations in political knowledge levels. In exploring the impact of political knowledge on group-level opinions, it is important to choose issues that are arguably relevant to the group characteristics in question. There is little a priori reason, for example, to expect men and women to differ systematically in their views regarding the trade or budget deficits. In the analysis presented here we looked at differences in opinions related to the proper scope of government in the area of social welfare, since theory and prior evidence suggests that women are more likely to draw on different values and experiences in evaluating such policies than are men (Shapiro and Mahajan 1986).[20] We also looked at gender differences in opinions about abortion, an issue of obvious relevance to women.

As a practical matter, the dearth of highly knowledgeable individuals in certain subgroups—for example, among poor and/or less educated women—imposes limits on what we can learn simply by looking at those individuals in a typical opinion survey. Further, because opinions are likely to be affected by a variety of personal and demographic factors other than political knowledge, and because these factors vary within groups, it is necessary to control for these potentially confounding effects. For each of the following analyses, we used multiple regression to estimate the impact of a set of 22 personal characteristics (for example, race, sex, age, education, income, and marital status) and political knowledge on the particular attitudes of interest. The regression model also included interaction terms for political knowledge and each of the personal characteristics. These interactions permit an estimation of how knowledge affects the relationship between personal characteristics and attitudes.[21] To simulate what the attitudes would be if all members of a group had a uniform level of knowledge, the regression coefficients from the model are used to compute an estimated attitude for each member of the group in the survey, using each person's actual data for all variables except political knowledge, which is imputed as either "uninformed" or "fully informed."[22]

For example, in the first analysis presented below, two sets of estimates were computed: one assumed that everyone scored 0 on the political knowledge scale, while the other assumed that everyone scored 28 (the highest possible score). Individuals were separated into four groups (married men, married women, single men, and single women). Each individual's scores on each variable were inserted into the equation, along with the appropriate imputed knowledge score (0 or 28, depending on which analysis was being conducted) and the corresponding interaction terms for knowledge with the other variables. This led to an estimated attitude score for each person. These estimates were aggregated (as means) for each group and then plotted on a graph. The opinion scale, arrayed along the vertical axis, is based on factor scores. Thus, the mean score for the sample is 0, and scores are based on their deviation from the sample mean (for example, a score of 1.0 is one standard deviation above the sample mean).[23]

The results of our first analysis are presented in Figure 1.3. Among the least informed citizens there are only modest differences in do-

Figure 1.3. **Impact of Knowledge on Opinion, by Sex and Marital Status.**

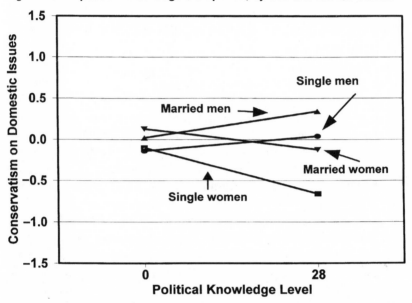

Source: 1992 National Election Study.
Note: Knowledge scale ranges from 0 (lowest possible score) to 28 (highest possible score).

mestic political opinion among members of four groups (married men, married women, single men, single women). As knowledge increases, however, both single and married men become slightly more conservative, while married women move slightly in the liberal direction and single women become quite a bit more liberal. These changes lead to a clear gender and marriage gap on domestic welfare issues among knowledgeable citizens. Significantly, a "fully informed" citizenry would have collective consequences, resulting in a public opinion environment that is more ideologically diverse and slightly more liberal (a shift of −0.05 on the standardized scale).

Knowledge also promoted greater gender differences on the issue of abortion (Figure 1.4). On a four-issue abortion index, the overall attitudes of men and women were about the same, but as women become more knowledgeable (other factors being equal) they also become more supportive of abortion rights. Significantly, knowledge also promotes greater support for abortion rights among men—a pattern that could result from more knowledgeable men believing that a woman's right to choose is also

Figure 1.4. **Impact of Knowledge on Opinion, by Sex.**

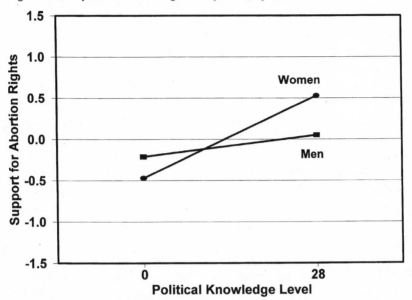

Source: 1992 National Election Study.
Note: Knowledge scale ranges from 0 (lowest possible score) to 28 (highest possible score).

in their own interest, or believing that the right to choose is legal and/or just regardless of their own interests. Although the effect for men is quite weak, it highlights the fact that increased knowledge need not always lead to movement in opposite directions among the groups in question. Nonetheless, because of the difference in the *rate* of change among women and men as knowledge rises, their *relative* position changes from one in which women are slightly more conservative than men to one in which women are considerably more liberal. The collective impact of a fully informed citizenry would be to shift the mean for attitudes on abortion in a liberal direction (from 0 to +0.30 on our scale).

Gender, Knowledge, and Issue-Consistent Voting

The formation of opinions based on an individual's (or group's) interests is only one step in the process by which citizens attempt to influence public policy. For opinions to result in real collective pressure on government, they must guide the citizen's political behavior, most typically (and perhaps consequentially) through the evaluation and selection of public officials. Political knowledge is critical to this process, because voters must be aware both of their own interests and of what the candidates and parties stand for. In short, there must be consistency between citizens' opinions on issues and the votes they cast.[24]

To gauge the extent of issue-consistent voting among men and women, we regressed the two-party vote choice in 1992 (using logistic regression) on three issue scales: the domestic issue index used above, a comparable index for foreign and military issues, and self-identified political ideology. The extent to which these attitudes allow us to predict the vote, as measured by the pseudo r-squared of the regression (Hagle and Mitchell 1992), is a simple measure of issue voting. The analysis was conducted separately for men and women, both for the whole sample and for individuals within each of four quartiles based on political knowledge level (Table 1.6).

The overall pseudo r-squared for men was 0.65; for women it was only 0.51. Thus, in the sample as a whole, men are somewhat more likely than women to use their political attitudes as a basis for choosing between candidates. But this difference is almost entirely a result of men's higher level of political knowledge: comparing men and women within each quartile of knowledge, the pseudo r-squares are much more similar. They are slightly higher for women in two quartiles, and higher for men in two. It is also noteworthy, in light of the analysis of the gender gap in opinions, that in the highest quartile of knowledge women were much more likely to vote for Bill Clinton than were men; in the lowest quartile of knowledge, women were less likely than men to do so.

Conclusion

In this chapter we have demonstrated that men are substantially better informed than women about national politics and government. This difference was seen in three national surveys covering a range of topics including civics, current issues, political leaders, and partisan alignments. In each of the surveys, the median score for men was near the seventy-fifth percentile for women. Furthermore, this gap has remained surprisingly consistent over time, though we found evidence of some reduction on some measures in very recent years.

Controlling for variables known to be associated with political

Table 1.6

Issue-Consistent Voting, 1992, by Sex and Political Knowledge

	Men	Women
All respondents	0.65	0.51
Lowest quartile of knowledge	0.12	0.15
2nd quartile of knowledge	0.51	0.46
3rd quartile of knowledge	0.78	0.72
Highest quartile of knowledge	0.80	0.82

Source: 1992 National Election Study.
Note: Entries are the pseudo r-squared statistics for logistic regression analyses predicting vote choice based on voters' issue positions.

knowledge—education, income, type of employment, political efficacy and engagement, and the like—reduced the gender difference in knowledge but did not eliminate it. Consistent with both political and gender socialization arguments, however, gender differences in knowledge are much smaller when the subject matter is arguably of special relevance to women. Perhaps most significantly, we found no evidence of a gender gap in knowledge of local politics, an arena in which both structural and psychological barriers to women are less formidable than at the national level, and in which the political agenda is likely to be seen as more relevant to women.

Finally, we presented evidence that political knowledge affects a citizen's ability to identify her and his interests. Equally important, knowledge is essential for citizens to connect their interests (in the form of their opinions) with their political participation. To the extent that women are less knowledgeable politically than are men, women will be less effective in pursuing their interests in the political system.

The application of political science's traditional criteria for political engagement to the matter of gender differences has occasioned considerable controversy (Carroll and Zerilli 1993). Many feminist scholars argue that mainstream political science ignores women in politics, and when it does not ignore them, finds their behavior deficient in one or more aspects (Goot and Reid 1984; Welch 1977; Sapiro 1983; Jones 1988; Morgen and Bookman 1988). A common thread through these critiques of political science is the arbitrary distinction between the public and private spheres. According to this view, as long as activities conducted within the private sphere are not regarded as political, women will continue to be judged as less political (and less politically sophisticated) than men. In turn, such judgments raise issues that ". . . have to do with changing women and adapting them to public life, rather than changing politics to accommodate the multiplicity and vitality of women's voices" (Jones 1988, 24).

This argument has obvious relevance to the analyses presented in this chapter. Our findings regarding knowledge of gender-relevant issues and knowledge about local politics can be viewed as empirical confirmation for feminist critiques of how national politics is defined and conducted. Nonetheless, the bulk of our findings suggests many of the normative conclusions derided by the feminist scholars cited above. Without denying the legitimacy of much of this feminist critique, we would argue that there are real consequences of women's relatively lower levels of knowledge regarding national, mainstream politics. Jane Mansbridge has argued persuasively that some political issues can be settled only through formal, legalistic, and adversarial processes (Mansbridge 1983). For these issues, traditional political methods and traditional political resources are necessary for effective action. In her recent book, *Fire With Fire*, Naomi Wolf writes:

> The late feminist poet Audre Lorde wrote that the master's tools would never dismantle the master's house. But the electoral process, the press, and money are among the master's tools . . . [I]t is *only* the master's tools that can dismantle the master's house. (1993, 54)

Knowledge of politics is essential for the effective use of the master's tools.

Notes

1. Portions of this chapter were adapted from the authors' earlier work on gender and knowledge published in *What Americans Know About Politics and Why It Matters* (1996). The data and analyses have been updated.

2. It should be noted, however, that much of this "information-processing" literature uses measures of political knowledge as an indicator of cognitive ability rather than of stored knowledge that is recalled for use in subsequent political decision making (see Lodge, McGraw, and Stroh 1989). Our own approach is to conceptualize "political knowledge" as a substantive *resource* rather than a cognitive trait.

3. An extended discussion of issues in the measurement of political knowledge in general, and the development of our national survey in particular, can be found in Delli Carpini and Keeter (1993).

4. More specifically, these items tapped two important aspects of "the rules

of the game" in the United States: political and economic processes (e.g., knowing how the veto process works, or knowing what a recession is); and individual rights (e.g., knowing what rights are protected by the First Amendment). They also tapped the two main components of "the substance of politics": domestic affairs (e.g., knowing what the "Superfund" is, or how much of the federal budget is spent on Social Security), and foreign affairs (e.g., knowing about the U.S.-Soviet arms agreement). And they tapped both the individual (e.g., knowing who your Senators are) and the organizational (e.g., knowing which party controls the House) aspects of "the people and players" of national politics. In addition (and following Berelson, Lazarsfeld, and McPhee 1954) these items attempted to gauge citizens' knowledge of the past in each of these three domains (knowing when women were granted the right to vote, knowing what the New Deal was, knowing the party of Harry Truman, and so forth). Finally, the questions varied in both their degree of difficulty (as demonstrated by the marginal frequencies) and their format (e.g., multiple choice, open-ended, and so forth). In addition, questions asked about facts that were either likely to be learned in the classroom or that required monitoring the changing political landscape.

5. The appropriateness of a simple additive index depends not only on the validity of the individual items from which the index is constructed, but also on the dimensionality of the construct to be measured. Elsewhere (Delli Carpini and Keeter 1992; 1993) we have reported on an extensive analysis of the dimensionality of political knowledge. Despite the reasonable assumption that citizens would manifest specialization in the types of political facts they know, our conclusion from examining several national surveys is that knowledge about national politics is a relatively undifferentiated and unidimensional phenomenon. While theoretically meaningful subdimensions of knowledge can be discerned (e.g., some citizens, principally partisans, are knowledgeable about matters relating to the political parties), a unidimensional model usually provides an adequate representation of the structure found in surveys of the mass public. The chief exception to this is knowledge of local politics, which, while related, appears to be relatively distinct from knowledge of national politics. This exception is of considerable importance to the study of gender and knowledge, as we discuss later in this chapter. Zaller's (1986) analysis of knowledge items on the 1985 NES pilot survey also concluded that a unidimensional model of knowledge is appropriate. For somewhat different perspectives, see Iyengar (1990) and Bennett (1990).

6. We examined this measure for evidence of a gender-of-interviewer bias. In the aggregate, female respondents received comparable ratings from male and female interviewers in the preelection survey, but received somewhat lower ratings from female than male interviewers in the postelection survey ($p < .05$). In any event, the potential magnitude of this bias would be small because men conducted only 13 percent of the interviews. However, the interviewer rating was very highly correlated with the rest of the knowledge scale (which was based on answers to factual questions).

7. Because the index uses items asked on both the preelection and postelection waves of the survey, the actual sample size for our analysis is 1,534. There are 1,714 total cases in the data set, but some respondents were not reinterviewed in the postelection wave.

8. The items are sorted by the odds-ratio, which shows the ratio of the odds that a man will correctly answer to the odds that a woman will do so. This statistic corrects for the "floor" and "ceiling" effects that occur when comparing percentage differences in very difficult or very easy items.

9. Nearly identical distributions were found using knowledge indixes constructed from the 1990 NES and 1991 NES pilot surveys (which included civics knowledge items), and from the 1992 NES survey.

10. See Delli Carpini and Keeter (1991) for a discussion of the data sets and the methodological issues involved making these comparisons over time.

11. Kessel (1992) has used the open-ended questions as a knowledge measure, and provides a defense of such use. Elsewhere, we found the open-ended items to be fairly strongly correlated with a knowledge scale similar to the 1988 NES index (Delli Carpini and Keeter 1993).

12. The model is linear and recursive, although we recognize that political knowledge not only depends upon but also influences some of the attitudinal variables, and that the effects on knowledge may not be linear in all instances.

13. The independent variables drawn from the 1996 NES data included sex, race (coded as black and nonblack), region (coded as south and nonsouth), age, education, politically impinged occupation, income, strength of party identification, political trust, efficacy (5 items), media use (4 items), attention to politics (2 items), and discussion of politics. Details about coding are available from the authors.

14. Truly capturing "structural and situational" differences through surveys is obviously a difficult task. For example, women and men, even those in similar structural situations, often do different things with their time, and much of the difference results from the sexual division of labor. The 1991 Virginia survey on reading and TV viewing habits (referred to earlier) found that a similar proportion of women and men reported engaging in other activities while watching television news or reading the newspaper. *What* they were doing was highly gender-specific, however: 32 percent of women were cooking, cleaning, or caring for children while watching television news, compared with only 12 percent of men (who were more likely to be eating or reading). Such differences presumably have consequences for the comparative level of political engagement of women and men.

15. Doris Graber observed substantial gender differences in her subjects' reported childhood socialization to politics, with men able to recall far more specific politically relevant incidents than women (Graber 1988, 134; for a related argument and evidence see Rapoport 1982; 1985; also see Jennings and Niemi 1981; Orum et al. 1974).

The "legacy" is not simply a matter of women's socialization, of course. Ample evidence exists that women continue to confront resistance from men when they take part in politics (e.g., Schumaker and Burns 1988; Mattei 1998). Such experiences also have socializing effects by lowering one's sense of efficacy.

16. We found similar patterns in other questions about abortion in the 1989 Survey of Political Knowledge.

17. We collected data from four surveys, including three we conducted in the Richmond, Virginia, metropolitan area. The most extensive of these was a 1991 survey of 804 residents in the city of Richmond. This survey included eight knowledge items, four on national and four on local politics. The local items included explaining how the city council and the mayor are selected, and naming the city manager and the superintendent of schools. Another Richmond city survey conducted in 1990 also included the item on how the mayor is selected, asked who was the incumbent, and asked about exposure to news of a dispute over the placement of a monument to civil rights leaders. A survey of suburban Chesterfield county (in the Richmond metro area) included four national knowledge items and four local items. The local items included naming the local U.S. representative

and county school superintendent, stating whether the county imposes an environmental impact fee on developers, and stating which party has a majority on the county Board of Supervisors. In addition to these local surveys, the 1987 General Social Survey conducted by the National Opinion Research Center at the University of Chicago asked respondents to name the head of their local school system, their U.S. representative, and their governor.

18. Given the similarities between women and African Americans in the obstacles each faced in achieving full rights of citizenship in the United States, much of what we have found about the gender gap in political knowledge may also apply to the race gap (Delli Carpini and Keeter 1996).

19. More controversially, these differences have also been attributed to socialization and even biological differences between men and women that lead the latter to be more "nurturing" in their approach to domestic social issues (see Tolleson-Rinehart 1992, 1–17).

20. The domestic issues index was a factor score scale of support for or opposition to government spending and action on seven domestic issues including government services and spending, health insurance, government guarantee of a job and good standard of living, government spending on food stamps, assisting the unemployed, assisting blacks, and helping the public schools. Alpha for the scale was .65. The adjusted r-squared of the regression predicting attitudes with personal characteristics and knowledge was .27.

21. See Bartels (1990) for a similar analysis of voting behavior. Our list of demographic and personal variables is quite similar to his.

22. Because the estimates are derived from a linear model, it is necessary to compute only the endpoints; all intermediate points will fall on a straight line connecting the two endpoints.

23. For a fuller discussion of the methodology for this analysis, see Delli Carpini and Keeter 1996, Appendix 5.

24. We recognize that there are many definitions of "issue voting." But all of them have in common the notion that issue voting requires citizens to choose candidates primarily on the basis of issues rather than candidate personal qualities, generalized feelings about the status quo, or idiosyncratic factors. We also do not deny the importance of candidate personal qualities as a criterion for casting a vote. We simply wish to demonstrate differences across groups in the extent to which vote choices are related to opinions on issues.

References

Barber, James David. 1973. *Citizen Politics*. 2nd ed. Chicago: Markham Publishing.

Bartels, Larry M. 1990. "Public Opinion and Political Interests." Paper delivered at the annual meeting of the Midwest Political Science Association, Chicago.

Bennett, Linda L.M., and Stephen Earl Bennett. 1989. "Enduring Gender Differences in Political Interest: The Impact of Socialization and Political Dispositions." *American Politics Quarterly* 17(1): 105–122.

Bennett, Stephen E. 1988. "Know-Nothings Revisited: The Meaning of Political Ignorance Today." *Social Science Quarterly* 69(2): 476–490.

———. 1990. "The Dimensions of Americans' Political Information." Presented at the annual meeting of the American Political Science Association, San Francisco.

Bennett, Stephen Earl, and Linda L.M. Bennett. 1992. "From Traditional to Modern Conceptions of Gender Equality in Politics: Gradual Change and Lingering Doubts." *Western Political Quarterly* 45(1): 93–111.

Berelson, Bernard R., Paul F. Lazarsfeld, and William N. McPhee. 1954. *Voting: A Study of Opinion Formation in a Presidential Campaign*. Chicago: University of Chicago Press.

Bourque, Susan, and Jean Grossholtz. 1984. "Politics an Unnatural Practice: Political Science Looks at Female Participation." In *Women and the Public Sphere: A Critique of Sociology and Politics*, ed. Janet Siltanen and Michelle Stanworth, pp. 55–76. London: Hutchinson.

Brady, Henry E., and Stephen Ansolabehere. 1989. "The Nature of Utility Functions in Mass Publics." *American Political Science Review* 83(1, March): 143–163.

Carroll, Susan J., and Linda M.G. Zerilli. 1993. "Feminist Challenges to Political Science." In *Political Science: The State of the Discipline II*, ed. Ada W. Finifter. Washington, DC: American Political Science Association.

Connolly, William E. 1972. "On 'Interests' in Politics." *Politics and Society* 2(4): 459–477.

———. 1983. *The Terms of Political Discourse*. 2nd ed. Princeton, NJ: Princeton University Press.

Converse, Philip E. 1962. "Information Flow and the Stability of Partisan Attitudes." *Public Opinion Quarterly* 26(4, Winter): 578–599.

Dahl, Robert A. 1989. *Democracy and Its Critics*. New Haven, CT: Yale University Press.

Darcy, R., Susan Welch, and Janet Clark. 1987. *Women, Elections, and Representation*. New York: Longman.

Delli Carpini, Michael X., and Ester Fuchs. 1993. "The Year of the Woman: Candidates, Voters, and the 1992 Elections." *Political Science Quarterly* 108(1): 29–36.

Delli Carpini, Michael X., and Scott Keeter. 1991. "Stability and Change in the U.S. Public's Knowledge of Politics." *Public Opinion Quarterly* 55(4): 583–612.

———. 1992. "An Analysis of Information Items on the 1990 and 1991 NES Surveys: A Report to the Board of Overseers for the National Election Studies."

———. 1993. "Measuring Political Knowledge: Putting First Things First." *American Journal of Political Science* 37(4): 1179–1206.

———. 1996. *What Americans Know About Politics and Why It Matters*. New Haven, CT: Yale University Press.

Erikson, Robert S., and Kent L. Tedin. 1995. *American Public Opinion*. 5th ed. Boston: Allyn and Bacon.

Fiske, Susan T., Richard R. Lau, and Richard A. Smith. 1990. "On the Varieties and Utilities of Political Expertise." *Social Cognition* 8(1): 31–48.

Gilligan, Carol. 1982. *In a Different Voice: Psychological Theory and Women's Development*. Cambridge, MA: Harvard University Press.

Glenn, Norval. 1972. "The Distribution of Political Knowledge in the United States." In *Political Attitudes and Public Opinion*, ed. Dan Nimmo and Charles Bonjean. New York: McKay.

Goot, Murray, and Elizabeth Reid. 1984. "Women: If Not Apolitical, Then Conservative." In *Women and the Public Sphere: A Critique of Sociology and Politics*, ed. Janet Siltanen and Michelle Stanworth, pp. 122–139. London: Hutchinson.

Graber, Doris. 1988. *Processing the News*. New York: Longman.

Hagle, Timothy M., and Glenn E. Mitchell II. 1992. "Goodness of Fit Measures for Probit and Logit." *American Journal of Political Science* 36(3): 762–784.

Hamilton, Alexander, James Madison, and John Jay. [1787–88] 1961. *Federalist Papers*. Garden City, NY: Anchor Books.

Iyengar, Shanto. 1990. "Shortcuts to Political Knowledge: The Role of Selective Attention and Accessibility." In *Information and Democratic Processes*, ed. John A. Ferejohn and James H. Kuklinski, pp. 160–185. Chicago: University of Illinois Press.

Jennings, M. Kent, and Richard G. Niemi. 1981. *Generations and Politics: A Panel Study of Young Adults and Their Parents.* Princeton, NJ: Princeton University Press.

Jones, Kathleen B. 1988. "Towards the Revision of Politics." In *The Political Interests of Gender: Developing Theory and Research with a Feminist Face*, ed. Kathleen B. Jones and Anna G. Jonasdottir, pp. 11–32. Newbury Park, CA: Sage.

Junn, Jane. 1991. "Participation and Political Knowledge." In *Political Participation and American Democracy*, ed. William Crotty, pp. 193–212. New York: Greenwood Press.

Kathlene, Lyn. 1994. "Power and Influence in State Legislative Policymaking: The Interaction of Gender and Position in Committee Hearing Debates." *American Political Science Review* 88(3): 560–576.

Kessel, John. 1992. *Presidential Campaign Politics.* Pacific Grove, CA: Brooks/Cole.

Lanoue, David J. 1992. "One That Made a Difference: Cognitive Consistency, Political Knowledge, and the 1980 Presidential Debate." *Public Opinion Quarterly* 56 (Summer): 168–184.

Leighley, Jan E., and Jonathan Nagler. 1991. "Socioeconomic Class Bias in Turnout, 1972–1988: Institutions Come and Go, But the Voters Remain the Same." Presented at the annual meeting of the American Political Science Association, Washington, DC.

Lever, Janet. 1976. "Sex Differences in the Games Children Play." *Social Problems* 23(4): 478–487.

———. 1978. "Sex Differences in the Complexity of Children's Play and Games." *American Sociological Review* 43: 471–483.

Lippmann, Walter. 1955. *Essays in the Public Philosophy.* Boston: Little, Brown.

Lodge, Milton, Kathleen M. McGraw, and Patrick Stroh. 1989. "An Impression-Driven Model of Candidate Evaluation." *American Political Science Review* 83(2): 399–419.

Luskin, Robert C. 1990. "Explaining Political Sophistication." *Political Behavior* 12: 331–361.

Mansbridge, Jane J. 1983. *Beyond Adversarial Democracy.* Chicago: University of Chicago Press.

Mattei, Laura R. Winsky. 1998. "Gender and Power in American Legislative Discourse." *American Journal of Political Science* 60(2): 440–461.

McGraw, Kathleen, and Neil Pinney. 1990. "The Effects of General and Domain-Specific Expertise on Political Memory and Judgment." *Social Cognition* 8(1): 9–30.

Miller, Warren E., and the National Election Studies. 1992 and 1996. *American National Election Study, 1992; 1996: Pre- and Post-Election Survey.* Conducted by the Center for Political Studies of the Institute for Social Research, The University of Michigan. Ann Arbor, MI: Inter-university Consortium for Political and Social Research.

Moon, David. 1990. "What You Use Depends on What You Have: Information Effects on the Determinants of Electoral Choice." *American Politics Quarterly* 18(1, January): 3–24.

Morgen, Sandra, and Ann Bookman. 1988. "Rethinking Women and Politics: An Introductory Essay." In *Women and the Politics of Empowerment*, ed. Sandra Morgen and Ann Bookman, pp. 3–29. Philadelphia: Temple University Press.

Neuman, W. Russell. 1986. *The Paradox of Mass Politics: Knowledge and Opinion in the American Electorate*. Cambridge, MA: Harvard University Press.

Niemi, Richard G., and Jane Junn. 1993. "Civics Courses and the Political Knowledge of High School Seniors." Paper presented at the annual meeting of the American Political Science Association, Washington, DC, September 2–5.

Orum, Anthony M., Roberta S. Cohen, Sherri Grasmuck, and Amy W. Orum. 1974. "Sex, Socialization and Politics." *American Sociological Review* 39: 197–209.

Palfrey, Thomas R., and Keith T. Poole. 1987. "The Relationship Between Information, Ideology, and Voting Behavior." *American Journal of Political Science* 31(3, August): 511–529.

Rapoport, Ronald B. 1982. "Sex Differences in Attitude Expression: A Generational Explanation." *Public Opinion Quarterly* 46(1): 86–96.

———. 1985. "Like Mother, Like Daughter: Intergenerational Transmission of DK Response Rates." *Public Opinion Quarterly* 49: 198–208.

Sapiro, Virginia. 1983. *The Political Integration of Women*. Urbana: University of Illinois Press.

Schumaker, Paul, and Nancy Elizabeth Burns. 1988. "Gender Cleavages and the Resolution of Local Policy Issues." *American Journal of Political Science* 32(4): 1070–1095.

Shapiro, Robert Y., and Harpreet Mahajan. 1986. "Gender Differences in Policy Preferences: A Summary of Trends from the 1960s to the 1980s." *Public Opinion Quarterly* 50(1): 42–61.

Sigelman, Lee, and E. Yanarella. 1986. "Public Information on Public Issues." *Social Science Quarterly* 67(2): 402–410.

Sniderman, Paul M, Richard A. Brody, and Philip E. Tetlock. 1991. *Reasoning and Choice: Explorations in Political Psychology*. New York: Cambridge University Press.

Taeuber, Cynthia. 1991. *Statistical Handbook of Women in America*. Phoenix, AZ: Oryx Press.

Tannen, Deborah. 1990. *You Just Don't Understand: Women and Men in Conversation*. New York: Ballantine Books.

Tolleson-Rinehart, Sue. 1992. *Gender Consciousness and Politics*. New York: Routledge.

Verba, Sidney. 1990. "Women in American Politics." In *Women, Politics, and Change*, ed. Louise A. Tilly and Patricia Gurin, pp. 555–572. New York: Russell Sage Foundation.

Weisberg, Herbert F. 1987. "The Demographics of a New Voting Gap: Marital Differences in American Voting." *Public Opinion Quarterly* 51(3): 335–343.

Welch, Susan. 1977. "Women as Political Animals." *American Journal of Political Science* 21(4): 711–730.

Wolf, Naomi. 1993. *Fire With Fire*. New York: Random House.

Zaller, John. 1986. "Analysis of Information Items in the 1985 NES Pilot Study." A Report to the Board of Overseers for the National Election Studies.

———. 1991. "Information, Values, and Opinion." *American Political Science Review* 85(4): 1215–1237.

———. 1992. *The Nature and Origins of Mass Opinion*. New York: Cambridge University Press.

2

Are Moral Voices Gendered?
Care, Rights, and Autonomy in Reproductive Decision Making

Eric Plutzer

> If men were angels, no government would be necessary. If angels were to
> govern men, neither external nor internal controls would be necessary. In
> framing a government which is to be administered by men over men, the
> great difficulty lies in this: you must first enable the government to control
> the governed; and in the next place oblige it to control itself.
>
> —James Madison, *Federalist 51*

James Madison's skepticism, especially that concerning the competency of citizens to govern themselves, was shared by the other founders and is an enduring dimension of U.S. political culture. As a result, a core component of American political thought is the belief that citizens require a structure of incentives and punishments, codified into law, in order to not only protect the fruits of their labor and pursue happiness but also to make wise personal choices and contribute to the collective good.

In spite of its influential pedigree, however, this pessimistic strain in American political thought has never held complete sway. The belief in human perfectibility and the potential for self-governance, as reflected in early Puritan efforts (e.g., Winthrop's sermon on Christian charity; the Mayflower Compact; New England town meetings) provide a continuing counterpoint to skepticism and lingering fears about self-governance. Indeed, writers from de Tocqueville to the present have observed that voluntary civic behavior is a distinguishing characteristic, and strength, of the American political system.

As a result, much debate about public policy in the United States is really an argument about the competency and capacity of citizens and political actors to make unregulated choices. For the most fundamental political choice, the vote, we are all familiar with the struggles to extend the franchise to African Americans (Fifteenth Amendment), women (Nineteenth Amendment) and those as young as eighteen years old (Twenty-sixth Amendment). In each instance, the debate concerned the competency of specific groups of citizens to choose wisely and responsibly. In each case skeptics relied on stereotypes and biases in coming to the conclusion that extending the franchise would have negative, even disastrous, consequences for American democracy.

Likewise, in the realm of public policy we ask if citizens can make competent and moral judgments in virtually any imaginable context. In some cases, such as laws that deter insider stock trading, false advertising, or environmental pollution, the regulations seek to eliminate the worst effects of unprincipled self-interest. In many others, especially those concerning alcohol, drugs, and sexuality, we debate whether citizens can make mature and sensible choices in the absence of laws and sanctions. In many instances, we divide the citizenry as when we restrict alcohol consumption and availability for those younger than twenty-one years of age but assume that older adults can make wise choices unfettered by the government.

In no policy area has the judgment of citizens been more scrutinized than in the case of abortion policy. Indeed, the forces fighting for unlimited freedom to abortion characterize the issue in terms of the competency of women (in consultation with their physicians) to make appropriate, moral choices without any interference from the state. Abortion opponents, in contrast, view the availability of legal abortion as a temptation to morally questionable women (and men) to engage in behaviors which are not merely wrong but which also poison the collective culture (see Luker 1984; Ginsburg 1984).

The abortion debate also taps into longstanding debates about women's competency as citizens and therefore echoes concerns voiced during the decades-long struggle for women's voting rights. Not only politicians, but (as Flammang 1997 documents) political scientists until well into the 1960s have viewed women as less competent than men to act responsibly in the civic arena, whether as voters or office holders. Indeed, the emergence of the field of women and politics was in large part a challenge to the practice within conventional political science to treat women as less able to make responsible choices. Although the pro-life movement would like to eliminate entirely the possibility of

choice, most regulations enacted by states have been intended by lawmakers to help women make *better* choices by requiring that they
consult with others, take more time to think over their decision, or
demonstrate their competence to choose on their own to a judge.

Seen in this light, the current abortion controversy raises a series of
related questions—questions that ultimately take us to core assumptions about the concepts of sex and gender, and their impact on the
U.S. political system.

- When faced with an unwanted or unexpected pregnancy, how do
  women (and men) actually think about the choices facing them?
- In what sense do moral considerations come into play when an
  individual makes an abortion choice? And what might this suggest
  about women's capacities for autonomy and the need for laws that
  regulate the availability of abortion in the United States?
- Is personal morality gendered? Here I raise the possibility that
  men and women hear a different "moral voice" than men. The
  assertion of multiple "moral voices" by Carol Gilligan in her land-
  mark *In a Different Voice* has influenced the field of gender and
  politics since its publication in 1982. Yet this influence has been
  quite superficial in empirical political research. I argue that the
  full implications of Gilligan's work for political science and especially for gender and politics have often been misunderstood
  and applied inappropriately.
- If the notion of a male (or masculine) and a female (or feminine)
  moral voice is valid, what implications should this have for the
  study of the gender gap, of women as political leaders, and for
  democratic theory?

In this chapter, I try to provide a preliminary answer to each of
these questions. I begin by briefly reviewing Gilligan's theory of a
different voice. I then report on a study that provides a window on
how women approached a specific moral dilemma—whether or not to
tell their partner or husband about their pregnancy and their consideration of abortion.

This study's unique data provide a more complex picture about gender and moral reasoning than most students of politics appreciate. I
argue that this more complex picture provides an opportunity to enrich
the field of gender and politics and I discuss implications for several

key research areas. In particular, the results speak to the ways in which we think about "gender gaps" of various kinds—differences in voting, differences in the legislative and leadership behaviors of men and women, differences in policy preferences.

Carol Gilligan's *In A Different Voice*

The 1982 publication of *In A Different Voice* was a watershed in gender politics. In order to understand why, it is essential to understand how developmental psychologists studied moral reasoning in the 1970s and 1980s. Psychologists would pose a hypothetical moral dilemma for each subject participating in a study. A typical (and the most famous) protocol is described by Gilligan as follows.

> . . . a man named Heinz considers whether or not to steal a drug which he cannot afford to buy in order to save the life of his wife . . . the description of the dilemma itself, Heinz's predicament, the wife's disease, the druggist's refusal to lower his prices, is followed by the question, "Should Heinz steal the drug?" The reasons for and against stealing the drug are then explored through a series of questions . . . designed to reveal the underlying structure of moral thought. (Gilligan 1982, 25–26)

Subjects' detailed answers are then carefully examined—usually by two or more coders—and scored on a six-point developmental scale developed by Lawrence Kohlberg. Gilligan reports that girls and women tended to score lower on measures of moral development than boys and men. Rather than try to "explain away" this "gender gap" (for example, by multivariate analyses that consider factors such as education, demographic variables, and the like) Gilligan shook up not only developmental psychology but all of the social sciences and humanities by arguing that the theory of moral development then in fashion, and Kohlberg's six-point development scale, was systematically biased against women and girls.

She argued that boys tended to be given higher scores on Kohlberg's six-stage developmental model because they were more likely than girls to use abstract reasoning and appeal to impersonal laws and rights as they tried to deal with hypothetical moral dilemmas. Girls, in comparison, tended to focus on how various solutions to ethical dilemmas would affect the lives and relationships of the people involved. Even quite intelligent girls would not follow the series of probing questions to what was regarded as the "best" and most mature way to reason through moral choices.

Gilligan argued that women tend to hear a different "moral voice," one that emphasizes care, attachments, and personal relationships. Moral reasoning is *gendered*, Gilligan explained, because of the different socialization patterns of men and women and, in particular, boys' drive for separation from their primary caregiver because this is usually the mother (this aspect of Gilligan's account derives largely from the work of Nancy Chodorow 1978). Gilligan argued that the feminine mode of moral reasoning, whose "moral voice" emphasized an ethic of care and the nurture of relationships, was as valid as abstract reasoning and appeals to impersonal rules, laws, and norms of justice.

It would be difficult to overstate the influence that Gilligan had on gender studies. Even in 1998, sixteen years after initial publication, the Social Science Citation Index shows 158 published articles citing Gilligan's 1982 book; since publication the total number of citations exceeds 5,000. Different aspects of Gilligan's efforts have resonated with different scholars. Perhaps most important among these was the charge that models and standards based on men and devised by male social scientists were invalid models to apply uncritically to women (Steurnagel 1987 develops this argument extensively in the context of political science). Second, the idea that men and women's thinking could be fundamentally different seemed to provide one compelling explanation for a variety of sex differences observed in daily life. As a result, Gilligan's theory was invoked as a potential explanation for almost every imaginable sex difference—everything from sex differences in corporate management styles to sex differences in the reasoning of judges (an extensive literature summarized by Susan Mezey's contribution to this volume). Third, many social scientists were inspired by the idea that by listening to women speak, and listening without an implicit male standard in mind, new and exciting ways of looking at the world could be developed.

The influence on political scientists who study gender and politics has been substantial. Reviewing every article published in the journal *Women and Politics* from 1984 to 1998 we find at least thirty-seven citing *In a Different Voice* (more than two every year). A similar number of articles citing Gilligan's work has appeared in political science's general journals as well.

However, the "use" of Gilligan by political scientists has been controversial. More than a decade ago, Virginia Sapiro observed that "Gilligan's name now seems to be invoked whenever anyone makes note of any gender difference in thinking" (1987, 22; a similar point is made by Tronto 1987, 88). If anything, a review of recent articles in political science's leading journals suggests an acceleration of this uncritical invocation of Gilligan's research.

In addition, Sapiro pointed to a fundamental misreading of Gilligan: the confusion between "modes of reasoning and the conclusions people reach as a result of their reasoning" (1987, 23). Sapiro recognized that, like the psychologists she criticized, Gilligan was unconcerned whether her subjects determined that Heinz should steal the drug or not. Either choice could be justified by an ethic of care, by an appeal to universal rights and justice norms, or even by less mature forms of moral reasoning.

By analogy, political scientists seeking to build on Gilligan's work should be unconcerned with sex differences in party identification or presidential voting (the "gender gap"), with differences in roll-call votes of male and female legislators, or other discrete outcomes. Rather, the potential for enriching empirical political research lies in the observation that citizens might employ different moral paths to reach the *same* conclusions. To my knowledge, no empirical study undertaken by political scientists has deliberately attempted to explore moral choices in this way. Moreover, it is *possible* that in some circumstances one mode of moral reasoning would lead to different choices than the other. But we currently have little basis for developing a systematic theory of when and where this might occur.

Yet these are exactly the types of studies that can integrate the study of gender and politics with questions of citizen competence that are so central to democratic theory. One "traditional" assumption is that women tend to be more emotional and less rational than men. If rationality is equated with "better" (at least in some circumstances) then this conclusion can be used to justify additional laws and regulations in domains of special relevance to women, such as reproductive choices and job discrimination.

In the remainder of this chapter, I report on a study completed in the mid-1980s that, although designed to answer specific policy questions, provides an opportunity to explore the modes of reasoning that women employ in a non-hypothetical context. This study was motivated by the consideration of laws that would have required women to notify the man who shared responsibility for the pregnancy. For many women, the choice to tell their partner was an easy one. But many women struggled with this choice and described their reasoning to counselor-interviewers who collected the data. These women's accounts provide an unusual window on difficult choices that many citizens and government officials believe should be strictly regulated.

"Did You Tell Your Partner?": The Hope Clinic Study

In the early 1980s, many state legislatures were debating laws that would place restrictions on women's reproductive decisions. Women seeking abortions might have had to get permission from their husband (if married), or their mother or father (if under eighteen) before terminating a pregnancy. Less stringent versions of these laws required only "consultation" or "notification," although some critics argued that in certain coercive settings (e.g., abusive relationships) consultation might be little different from getting permission. Outside of state legislatures, pro-life attorneys were offering "Father's Rights Litigation Kits" to men intent on preventing their wives, girlfriends, or acquaintances from terminating pregnancies that these men shared responsibility for creating. Articles in well-known magazines, ranging from *Glamour* (Weiss 1989) to the *New York Times Magazine* (Black 1982), focusing on men's rights and men's perspective in the abortion choice were popular at the time. Sociologists Arthur Shostak and Gary McClouth wrote a book (1984) documenting the dynamics and emotions of men's abortion experiences and the authors were invited to appear on major talk shows.

It was in this context that Barbara Ryan, Anne Baker, and I undertook a large study of women who had chosen abortion as their desired outcome. The study was carried out with the cooperation of the management and staff of the Hope Clinic For Women, a full service family planning center in Granite City, Illinois. Granite City is a medium-sized industrial city ten miles east of St. Louis. A majority of the clients of the clinic came from towns and cities within the St. Louis metropolitan area. For a variety of reasons, including limited abortion services in bordering states (especially second trimester procedures), clients also traveled from Indiana, Iowa, Kentucky, and Tennessee.

A three-part survey was administered to patients at the clinic from January through August 1984. The first part of the survey was a brief self-administered questionnaire, which 2,337 patients completed in the waiting room. This part of the questionnaire contained most of the basic background and demographic questions and did not include any sensitive questions.

The second part of the questionnaire was administered by clinic counselors during the routine pre-procedure counseling session. The purpose of this counseling session, on the day of the planned procedure, is to ensure that the woman has no second thoughts, that she is psychologically prepared, and to make sure that she is not being coerced by anybody into a decision she opposes. As a result, this counseling session would normally include questions about the co-conceiver and the woman's discussions and interactions with him. Consequently, the study questions could be incorporated into the normal flow of discussion. The counseling sessions normally lasted from fifteen to forty minutes and were extended by no more than five or ten minutes as a result of the study. This portion of the survey ascertained information concerning the interaction between the client and the co-conceiver and her perceptions of that interaction. The third part of the questionnaire was self-administered at the close of the counseling session and asked a series of attitude questions that were deemed too sensitive to be completed in the waiting room in the company of close friends or relatives.

All clinic clients during the study period completed the first part of the survey while a sample of 506 was selected to complete the latter two parts. For the purpose of this chapter, we can treat those data as two subsamples: one that includes *every* woman who did not tell the co-conceiver ($N = 243$) and a second subsample ($N = 263$) that includes approximately one in every nine women who did inform the co-conceiver about the pregnancy (for details on the sampling procedures, see Ryan and Plutzer 1989).

In reporting on the study, we use the term *co-conceiver* because, as I will show shortly, the men who shared responsibility for the pregnancy are so diverse that they cannot be easily subsumed by terms like "partner," "lover," or "significant other."

The data I report here are based primarily on open-ended questions. However, the answers were not recorded verbatim but rather through the use of a long list of pre-coded answers which were anticipated on the basis of two extensive pre-tests and lengthy discussions with the counseling staff of the clinic. Multiple responses were permitted in all

open-ended questions. While open-ended questions entail certain limitations, we preferred them because they permitted the women we studied to speak for themselves, without having to conform to choices
given to them by the researchers. The method of coding, however,
permits us to meaningfully classify the large number of responses.

All participants were provided with study information in writing
when they arrived and then again orally as the counseling session began. All women were told that participation was voluntary but only 4
percent declined to participate. The 96 percent response rate is high,
perhaps too high, indicating that in a clinical setting patients do not
feel they have the power to decline, but consistent with response rates
approaching 100 percent in similar studies (e.g., McCormick 1975;
Zimmerman 1984).

Study Participants and Their Choices

Before moving to a discussion of the two subsamples it is helpful to
describe some characteristics of the larger sample of all women obtaining an abortion at Hope Clinic, described in Table 2.1. On most
important background characteristics, the larger sample of 2,337
women closely resembles estimates of the national profile of abortion
patients. About two-thirds of the clinic's clients had never been married
while a little more than a fifth were divorced or separated. Only 12
percent of the clinic clients were married at the time of their abortion.
Among those who were unmarried, most were in fairly close relationships including those engaged to be married (8.3 percent), living together (9 percent), or "going steady" (41.3 percent). A smaller group
of about 13 percent had recently broken up with the man involved.
This group includes those who divorced after conception, those with
broken engagements, those who had moved apart after living together,
and those who had previously "gone steady" but had since broken up.
Only 14.2 percent described their relationship as casual and consensual
(about half of these had broken up).

An extended portion of the interview concerned the decision to tell
or not tell the partner or co-conceiver about the pregnancy. We also
asked about any discussion of the abortion or abortion alternatives. In
all, 89.5 percent of the women told the co-conceiver of the pregnancy
and 82.5 percent of the men knew of the woman's decision to have an
abortion. The small discrepancy between the two figures is based in

Table 2.1

Respondent's Marital Status and Current Relationship with Co-conceiver
(percent)

Marital status	
Never married	65.5
Divorced/Separated	22.3
Married	12.0
Widowed	0.3
Weighted N = 505	
Current relationship with co-conceiver	
Going steady	41.3
Married	11.3
Living together	9.0
Engaged	8.3
Casual relationship; no longer seeing one another	8.1
Had gone steady; no longer seeing one another	7.6
Casual/dating and still seeing one another	6.1
Living together; no longer seeing each other	2.0
Ex-husband	1.8
Had been engaged; no longer seeing one another	1.4
Divorced after conception	1.2
Raped (those not classified in other categories)	0.9
Extramarital affair	0.8
Weighted N = 497	

part on some women's decision not to tell the co-conceiver about the abortion (at least not until after the procedure) and the tendency for some men to leave the woman on learning of the pregnancy.

The nature of the relationship was a crucial factor in determining the likelihood of confiding. Table 2.2 reports the percentage of women who told their partner, broken down by a detailed classification of relationships. The categories are ordered from most to least likely to tell and this reveals that women who were no longer involved and those in casual relationships were least likely to inform the man involved. Even so, most women in every category confided and discussed the situation with the co-conceiver. We then asked women a series of questions about why they made the choice they did and whether they had mixed feelings along the way. These questions, admittedly, only scratch the surface of the ethical considerations that characterized these women's choices. As in all studies that are carried out in a clinical setting, our main concern was for the well-being of the patients. As a result, we felt that probes to elicit longer responses and more detailed

Table 2.2

Percent Telling About Pregnancy by Current Relationship

Living together	98.6
Engaged	97.4
Going steady	95.5
Married (told husband)	95.4
Ex-husband	95.2
Had been engaged; no longer seeing one another	87.4
Living together; no longer seeing each other	85.1
Divorced after conception	82.2
Casual/dating and still seeing one another	80.1
Had gone steady; no longer seeing one another	77.0
Casual relationship; no longer seeing one another	70.9
Extramarital affair (told husband)	—
Raped (excluding those counted in above categories)	—
All rapes (includes cases counted in above categories)	73.9
Weighted $N = 497$	

Note: Percentages for cells with five or fewer cases are not reported.

recollections would place an unreasonable burden on the women who participated in the study. Nevertheless, the answers provide a rich description of the variety of moral points of view that women considered during the decision-making process.

Women Who Told the Man Involved

Regardless of the choice made, we were interested in learning the reasons for that decision. We asked those who did tell, "What were your main reasons for telling him?" We allowed women to give multiple answers and the percentages of women mentioning each response are contained in Table 2.3.

What we find here is evidence of both "moral voices" and corresponding ethics. More than half (58.6 percent) of the women couched their answer in terms of the co-conceiver's "right to know." In addition, more than one-third said they felt it was "his responsibility also." These answers, focusing on rights and responsibilities, would seem to correspond most closely with Kohlberg's notion of high moral reasoning, which Gilligan claims is more characteristic of masculine thought and derives from the need for separation that characterizes male socialization.

Table 2.3

Reasons for Telling Co-conceiver (percent)

His right to know	58.6
It's his responsibility also	34.9
Why not? Why wouldn't I? I tell him everything	24.5
Needed his emotional support	19.5
Needed his financial support	16.5
Wanted to know how he felt	15.7
Needed somebody to talk to	11.9
He'd find out anyway	4.2
Hoped he would help with abortion arrangements	3.4
He knew first; was certain I was pregnant	2.7
Angry at him	2.3
Wanted him to know (to feel guilty, etc.)	1.1
Impulse	1.1
Other misc. answers	6.9
Women who told co-conceiver, $N = 261$	

On the other hand, almost 20 percent of the women mentioned, as one reason they told the co-conceiver, their need for his emotional support. In addition, almost 15 percent of the women reported that one of the reasons they told was they wanted to know how the co-conceiver felt; approximately 12 percent needed someone to talk to. These responses (about 30 percent of all confiders mentioned at least one of them) evoke Gilligan's description of an ethic of care and nurturance that derives from socialization patterns which emphasize interpersonal attachments.

Women Who Told But Had Mixed Feelings

Among those who told, sixty-one women, or 23 percent, reported having some mixed feelings about the decision. Counselors asked these women, "What reasons did you think of for not telling him?" As in all open-ended questions, interviewers were instructed to check all responses that were mentioned. The answers are reported in Table 2.4.

The most frequent type of response was an unqualified "I was afraid" (26.2 percent). Often this answer was followed by clarification such as fear of the co-conceiver's anger or verbal abuse (14.8 percent); fear of his physical abuse (8.2 percent); afraid that he would blame her for the pregnancy (11.5 percent); that he would leave and the re-

Table 2.4

Reasons Considered for Not Telling the Co-conceiver (percent)

Fear of unknown; general fear	26.2
He'd want her to have the baby	21.3
Protecting him from crisis	21.3
Fear of his anger/verbal abuse	14.8
He didn't need to know	14.8
Fear he wouldn't care	11.5
Fear he'd blame her for pregnancy	11.5
Fear of his physical abuse	8.2
Other answers, misc.	8.2
Fear he'd leave; relationship would break up	6.6
Broke up since conception	4.9
Man raped her	4.9
He would deny paternity	4.9
To avoid his influence	4.9
He'd want to get married	3.3
Felt ashamed	3.3
Fear legal revenge (e.g., custody problems)	3.3
Fear he would tell others (or use info against her)	1.6
Wants to reconcile with husband or boyfriend (not co-conceiver)	1.6
He is married (to somebody else)	1.6
Women who did tell but had mixed feelings, $N = 61$	

lationship would end (6.6 percent); or that he would seek legal revenge (3.3 percent).

Together, these can be seen as motivations for self-preservation and at least one of these was mentioned by 45 percent of the women who confided despite mixed feelings. In the few cases in which women mentioned the possibility of physical abuse, self-preservation is quite literal. In others, women are concerned with their psychological well-being and the emotional stability of the relationship. Such concerns are also reported by some of Gilligan's subjects but Gilligan is not entirely clear on where this type of thought might fit in either her or the more traditional conception of moral development.

The second most common type of response involved concern for the well-being of the partner. Twenty percent of the ambivalent confiders recounted a concern to protect their partners from a crisis of some kind. For example, in one case a woman's husband was struggling through a difficult stint in medical school and she considered sparing him the additional burden of dealing with an unplanned pregnancy. In almost all of these cases, the women were swayed by the man's right to know, seeing this as outweighing any harm that might result. Thus, these sixty-one ambivalent women overcame their fears about their own well-being or concerns about their partners and responded to the voice of rights and responsibility.

Women Who Chose Not to Tell

When clinic clients indicated that they did not tell the co-conceiver about the pregnancy, counselors asked: "What were your main reasons for not telling him?"

Responses are reported in Table 2.5 and here we see a greater variety of rationales than for women who chose to confide.

The dominant concern expressed by these women seems to be maintaining autonomy and self-preservation. More than one-third of the women mentioned, as at least one of the reasons for not telling, their assumption that the co-conceiver would want her to have the baby. In addition, the belief that the male would want to get married was mentioned by more than 17 percent of the women. In addition, we again see a wide range of fears and concerns; these include physical abuse (6.6 percent), verbal abuse (13.3 percent), and the fear he would tell others or somehow use the information against her (16.1 percent). Overall, 36 percent of the women who did not tell mentioned at least one of these fears as a reason for not telling.

The second major explanation invokes the context of the relationship. Breaking up since conception accounted for one-fourth of the responses clients gave as a reason for not telling; nearly one-third of the women felt the co-conceiver "did not need to know." Here we see evidence that women regarded the "right to know" as being conditional not only on shared responsibility for the pregnancy, but on the closeness of the relationship.

It is important, however, to remind ourselves of the general pattern of responses reported earlier in Table 2.2: that even in the most casual relationships and in all categories of broken relationships, roughly 80 percent of women confided anyway. We also see among this group of women a small group, 15 percent, who did not tell in order to protect the male from crisis—the clearest evidence of Gilligan's ethic of care.

Table 2.5

Reasons for Not Telling the Co-conceiver (percent)

He'd want her to have the baby	35.5
He didn't need to know	31.0
Broke up since conception	25.2
He'd want to get married	17.4
Fear he would tell others (or use info against her)	16.1
Protecting him from crisis	14.9
Fear of his anger/verbal abuse	13.3
Fear of unknown; general fear	9.1
Fear of his physical abuse	6.6
Fear he'd blame her for pregnancy	6.6
Fear he wouldn't care	6.2
Felt ashamed	4.5
Man raped her	4.5
Fear he'd leave; relationship would break up	4.1
Couldn't tell (e.g., co-conceiver unknown)	2.5
Wants to reconcile with husband or boyfriend (not co-conceiver)	1.7
Fear legal revenge (e.g., custody problems)	1.2
One-night stand	1.2
To avoid his influence	1.2
Other answers, misc.	3.7
Women who did not tell, $N = 242$	

Women Who Did Not Tell But Had Mixed Feelings

Of those women who did not inform the man about the pregnancy, 37 percent expressed mixed feelings. Counselors asked these clients, "What were some of the main reasons you thought of for telling him?" These data are reported in Table 2.6.

The most frequent response, mentioned by more than half the women with mixed feelings, was "his right to know." That it was "the male's responsibility also" was a response one-fourth of the women gave for having mixed feelings about not telling. Thus, the voice of rights and responsibilities played a major role in the dilemma faced by these women.

On the other hand, a substantial number of these women were tempted to tell because of concerns related to the quality of the relationship. One-fourth of the women with mixed feelings about their decision to tell reported a desire to know how the co-conceiver felt. Needing his emotional support was reported by almost 14 percent of the women, and 11.5 percent felt a need for somebody to talk to. Here

Table 2.6

Reasons Considered for Telling the Co-conceiver (percent)

His right to know	55.1
It's his responsibility also	23.0
Wanted to know how he felt	23.0
Needed his financial support	18.4
Needed his emotional support	13.8
Needed somebody to talk to	11.5
He'd find out anyway	4.6
Hoped he would marry me	3.4
Hoped he would help with abortion arrangements	2.3
Other responses	9.0
Women who did not tell co-conceiver but had mixed feelings, $N = 87$	

we see reasons that appear to be similar to those that are characteristic of the ethic of care—except that these women could be accused of being selfish.

Summary and Implications

The women who took part in the Hope Clinic study are representative of the roughly 1.1 to 1.4 million who have terminated a pregnancy each year since the early 1980s (Centers for Disease Control 1996). For many of these women—most especially those who were married, engaged, or living together—the decision to discuss the pregnancy was hardly a dilemma at all. But for many other women, the decision to bring the man involved into the discussion is a moral choice. The man's right to know or the man's responsibility for the consequences of his actions—abstract principles that can be applied to many moral dilemmas and across a wide range of circumstances—weigh heavily on the minds of most of these women. That is, in this particular context the voice of rights and responsibilities speaks quite loudly and most often decisively.

Even women who elect not to tell are pulled by the voice of rights and principles. Unlike the carefully crafted hypothetical dilemma of Heinz, his wife, and the pharmacist, real-life dilemmas may by their nature invoke one mode of reasoning more than others. As Sapiro observed, "People do not reason similarly in all situations, and some of the context-driven patterns [in reasoning mode] are gender relevant"

(1987, 23). Ironically, this particular context of reproductive decision making may be inherently structured in a way that enhances the salience or "volume" of the ethic of rights and responsibilities—which Gilligan and others associate with men and masculinity.

It therefore seems likely that men and women each carry with them the ability to reason in all ethical modes; and the particular mode invoked may be subject to manipulation and socialization. Indeed, many women concerned with control of their bodies and self-preservation nevertheless were persuaded by the idea that the co-conceiver had a right to know. This suggests that any analysis of ethical reasoning must be placed in the context of politics and culture. There are many rights that citizens do not claim (e.g., many citizens eligible for food stamps do not take advantage of this opportunity). And there are other rights, such as the right to have an attorney present during questioning by police, which were once so rarely understood that the Court required that they be explained in every instance in which they might be applicable. Today, more people are cognizant of this right and so we might expect it to be invoked routinely by those in police custody. Thus, the simple frequency with which a particular explanation is provided may say more about the culture than the reasoning style or capacity of the individual making the choice.

Although a concern with rights and responsibilities is prevalent, we see that the mode of thinking is nevertheless varied. Both moral voices are present in the minds of many women. Closer analysis of the data shows, for example, that among the women who did not tell and had mixed feelings, about 25 percent simultaneously invoked the ethic of care (e.g., sparing him from crisis) *and* the ethic of rights and responsibilities in explaining their thinking. Similarly, about a fifth of all women who told their partner gave multiple answers that reflected both modes of reasoning. These percentages almost surely understate the true proportion of women hearing both moral voices because the survey did not include explicit probes to encourage lengthy answers and multiple responses. This substantial degree of overlap should lead us to be skeptical of theories that posit essential differences between men and women. And it speaks for efforts such as Tronto's (1993) to consider how normative political theory might derive from Gilligan's ethic of care and nurturance without associating that ethic with women and femininity.

We also see in this analysis that the mode of thinking is loosely linked with the choice made—the invocation of a rights-based explanation is more associated with telling than with withholding information. In this sense, the dilemma is fundamentally different from that confronting Heinz because the decision to steal the drug (or not) can be reached through either mode of reasoning. The association between mode of reasoning and outcome is an empirical question and the answer is likely to differ in specific settings.

This should lead us to eschew hypothesizing *specific* gender gaps simply on the basis of an assumption of different modes of reasoning. It also suggests that structures of power, law, and tradition may be crucial in determining both the dominant mode of reasoning for some dilemmas, and the association between mode and outcome in others.

Indeed, we see in the data reported evidence that the way in which women reason through ethical choices depends on context. In close relationships, the "rights" of the man loom larger, but so also does the consideration that telling the man might not be the "caring" thing to do. Indeed, this suggests that the original dilemma faced by Heinz is not a neutral story but may contain elements that specifically evoke the ethic of care. We can ask ourselves how the responses of Gilligan's subjects might have differed if the person needing the expensive drug were Heinz's girlfriend, his neighbor, co-worker, or simply a stranger who confided her illness to Heinz.

The loose connection between mode of reasoning and outcome also helps place much previous literature in context. The literature on judicial decision making reviewed by Mezey in her contribution to this book serves as a good example. Many of the studies of judges were inspired by Gilligan's insights but the scholars then used a variety of different indicators for gender differences. These ranged from the actual vote (with or opposed to a particular majority), the likelihood of dissent, or the type of representation. None of these indicators is very similar to the central phenomena in Gilligan's own research: personal accounts that explain moral choices. When the mode of reasoning is highly correlated with the choice made, then looking at choices (e.g., voting with the liberal majority on a particular court) may tell us something about the moral reasoning that preceded the choice. But when situations are such that different modes can be used to get to the same outcome, then this kind of reverse reasoning is likely to give us invalid conclusions.

The Hope Clinic study also shows us that strictly moral reasoning often is complicated by imperatives toward self-preservation. This suggests an important place for discussions of *power* in studies of different modes of moral reasoning. Such concerns may not manifest themselves in the types of hypothetical scenarios on which much psychological research is based (although they are quite prominent in Gilligan's study of women who confronted an abortion dilemma). In the case of abortion restrictions in particular, a sensitivity to women's autonomy is crucial because proposed legislation may be couched in terms of rights (the rights of husbands or parents, for example), yet the effect of the law may be to reduce women's autonomy with respect to actions they might take to preserve their physical or mental health, or the quality of their intimate and familial relationships. In relationships characterized by physical or verbal abuse, these laws would have the effect of increasing the power that abusive men hold over women.

Finally, the data from this study speak to the policy questions that introduced the chapter. These data were collected in a time and place completely free of government regulations intended to promote consultation and better decision making. Had the married women been subject to a law requiring spousal notification, we see that 93 percent were in complete compliance; in research reported previously, Ryan and I show that most of the married women who did not tell their husbands provided reasons that would have qualified for a judicial bypass (Plutzer and Ryan 1987). For women in other types of long-term relationships (engaged, living together, going steady) who comprise more than 60 percent of the single women seeking abortions, we see similarly high rates of confiding.

The reasons given by these women are again frequently of the type that would make them exempt from most proposed laws. Yet even when the reasons might be deemed questionable by some, we see evidence of considerable thought and the weighing of rationales which derive from different ethical perspectives. In this sense, and given the fundamental legality of abortion, the data weigh in favor of considerable autonomy for women since they invoke the same types of concerns that would be considered by a judge who was asked to authorize an exemption from a notification requirement.

It, of course, is true that the strong proponents of abortion regulation support any laws that hinder abortion access and increase the costs to women of obtaining and physicians of providing abortion services. But most of these laws could only pass with assistance of "moderate" legislators who see the laws as providing prudent reforms that help women and physicians to make better choices. Indeed, Stetson's chapter in this volume points to key changes in rhetoric which have changed the legislative landscape in the United States. These changes are dramatic in outcome but only involve small shifts of legislators positioned near the middle of the political spectrum. As a result, the conclusion that women appear to reason through these choices carefully and use the same considerations relevant to the so-called judicial bypass, may persuade some centrists that such regulations are unnecessary or even harmful.

In a more general sense, examining the way that men and women reason through real decisions could make a substantial contribution to the way we evaluate regulations of various kinds. Similarly, such a mode of inquiry can be especially useful whenever it is claimed that one group, such as women, is somehow less able to act responsibly and carry out political and personal choices in a free society.

References

Black, Pamela. 1982. "Abortion Affects Men, Too." *New York Times Magazine*, (28 March), Sec. 6, Pt. 1.

Centers for Disease Control and Prevention. 1996. "Abortion Surveillance, 1992." *Morbidity and Mortality Weekly Report* 45 (May 17, 1996, No. SS-3). Washington: U.S. Government Printing Office.

Chodorow, Nancy. 1978. *The Reproduction of Mothering*. Berkeley: University of California Press.

Flammang, Janet A. 1997. *Women's Political Voice: How Women Are Transforming the Practice and Study of Politics*. Philadelphia: Temple University Press

Gilligan, Carol. 1982. *In a Different Voice*. Cambridge: Harvard University Press.

Ginsburg, Faye. 1984. "The Body Politic: The Defense of Sexual Restriction by Anti-abortion Activists." In *Pleasure and Danger: Exploring Female Sexuality,* ed. Carole S. Vance, pp. 173–178. Boston: Routledge and Kegan Paul.

Luker, Kristen. 1984. *Abortion and the Politics of Motherhood*. Berkeley: University of California Press.

McCormick, E. Patricia. 1975. *Attitudes Toward Abortion*. Lexington, MA: Lexington.

Plutzer, Eric, and Barbara E. Ryan. 1987. "Telling Husbands About an Abortion: An Empirical Look at Constitutional and Policy Dilemmas." *Sociology and Social Research* 71 (April): 183–189.

Ryan, Barbara, and Eric Plutzer. 1989. "When Married Women Have Abortions: Spousal Notification and Marital Interaction." *Journal of Marriage and the Family* 50 (February): 41–50.

Sapiro, Virginia. 1987. "Reflections on Reflections: Personal Ruminations." *Women and Politics* 7 (Winter): 24–25.

Shostak, Arthur B., and Gary McLouth, with Lynn Seng. 1984. *Men and Abortion: Lessons, Losses, and Love*. New York: Prager Publishers.

Steurnagel, Gertrude A. 1987. "Reflections on Women and Political Participation."
Women and Politics 7 (Winter): 3–13.

Tronto, Joan. 1993. *Moral Boundaries: A Political Argument for an Ethic of Care.*
New York: Routledge.

———. 1987. "Political Science and Caring: Or, The Perils of Balkanized Social
Science." *Women and Politics* 7 (Fall): 85–97.

Weiss, Michael J. 1989. "Equal Rights: Not for Women Only." *Glamour* (March):
276–277, 317–322.

Zimmerman, Mary K. 1984. "It Takes Two: An Examination of Contraceptive
Risk Taking and the Role of the Male Partner." Paper presented at the annual
meetings of the Midwest Sociological Society, Chicago.

3

Gender and Political Participation

M. Margaret Conway

Introduction

After two centuries of struggle to obtain equal rights, do women participate in politics at rates equal to men? To what extent do women's gender role orientations influence their patterns of political participation? To answer these questions we must first consider women's and men's patterns of political participation, then compare participation patterns among women on the basis of their gender role orientations.

A brief history of women's political participation provides background for this analysis. Until early in the twentieth century, women in the United States were denied political rights. The struggle for political rights for women began in America in the colonial period. One very early demand for political rights occurred in 1638 when Margaret Brent, a wealthy and highly respected Maryland landowner, petitioned the Maryland colonial assembly for the right to vote. She requested not one vote, but two—one as a person who met the Maryland colony's property owning requirements for the franchise, and one as the administrator of the estate of Leonard Calvert, the recently deceased governor of the Maryland colony and the brother of Lord Baltimore, the colony's proprietor. The colonial assembly responded to her request for the right to vote with a resounding no. Lord Baltimore was furious that Margaret Brent had requested the right to vote, and she was so angry at being denied the right to vote that she moved to Virginia where she became one of the wealthiest landowners in the American colonies. In some colonies a few women voted; as the colonies became states in the newly created United States of America, they drafted new laws and constitutions with the norms against political rights for women being entrenched in legal documents (Flexner and Fitzpatrick 1996).

Women's acquisition of political rights was a major focus of the first women's movement at the Seneca Falls, New York, convention held in 1848. A small group of women, whose members included Elizabeth Cady Stanton and Lucretia Mott, organized a local meeting to discuss the status of women and placed an announcement in the local paper inviting local residents to attend. The organizers drafted a Declaration of Sentiments and proposed twelve resolutions for adoption by the convention. The only controversial resolution asserted that women should have the right to vote. Stanton's husband considered the proposal so outrageous that the assembly and its supporters would be subject to public ridicule and their resolutions devalued as a consequence. Undeterred, Mrs. Stanton insisted that the right to vote must be included, as it was the key to obtaining all other rights. Also opposing the inclusion of the demand for political rights were Lucretia Mott and her husband James Mott; both believed that including political rights in the resolutions would be too controversial. The voting rights resolution was the only one that did not pass unanimously. Furthermore, many attending the meeting declined to sign the document containing the set of resolutions because that document contained the voting rights resolution (Flexner and Fitzpatrick 1996).

Prior to the ratification of the federal constitutional amendment, several states enfranchised women to vote in some or all elections. The first was Kentucky in 1838, which granted widows with school age children and living in rural areas the right to vote in school elections. By 1918, fifteen states had enfranchised women for all elections, and by 1920, an additional twelve states had enfranchised women for presidential elections (Stucker 1977). The struggle for women's right to vote culminated in 1920, when the Nineteenth Amendment to the United States Constitution guaranteeing women the legal right to vote in all elections was ratified by a sufficient number of states.

Beginning with the elections held in 1920, many supporters of woman suffrage were disheartened by the low levels of voting turnout among women. Those who had struggled for so many years to win women the right to vote could not understand why women's levels of participation in almost all other forms of political activity would continue to be lower than those of men.

In this chapter, comparisons are first drawn between the levels of participation of men and women in a variety of political activities. Then the analysis turns to a comparison of participation levels among women who have different gender role orientations. Explanations for participation rates among women are examined; these include not only differences in gender role orientations, but also a variety of other possible influences on participation patterns. Finally, the relative effects of gender role orientations and other explanatory variables are considered.

Patterns of Participation

Individuals may engage in many different types of political activity. The focus here is on three types of election related activities: voting; contributing money to a political party or a candidate; and engaging in one or more types of campaign activities.

As Tables 3.1 and 3.2 illustrate, not until sixty years after the ratification of the Nineteenth Amendment did women vote in presidential elections at rates equal to men. Not until 1986 did women's voting turnout in midterm elections equal that of men. These patterns underestimate, however, the impact of women's electoral participation, as women outnumbered men in the voting age population by more than 8.9 million in 1980 and by 8.4 million in 1996. Even with equal rates of turnout, women's impact on electoral outcomes would be magnified by their larger share of the voting age population. Furthermore, for several decades women's and men's vote choices have diverged, with women more likely to support Democratic party candidates while men have been more likely to support Republican party candidates (Clark and Clark 1996; 1999).

In addition to voting, citizens may engage in a variety of campaign activities. These include attempting to persuade others how to vote, displaying campaign signs or wearing campaign buttons, attending political meetings or campaign rallies, and working for a candidate or party. The measure of campaign participation sums the number of campaign activities in which individuals engage. As Table 3.3 indicates, from 1964 to 1996 a greater proportion of men than of women reported taking part in at least one campaign activity. For example, in 1996 39 percent of the men and 30 percent of the women participated in at least one campaign activity.[1] Men were also more likely than women to be involved in more than one type of campaign activity.

A different form of political activity is contributing money to a party or candidate. Since 1964 men are also more likely to give money to a party or candidate.[2] Between both men and women, however, the pro-

Table 3.1

Patterns of Voting Turnout by Sex, Presidential Election Years
(percentage)

Year	Men	Women
1968	70	66
1972	64	62
1976	60	59
1980	59	59
1984	59	61
1988	56	58
1992	60	62
1996	53	56

Source: U.S. Department of Commerce, Bureau of the Census, Current Population Reports, *Voting and Registration in the Election of November 1996.* Series P20-504, July 1998, Table 1.

portion engaging in this type of political activity is quite low. In 1996, only 8 percent of men interviewed report contributing to political parties, 7 percent to candidates, and 6 percent to political groups. Five percent of the women contributed to political parties and to candidates, while 4 percent gave money to political groups, as we see in Table 3.4.

For two of the three types of electoral activities (contributing money and engaging in campaign activities), men were more active than women in 1996. However, no significant differences occurred in levels of voting turnout.

What inhibits women's levels of political participation? A number of explanations for differences have been examined in other research. Gender differences in participation may occur because of sex role socialization. Women may learn, perhaps as children, that "politics is a man's business." Indeed research on the political socialization of children conducted in the 1960s suggests girls learned a passive orientation toward politics (Greenstein 1965; Hess and Torney 1967). However, the increasing number of women elected to public office and especially to very visible offices such as U.S. Senator and Representative provides an alternative pattern of role models. Life experiences as adults (observing women in leading political roles) could result in resocialization, with women learning that politics is also women's business (Verba, Burns, and Schlozman 1997).

A second explanation for patterns of participation focuses on resources available to support, either directly or indirectly, political par-

Table 3.2

Patterns of Voting Turnout by Sex, Midterm Election Years (percentage)

Year	Men	Women
1966	58	53
1970	57	53
1974	46	43
1978	47	45
1982	49	48
1986	46	46
1990	45	45
1994	45	45

Sources: U.S. Department of Commerce, Bureau of the Census. http//www.census.gov/population/socdemo/voting/history//vot01.txt

ticipation. These resources include educational attainment. The cognitive skills acquired through education facilitate acquiring the information necessary to evaluate policy options and leadership alternatives in order to make informed vote choices. For example, higher levels of educational attainment provide both skills and information. Educational attainment also structures placement in social networks, with those with higher levels of educational attainment tending to be more active in organizations in which political matters are discussed and formal and informal efforts at political mobilization occur (Brady, Verba, and Schlozman 1995; Verba, Schlozman, and Brady 1995; Rosenstone and Hansen 1993).

Two other resources that structure participation patterns are income and occupation. Income both directly and indirectly facilitates participation. Those who give money to political causes must have disposable income available. Those with higher incomes also have a higher probability of receiving requests to contribute to political campaigns. Some occupations enhance knowledge relevant to politics and government and facilitate the development and honing of skills useful in political activity.

A third explanation for patterns of political participation emphasizes the social contexts within which individuals live and work. The workplace, the family, the neighborhood, and social and religious organizations influence time demands, communications patterns, and peer

Table 3.3

Percent Participating in at Least One Campaign Activity, Presidential Election Years (percentage)

Year	Men	Women
1964	45.7	37.4
1968	47.7	35.4
1972	44.0	35.3
1976	47.3	37.3
1980	44.5	37.1
1984	41.1	36.5
1988	39.9	30.5
1992	49.3	38.2
1996	39.5	30.5

Sources: Calculated from American National Election Studies Cumulative File, 1952–1992; American National Election Studies, 1996 File.

pressures (Lake and Huckfeldt 1998; Verba, Schlozman, and Brady 1995).

Age differences exist in patterns of political participation. The differences may be due to the time and task demands associated with places in the life cycle, with both interest in politics and opportunities to participate varying at different stages of the life cycle. Research also suggests that significant generational differences in political activity exist (Bennett and Rademacher 1997; Miller and Shanks 1996). In research that traced patterns of voting turnout among three generations of the American electorate from 1952 to 1992, with the electorate divided into Pre–New Deal, New Deal, and Post–New Deal generations, Warren Miller and Merrill Shanks (1996) discovered significant differences in voting turnout among these three generations. The differences remained after controls for level of educational attainment, race, social connectedness, and several types of political beliefs were applied.

Other research contrasts initial voting turnout rates in the first election for which Early Baby Boomers (those born between 1946 and 1954), Late Baby Boomers (those born between 1955 and 1964), and Generation Xers (those born after 1964) were eligible to vote (Bennett and Rademacher 1997). Initial turnout rates were substantially higher among the Early Baby Boomers in the first election for which they

Table 3.4

Percent Contributing Money During Presidential Election Campaigns

Year	Men	Women
1972	12	9
1976	21	14
1980	9	8
1984	9	7
1988	10	8
1992	9	6
1996	12	7

Sources: American National Election Studies Cumulative File, 1952–1992; American National Election Studies, 1996.

were eligible to vote than they were for the two subsequent generations in their respective first elections for which they were eligible. Therefore, generational differences appear to exist at least in voting turnout.

Are there gender differences in patterns of participation among generations? The 1996 electorate has been grouped into four generations (birth cohorts). The birth cohorts, their ages, and the generation labels used in the discussion are:

Birth cohort	Age in 1996	Generation label
1963–1978	18 to 33	Generation X
1948–1962	34 to 48	Baby Boomers
1925–1947	49 to 71	Silent Generation
1924 and earlier	72 or older	Oldest Generation

In each generation, men are more likely than women to participate in each type of political activity (voting, campaigning, and contributing money). As Table 3.5 demonstrates, differences in voting turnout by generation existed in 1996, but they are not large enough to be statistically significant. In contrast, significant generational differences existed in participation in campaign activities among men and women, with the oldest and youngest cohorts being less likely to participate in even one campaign activity. Among both men and women, the silent generation is the most active cohort. Differences exist in the proportion of men and women contributing money, with the differences being largest among baby boomers and the oldest generation.

Table 3.5

Generational and Gender Differences Among Participants in Three Types of Political Activities, 1996

Generation	Percent voting		Percent engaging in at least one campaign activity		Percent contributing money to a candidate	
	Men	Women	Men	Women	Men	Women
Generation X	61	64	34	26	6.4	3.0
Baby boomers	80	75	40	30	8.8	4.1
Silent generation	84	76	44	36	14.1	12.4
Oldest generation	88	81	34	27	18.4	9.4

One possible explanation for generational differences in participation among women is that the type and level of participation is influenced by their gender role orientations. One might expect that those with a feminist orientation would be more active, supporting the party, candidates, and issues that are perceived as supportive of equal roles for women.

How can women's gender role orientations be measured? One method uses a measure of gender consciousness, with gender consciousness defined as "one's recognition that one's relationship to the political world is at least partly but nonetheless particularly shaped by being female or male. This recognition is followed by identification with others in the group of one's sex, positive affect toward the group, and a feeling of interdependence with the group's fortunes" (Tolleson-Rinehart 1992, 32). If gender consciousness influences political orientations, then political beliefs, attitudes, and activities would be expected to be different between women who operate within the context of this cognitive structure and those who do not. However, gender consciousness need not take one form. Different cognitive structurings may develop. Indeed, women who support a patriarchal culture and traditional definitions of women's roles would have a quite different set of gender role orientations than would women whose role orientations are based on modern feminism. Thus, while gender consciousness is one type of organizing schema, it can vary in its contents, depending on the beliefs and value structure of the individuals.

In their examination of subjective group identification, Gurin, Miller, and Gurin (1980) define four components of group consciousness. Those are a sense of belonging to a group; a preference for group members and dislike of nongroup members; evaluative assessments of the group's resources, power, and status relative to those of other groups; and attributions of responsibility for the status of the group. (See also Miller et al. 1981; Gurin 1985.) Gender consciousness could be manifested in the relationship between group identification and political beliefs, attitudes, and activities. To summarize, the argument being made is that many different varieties of gender group consciousness are possible. These result from differences in the group cultures in which women's lives are imbedded. For example, feminism is one type of gender consciousness; antifeminism would be another. Unfortunately, the measures needed to assess different types of gender consciousness among women rarely exist. It is possible to measure one type of gender consciousness, that which is generally referred to as feminist consciousness. Several different measures of feminist consciousness have been used.

One way to measure feminist consciousness is to evaluate responses to survey items assessing individuals' closeness to various groups. The survey respondents are presented with a list of groups and asked to indicate whether or not they feel close to each group. The survey item asks if members of the group are "people who are most like you in their ideas and interests and feelings about things." In surveys prior to 1996, individuals also were asked to indicate to which group they felt closest. That permitted creating a scale of group closeness that ranged from 0 (not close at all) to 1 (close) to 2 (closest). Women's assessments of the extent to which they felt close to other women could be used as a measure of feminist consciousness (Tolleson-Rinehart 1992). Unfortunately, the "closest" question was not included in the 1996 American National Election Studies (NES) survey. Therefore that measure cannot be used to analyze patterns of feminist consciousness in 1996.

An alternative measure of feminist gender consciousness uses evaluations of feelings toward women as a group (Cook 1999). Because individuals vary in how positively they rate all groups, with some rating all groups very positively and others rating all groups more negatively, the scoring system must take into account differences in how individuals rate all groups. A mean rating score is created by summing the ratings given several groups, then dividing the summed score by number of groups.[3] The average rating given to all groups is then sub-tracted from the rating given to women as a group. Those who score women 10 percent or more above their mean rating for all groups are evaluated as giving women a positive score and categorized as feminists. Those who score women 10 percent or more below the average score for the groups are scored as giving women a negative evaluation and labeled nonfeminists. Those rating women within 9.99 percent of their mean rating of comparison groups are scored as giving women a neutral rating and labeled as potential feminists.[4]

Another measure of gender role orientations uses support for an equal role for women in society and politics. The hypothesis to be tested here is that women who are more supportive of an equal role for women in society and politics would be more likely to participate in politics. Using this measure, we can determine whether women's levels of participation across time have increased as more women support equal roles for women. We can also compare among groups of women at one point in time, examining differences in participation levels between those who support and those who oppose equal roles for women.

Whatever measure of gender role orientations is used, a pattern of changing support over time for the women's movement and for equal roles for women in politics and society is evident. Using an index based on three items in the national sample–based General Social Survey, Bennett and Bennett (1999) find such a trend present from 1974–1975 through 1994–1996. The same trend is evident using responses to the feeling close to women item and the thermometer scales rating of the women's movement in the biennial American NES. Across time both men and women are increasingly positive in their assessments of the women's movement (Cook 1999; Conway, Steuernagel, and Ahern 1997). In 1996, only 14 percent of the women and 19 percent of the men surveyed evaluated the women's movement negatively. Using the measure of support for equal roles, both men and women also are more likely to support equal roles for men and women in society and politics when questioned specifically about that. By 1996, 77 percent of both men and women endorsed equal roles, with only 10 percent of the men and 12 percent of the women opposing that idea, as we see in Table 3.6.

Given the high support for equal roles for women and high levels of positive evaluation of the women's movement, we might expect that

Table 3.6

Support or Opposition to Equal Role for Women by Generation and Gender, 1996 (percent)

Generation	Strongly support	Support	Neutral	Oppose	Strongly oppose
Men[a]					
Generation X	52	33	10	4	2
Baby boomers	47	32	12	7	2
Silent generation	44	31	16	7	2
Oldest generation	30	33	15	17	5
Women					
Generation X	63	20	8	5	3
Baby boomers	63	21	9	5	2
Silent generation	42	30	12	9	7
Oldest generation	35	25	18	17	5

[a]Chi square tests indicate differences between men and women are significant for Generation X and the Baby Boomers, but not for the two older generations.

gender role orientations would contribute little to explaining patterns of political participation. However, generational differences may exist in patterns of support for equal roles and approval of the women's movement, with those socialized when equal roles for women received less positive evaluation being less supportive. As Table 3.7 indicates, that is indeed the pattern. Examining just 1996 and using responses to the feeling thermometer rating scale, support is highest among younger women.

To summarize, both gender and generational differences exist in patterns of support for equal roles for women and for the women's movement. Men and women also differ in the number of types of campaign activities in which they engage and in the number of different types of campaign contribution recipients (parties, candidates, and political groups) to which they give. However, do gender orientations and generation have an impact on these types of political action when controls for other variables are included in a multivariate analysis?

As Table 3.8 indicates, when socioeconomic resources and characteristics, indicators of political engagement, contacts from political

Table 3.7

Generational Differences in Percent Support for the Women's Movement, 1996

	Men			Women		
	Not feminist	Potential feminist	Feminist	Not feminist	Potential feminist	Feminist
Generation X	22	28	50	8	21	71
Baby boomers	27	25	48	16	22	62
Silent generation	27	23	50	21	28	51
Oldest generation	18	32	49	26	27	48

Note: Entries based on computed scores.

Table 3.8

Regression Analyses, Number of Types of Campaign Contributions Made and Types of Campaign Activities Performed, 1996

	Number of types of campaign contributions made	Number of types of campaign activities performed
Care who wins	—	−.144**
Clergy stated views	−.131*	.232*
Contacted by religious group	.113***	.177*
Contacted by presidential campaign	—	.260***
Education	.022**	—
Family income 1995	.005**	.008*
High status occupation	—	−.109*
Race	—	—
Sex	−.050*	—
Employed	—	—
Group involvement	.040***	.093***
Follow politics	.040**	.199***
Generation	.031*	—
Support for women's movement	—	—
Support for equal role	—	—
Adjusted R²	.133	.197
N of cases	1,223	1,226

Note: Entries are OLS regression coefficients. *p < .10. **p < .05. ***p < .01.

mobilizers, and political attitudes are included in regression analyses, generation effects are not significant in explaining the number of types of campaign activities in which individuals engage, but they are when examining the types of campaign contributions individuals make. Furthermore, while several measures of political mobilization, resources, and political engagement are statistically significant, the measures of gender role orientations used in this analysis are insignificant. Should we conclude from this that gender role orientations do not influence political participation patterns? The answer is no. Only one type of gender role orientation (feminism) is measured. Furthermore, although two different measures of feminist gender consciousness are used, both measures are limited in their ability to discriminate the intensity with which gender role orientations are held. Also lacking are direct measures of the connections the respondents draw between their gender role orientations and gender related issue stands taken by political candidates, parties, or groups in the various electoral contests on the ballot in 1996. Better measures of both gender role orientations and of the gender role–relevant perceptions of candidates, parties, groups, and issues are needed. Furthermore, measures of gender role orientation are needed that can assess a variety of orientations that exist and that could be activated to stimulate various types of political participation.

Notes

1. The variables necessary to compute this measure are not available in the American National Election Studies prior to 1964.

2. Measures of giving both to political parties and to candidates are not available before 1964 in the American National Election Studies.

3. The four groups used were liberals, conservatives, big business, and labor unions.

4. Unfortunately the terms used as an indicator of the women's movement have varied across time. In the American National Election Studies from 1972 to 1984 the group label "women's liberation movement" was used. In the 1988 and 1992 surveys the term "feminists" was used, and in 1992 and 1996 the reference group was the women's movement.

References

Bennett, L.L.M., and S.E. Bennett (1999). "Changing Views About Gender Equality in Politics: Gradual Change and Lingering Doubts." In *Women in Politics: Outsiders or Insiders?*, ed. L.D. Whitaker, pp. 33–44. Upper Saddle River, NJ: Prentice Hall.
Bennett, S.E., and E.W. Rademacher (1997). "The 'Age of Indifference' Revisited:

Patterns of Political Interest, Media Exposure, and Knowledge Among Generation X." In *After the Boom*, ed. S.E. Craig and S.E. Bennett. Lanhan, MD: Rowman and Littlefield.

Brady, H., S. Verba, and K.L. Schlozman (1995). "Beyond SES: A Resource Model of Political Participation." *American Political Science Review* 89(2): 271–294.

Clark, C., and J. Clark (1999). "The Gender Gap in 1996: More Meaning than a 'Revenge of the Soccer Moms.' " In *Women in Politics Outsiders or Insiders*, ed. L.D. Whitaker, pp. 68–84. Upper Saddle River, NJ: Prentice Hall.

Clark, J., and C. Clark (1996). "The Gender Gap: A Manifestation of Women's Dissatisfation with the American Polity?" In *Broken Contract?* ed. S.C. Craig, pp. 167–182. Boulder, CO: Westview Press.

Conway, M.M., G.A. Steuernagel, and D.W. Ahern (1997). *Women and Political Participation*. Washington, DC: CQ Press.

Cook, E.A. (1999). "The Generations of Feminism." In *Women in Politics: Outsiders or Insiders?*, ed. L.D. Whitaker, pp. 45–55. Upper Saddle River, NJ: Prentice Hall.

Flexnor, E., and E. Fitzpatrick (1996). *Century of Struggle*. Cambridge, MA: Harvard University Press.

Greenstein, F. (1965). *Children and Politics*. New Haven: Yale University Press.

Gurin, P. (1985). "Women's Gender Consciousness." *Public Opinion Quarterly* 49(2): 143–163.

Gurin, P., A.H. Miller, and G. Gurin (1980). "Stratum Identification and Consciousness." *Social Psychological Quarterly* 43(1): 30–47.

Hess, R.D., and J.V. Torney (1967). *The Development of Political Attitudes in Children*. Chicago: Aldine.

Lake, R.L., and R. Huckfeldt (1998). "Social Capital, Social Networks, and Political Participation." *Political Psychology* 19(3): 567–565.

Miller, A.H., P. Gurin, G. Gurin, and O. Malanchuk (1981). "Group Consciousness and Political Participation." *American Journal of Political Science* 25(3): 494–511.

Miller, W.E., and J.M. Shanks (1996). *The New American Voter*. Cambridge: Harvard Universitiy Press.

Rosenstone, S.J., and J.M. Hansen (1993). *Mobilization, Participation, and Democracy in America*. New York: Macmillan.

Stucker, J.J. (1977). "Women as Voters: Their Maturation as Political Persons in American Society." In *A Portrait of Marginality*, ed. Marianne Githens and Jewel L. Prestage, pp. 264–283. New York: David MacKay Company.

Tolleson-Rinehart, S. (1992). *Gender Consciousness and Politics*. New York: Routledge.

Verba, S., K.L. Schlozman, and H.E. Brady (1995). *Voice and Equality*. Cambridge, MA: Harvard University Press.

Verba, S., N. Burns, and K.L. Schlozman (1997). "Knowing and Caring About Politics: Gender and Political Engagement." *Journal of Politics* 59(4): 1051–1072.

Part Two
Public Policy

4

Gender and Tax

R. Michael Alvarez and Edward J. McCaffery

Introduction

Given the stakes involved, there has been surprisingly little empirical analysis of gender-based differences in attitudes toward specific aspects of taxation. Most of the literature on the so-called gender gap in political behavior has focused on the effects of gender on voting behavior in presidential or congressional elections (Chaney, Alvarez, and Nagler 1998; Mattei and Mattei 1998).[1] When this literature has looked at attitudes on particular issues, it typically has been concerned with the impact of possibly gender-diverse policy preferences on voting behavior. Such analysis tends to use rather general attitudes toward questions of public interest as its input.

What is missing is a focus on gender-specific attitudes toward particular features of substantive law, independent of the impact on electoral outcomes, as a way of helping to explain certain persistent structural biases in the law. Tax is of particular interest and importance in this regard. The U.S. tax system is big and coercive and has deep effects on matters of concern to men and women, such as decisions to marry, to bear children, to be a one- or a two-earner family, and so forth. Present law, for example, contains a pattern of "marriage penalties," whereby income taxes of two-earner couples increase on marriage, and "marriage bonuses," whereby taxes of one-earner couples decrease on marriage (McCaffery 1997). Such biases raise a host of questions for gender-oriented researchers. Do men and women share similar attitudes toward the relevant questions of tax policy and design? Are they equally likely to make their preferences known to lawmakers? Are they equally well informed, or not? Are there institutional barriers to greater gender equity in tax? Do politicians target their advertising and educational outreach efforts to attempt to appeal differently along gender-based lines?

This chapter points to work to be done in this important dimension of the interplay between gender and the law. It addresses two puzzles. The first is a theoretical one. Scholars have long postulated that women support redistributive tax policies more than men do (see for example Kornhauser 1987; see also Welch and Hibbing 1992). This assumption has found at least casual substantiation in national polling data suggesting that men are more likely than women to consider tax reduction as an important issue and in empirical analysis of the determinants of the gender gap in presidential elections (Chaney, Alvarez, and Nagler 1998). This latter work has corroborated a longstanding theme in the empirical gender gap literature, namely that men tend to vote on the basis of narrow "pocketbook" issues, whereas women are influenced by broader questions of national and international social justice (Welch and Hibbing 1992), or, somewhat equivalently, that women are more "compassionate" than men (Gilligan 1982). At the same time, recent work has found, not surprisingly, that the gender gap is a highly complicated social phenomenon, with no one "simple explanation" (Chaney, Alvarez, and Nagler 1998, 333).

The assumption of women's greater support for progressive taxation, however, has been called into question. A recent survey suggests that when directly asked questions about the fairness of social spending and redistributive taxation, men and women show "little difference" in their attitudes (Turnier, Conover, and Lowery 1996, 1315). This study draws support from recent polling data suggesting very similar attitudes of men and women toward broad questions of tax policy, and from the more general finding that men's and women's policy preferences across a range of issues are not necessarily "substantially different" (Chaney, Alvarez, and Nagler 1998, 314).

The second puzzle is one of practical politics. The substantive tax laws in the United States continue to reflect a strong bias against modern, two-earner families—a bias that easily can be understood as directed primarily toward women (McCaffery 1997). Features such as mandatory joint filing under the income tax, severely limited tax relief for the costs of paid third-party child care, and the absence of a secondary-earner exemption under the Social Security system mean that working married mothers face extremely high marginal and effective tax rates. The average working wife sacrifices two-thirds of her salary to taxes and work-related expenses, and many women can even lose money, in a cash flow sense, by working outside the home (Hanson and Ooms 1991; McCaffery 1997).

Principal features of substantive tax law causing this effect were put in place in the 1930s and 1940s.[2] Since that time, there has been a dramatic increase in the incidence of working married mothers: fewer than 10 percent of married mothers of young children engaged in paid work in 1940; more than 65 percent now do.[3] A simple interest group model of politics would predict that as women have been both working more and exercising increasing political power, tax policy would change to lessen the structural burdens on working wives. But the trend has gone in precisely the other direction. The bias against two-earner families has become more severe as the structural features contributing to it have grown in magnitude. Meanwhile, women and feminist groups have not exerted significant influence over tax policy at the national level; indeed, salient issues such as the marriage penalty have been used by conservative social forces to continue to reward more traditional, single-earner families, as we explore further below.

Our analysis in this chapter suggests a possible single answer to both of these puzzles. While there is reason to believe that men and women may indeed share similar primary or "first order" attitudes toward matters of tax, the weighting or "second order" preferences that men and women put on the importance of tax issues seems to have marked differences. This central finding reconciles the apparent paradox in the theoretical literature. Women and men will often answer direct questions about their attitudes toward matters of tax similarly, while continuing to show a marked gender gap in their actual voting behavior when tax is one of several issues to be considered.

The results on first order preferences also appear to be subject to a strong framing effect, whereby answers to questions of tax are highly dependent on the form of the question (Kahneman and Tversky 1979). Linking tax cuts to decreased social spending, for example, seems to exacerbate a gender gap, because it draws attention to the more "sociotropic" attitudes of women, as opposed to the more "egocentric" attitudes of men (Welch and Hibbing 1992; Chaney, Alvarez, and Nagler 1998). This is consistent with the salience or weighting hypothesis. Men are more likely to take their antitax attitudes as an "anchor," whereas women are more likely to take their pro–social spending positions that way. This divergent weighting of similar first order preferences leads to a gender gap, but only when positions are brought into trade-off.

The central finding also helps to explain the persistence of gender bias in practical tax policy. The divergent weighting or salience of tax issues for women and men suggests that it is a successful political strategy to pitch tax-oriented reforms toward men, and spending or social justice–oriented reforms toward women. Contemporary tax politics seems to bear out this hypothesis, and we conclude this chapter by outlining a future research agenda in this important area of the politics of gender in America.

Empirical Results and Analysis

Evidence on First Order Preferences

Professors Turnier, Conover, and Lowery recently set out to test the hypothesis that men and women differed in their attitudes toward taxation. Using an extensive national telephone poll, Turnier and colleagues asked respondents to self-identify as men or women, Democrat or Republican, feminist or not. They asked a series of six questions on the fairness of supporting various causes with taxpayer money: care for abused spouses, the homeless, AIDS patients, and the like.

In order to determine attitudes toward tax, Turnier and colleagues asked two questions:

> The federal income tax is based on the principle that people with higher incomes not only pay more taxes but also a greater percentage of their income in taxes. Do you think this is very fair, somewhat fair, somewhat unfair or very unfair?

And:

> Some say that capital gains—that is the profits people make from the sale of investment property, stocks and so forth—should be taxed at a lower rate than their income from wages and interest. Do you strongly agree, disagree, strongly disagree or have no opinion?

Based on their answers to these two questions, the authors studied the impact of gender on "tax fairness issues" and found it to be "very weak." More specifically, "by a very narrow margin, women indicated greater support for progressive taxation; however, by a slightly wider margin, men indicated greater support for eliminating capital gains preferences" (Turnier, Conover, and Lowery 1996, 1312).

We put aside questions as to the study's methodology and conclusions, although we note that it is somewhat difficult to ascertain the "fair" position on a complex issue such as capital gains (for other criticisms of the Turnier study, see Kornhauser 1997). The Turnier study draws some support from a National Monitor Survey conducted in October 1997. A national telephone poll of 1,000 regular voters asked a question on federal budget and tax policy, specifically whether the respondent agreed with one of three positions:

- A tax cut is a good idea but it should be across the board so that all taxpayers get a break;
- A tax cut is a good idea if it is targeted toward families and some eligibility is based on people applying that money directly toward savings for their children's education and their own retirement; or
- There is no need for a tax cut and balancing the budget and assuring that federal programs are fully funded is more important.

The results of this question were sorted between men and women, and a further subset of working women was broken out. These results show virtually no gender gap, as Figure 4.1 illustrates. Across-the-board tax cuts were favored by 50 percent of men and 51 percent of women (48 percent of working women); targeted tax cuts were favored by 31 percent and 34 percent (36 percent), respectively, showing no significant gender gap.

This result—that men and women are close in their general political preferences—is a central finding of recent gender gap research (Chaney, Alvarez, and Nagler 1998). The evidence on gender-based differentials in first order preferences still remains unclear, however, in part because of the framing effect we explore further below. Nonetheless, even assuming that the Turnier study is correct and that men and women share similar first order preferences about tax, the analysis of the empirical dimensions of political attitudes on gender and tax is far from over.

Figure 4.1. **Attitudes on Type of Tax Cut, 1997.**

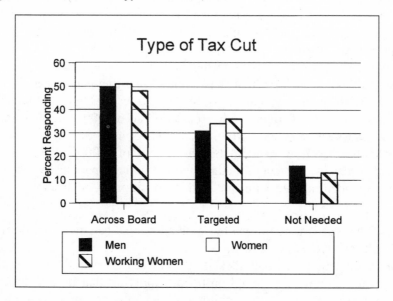

Evidence on Second Order Preferences

The same October 1997 National Monitor Survey that generated Figure 4.1 included a question linking federal budget and tax policy:

> Do you feel that future budget surpluses should be used to reduce the deficit or used to continue to provide tax relief for working families?

Surprisingly, this question generated a pronounced gender gap among the very same pool of respondents, as Figure 4.2 shows. Men preferred deficit reduction by 52 percent to 40 percent; women in contrast preferred tax relief for working families, and by an even larger margin, 54 percent to 38 percent. It is interesting to note that, in both questions, the preferences of working women and women overall were closely aligned. On the use of the surplus, working women were slightly more likely (57 percent to 36 percent as opposed to 54 percent to 38 percent) to prefer tax cuts, but were far closer to all women than to men.

The stark reversal between Figure 4.1 and Figure 4.2 shows that gender-based attitudes toward tax are susceptible to either the choice

Figure 4.2. **Attitudes on Use of Government Surplus.**

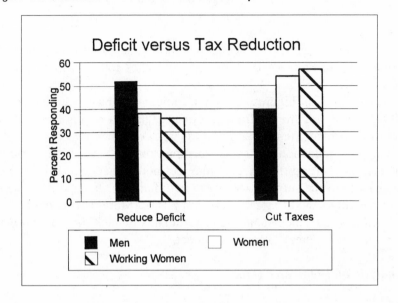

set, a framing effect, or both. Whereas the Turnier study and Figure 4.1 show that men and women sometimes have virtually indistinguishable primary attitudes toward questions of tax, Figure 4.2 shows that men and women can differ dramatically when a question of tax is posed in trade-off terms. This result might obtain because men and women attach different weights to the importance of tax vis-à-vis other issues, or because of a framing effect, with the precise determinants of either not altogether clear from the survey. Figure 4.1 reflects a choice between general, targeted (to families), and no tax reduction, and it generates a strong preference among both genders for general reduction. Figure 4.2 reflects a choice between targeted and no tax reduction, and it generates a pronounced gender gap, with women preferring the tax cut and men preferring the deficit reduction that comes from no tax cut. This might indicate a different ranking among choices for men and women, with men ranking the choices as:

general tax reduction > deficit reduction > targeted tax reduction for families

and women ranking them as:

general tax reduction > targeted tax reduction for families >
deficit reduction.

Including the general tax reduction option makes for no noticeable
gender gap in Figure 4.1; eliminating it makes for the gap evident in
Figure 4.2.

The reversal in Figures 4.1 and 4.2 might also have been caused, in
whole or in part, from a framing effect generated by the fact that the
question behind Figure 4.2 more clearly combines two distinct elements—tax reduction and social spending on one side of the question.
Women supporting the tax cuts may be more concerned that some of
the benefit of the surplus is going to help families, as opposed to more
affirmatively supporting tax reduction per se. More precise research is
needed to better understand the determinants of such inconsistent gender gaps as Figures 4.1 and 4.2 reflect.

Analysis of 1996 Voter Data

We wanted to get a better feel for the relative "politicization" of tax
issues—how men and women weight the general issue of taxation in
their political behavior. To do so, we turn to the most recent national
election—the 1996 elections for president, U.S. Senate, and U.S.
House. Tax was a very important issue in these campaigns. Bob Dole
ran on a platform of across-the-board income tax rate cuts; other Republican candidates, picking up on the *Contract with America* and
polling data suggesting that fundamental tax reform was a compelling
political issue, were even more aggressive in calling for tax reform and
reduction. Bill Clinton and the Democrats, in contrast, ran on a more
moderate tax-cutting platform, emphasizing the need to preserve social
spending on such programs as Social Security and education. The 1996
elections thus provide an excellent vehicle for examining the ways in
which tax issues influence the political behavior of men and women.

Our empirical analysis of the 1996 national elections uses exit poll
surveys taken on Election Day; specifically, we use the Voter News
Service (VNS) General Election Exit Polls 1996. The VNS exit poll
was conducted in all fifty states and the District of Columbia on Election Day. In our work we use only the national exit poll sample, not
the separate state samples. The VNS national exit poll contained a wide
variety of important survey questions, most specifically questions ask-

ing for the voter's presidential, Senate, and House candidate choices and for the voter's assessment of the most important issue facing the nation. Voters were given a list of seven issues and they could check one as being most important.

In Table 4.1 we provide the distribution of responses to this most important issue question, first for the complete sample (6,832 voters), then for men (3,184 voters) and for women (3,552) voters. The issues are given in the left column of Table 4.1. In the full sample column, the percentages given are for the column—that is, they show the proportion of total voters who thought each issue was the most important one facing the nation. In the full sample, the most important issues were the economy and jobs (26.6 percent), Social Security and Medicare (17 percent), and education (15.6 percent). Taxes were said to be the most important issue by 4.8 percent of the voters in this exit poll.

The third and fourth columns of Table 4.1 list the numbers of men and women voters, respectively, who said that each issue was the most important. In these columns, the percentages are for the row—that is, they show what proportion of voters identifying an issue as most important were men or women. For the three overall most important issues in the 1996 elections, as identified by the first column, we see that women were slightly more likely than men to say that the economy and jobs was the most important issue but that women were much more likely than men to list Social Security and Medicare and education as most important.

On the tax issue, men were much more likely than women to say that it was the most important issue—56 percent of those who ranked tax as the most important issue were men, significantly disproportionate to men's representation in the full sample. The relatively greater weight attached to taxes by men as opposed to women is consistent with a view of second-order ranking of preferences that has men being more egocentric, and women more sociotropic, tax being a classic "pocketbook" issue.

While men were more likely than women to think that taxation was the most important issue in the 1996 election, however, this does not necessarily imply that taxation was a less important component in voting decisions for women than for men. To assess the relative importance of taxation in political behavior for men and women, we estimated a series of voter choice equations, one for the presidential race, one for the Senate race (if there was one in the voter's state), and

Table 4.1

Distribution of 1996 Most Important Issue by Gender

	Full sample		Men		Women	
Issues	%	N	%	N	%	N
Foreign policy	13.33	911	57.05	514	42.95	387
Medicare/Social Security	17.02	1,163	38.97	440	61.03	689
Taxes	4.83	330	56.03	172	43.97	135
Crime and drugs	14.37	982	55.48	542	44.52	435
Economy and jobs	26.6	1,817	48.81	881	51.19	924
Education	15.59	1,065	36.07	382	63.93	677
Budget deficit	8.26	564	45.34	253	54.66	305
Total		6,832	46.60	3,184	51.99	3,552

one for the House race. In these voter choice models, we had a binary dependent variable (1 for a Democratic vote, 0 for a Republican vote) that required the use of an appropriate statistical technique. Here we used binary probit models (see Chaney, Alvarez, and Nagler 1998 for a fuller description of methodology).

For each race, we began by estimating the effect of a series of political issues, partisanship, ideology, economic perceptions, abortion prefer-ences, and gender on vote choice for the entire sample. We then stratified the sample by gender, and reestimated the probit models for men and women separately. This procedure allowed us to examine the impact of each of these different factors on the voting decisions of men and women.

We report the results for the presidential election in Table 4.2, for the Senate in Table 4.3, and for the House in Table 4.4. Beginning with the presidential voting equation set out in Table 4.2, we see that for the full sample the model performed as one would expect: Dem-ocratic voters were much more likely to vote for Clinton, Republicans for Dole; liberals were much more likely to support Clinton, conser-vatives to support Dole, and so on.

For the various most important issues, all but foreign policy were statistically significant, most at a high level. Voters who believed that Social Security and Medicare, the economy and jobs, and education were the most important issue were significantly more likely to support Clinton. On the other hand, those who believed that taxes or the budget deficit were the most important issue were more likely to support Dole. Voters whose personal finances had improved, or who thought the na-tional economy was much improved, were more likely to support Clin-

Table 4.2

1996 Presidential Voting by Gender

	Full sample	Men	Women
Constant	.90**	.65**	1.2**
	.20	.29	.28
Democrats	.96**	1.2**	.73**
	.08	.11	.11
Republicans	−.97**	−.71**	−1.3**
	.08	.11	.11
Liberals	.50**	.51**	.49**
	.09	.13	.12
Conservatives	−.60**	−.65**	−.59**
	.08	.10	.11
Tax	−.39**	−.37**	−.48**
	.12	.17	.19
Social Security	.60**	.66**	.59**
	.11	.17	.13
Foreign policy	−.13	−.12	−.15
	.17	.21	.28
Deficit	−.22**	−.22*	−.20*
	.10	.14	.14
Economy and jobs	.42**	.36**	.50**
	.09	.13	.13
Education	.71**	.63**	.76**
	.11	.18	.14
Personal finances	.22**	.22**	.23**
	.04	.06	.06
National economy	−.26**	−.21**	−.32**
	.05	.07	.07
Abortion	−.28**	−.27**	−.28**
	.03	.05	.05
Gender	−.05		
	.06		
Chi-square	2,277.9	1,055.8	1,218.9
Sample size	3,244	1,522	1,722

Notes: A positive number indicates a likelihood to vote Democratic; a negative, Republican. $*p < .10.$ $**p < .05.$

Each column presents one probit equation, with the model coefficients given for each variable, followed by either one * or two ** to indicate differing levels of statistical significance and each coefficient's standard error.

Table 4.3

1996 U.S. Senate Voting by Gender

	Full sample	Men	Women
Constant	.45**	.06	.92**
	.23	.32	.33
Democrats	.70**	.69**	.67**
	.08	.12	.12**
Republicans	−.82**	−.66**	−1.0**
	.09	.13	.14
Liberals	.26**	.34**	.18*
	.09	.14	.13
Conservatives	−.52**	−.52**	−.54**
	.09	.12	.13
Tax	−.32**	−.28*	−.35*
	.15	.20	.24
Social Security	.13	.25*	.03
	.12	.19	.17
Foreign policy	.01	.15	−.25
	.20	.24	.41
Deficit	−.20**	−.11	−.27*
	.11	.15	.17
Economy and jobs	.17*	.27**	.09
	.10	.14	.15
Education	.30**	.47**	.18
	.12	.20	.16
Personal finances	.15**	.16**	.14**
	.05	.07	.07
National economy	−.17**	−.08	−.25**
	.06	.07	.08
Abortion	−.13**	−.12**	−.15**
	.04	.06	.05
Gender	.04		
	.07		
Chi-square	839.6	369.6	465.9
Sample size	1,835	884	951

Notes: A positive number indicates a likelihood to vote Democratic; a negative, Republican. * p < .10. **p < .05.

Each column presents one probit equation, with the model coefficients given for each variable, followed by either one * or two ** to indicate differing levels of statistical significance and each coefficient's standard error.

Table 4.4

1996 U.S. House Voting by Gender

	Full sample	Men	Women
Constant	.51**	.38*	.74**
	.81	.27	.25
Democrats	.78**	.90**	.65**
	.07	.09	.09
Republicans	−1.1**	−1.0**	−1.2**
	.07	.10	.10
Liberals	.35**	.32**	.37**
	.07	.11	.10
Conservatives	−.43**	−.47**	−.39**
	.07	.10	.10
Tax	−.28**	−.19	−.39**
	.12	.16	.18
Social Security	.44**	.54**	.36**
	.10	.15	.13
Foreign policy	−.12	−.12	−.07
	.16	.20	.26
Deficit	−.03	.02	−.06
	.09	.12	.13
Economy and jobs	.28**	.34**	.23**
	.08	.11	.11
Education	.45**	.54**	.38**
	.10	.15	.12
Personal finances	.10**	.08*	.11**
	.04	.06	.05
National economy	−.16**	−.14**	−.17**
	.04	.06	.06
Abortion	−.16**	−.15**	−.17**
	.03	.05	.04
Gender	.10**		
	.06		
Chi-square	1,915.5	924.5	961.2
Sample size	3,364	1,616	1,748

Notes: A positive vote indicates a likelihood to vote Democratic; a negative, Republican. *p < .10. **p < .05.

Each column presents one probit equation, with the model coefficients given for each variable, followed by either one * or two ** to indicate differing levels of statistical significance and each coefficient's standard error.

ton, as were pro-choice voters. Notice that once we control for all of these different determinants of voter choice, we see little evidence for an independent impact of voter gender.

This does not mean, however, that gender was not a significant factor in voting behavior—only that, if it was, it was captured in the attitudes toward different issues. Indeed, we see strong evidence of significant gender-based heterogeneity in the last two columns of Table 4.2. Some of these differences verify past findings in the literature; women place more weight on the state of the national economy than men, while men and women in 1996 placed roughly equal weight on the state of their personal finances. Women place more weight on education, which has typically been called a "woman's issue," while the weights of abortion are almost equivalent between male and female voters. Women also relied more heavily on the importance of the economy and jobs than did men, while men more heavily weighted Social Security. Last, of importance for our analysis, women weighted tax more heavily in their vote choice as an issue than did men.

Tables 4.3 and 4.4 present the same type of model, but for voter choice in the Senate and House. The general outline of the results in each congressional election model are very similar to those for the presidential election. While the signs of almost all of the coefficients are the same across these two races for the full sample models, we see that some of the issues are statistically insignificant in each model: Social Security and Medicare and foreign policy, for example, are statistically insignificant in the Senate voting model; foreign policy and the budget deficit are statistically insignificant in the House voting model.

Importantly, in both congressional election models, the tax issue is a strong predictor of voter choice. It is negative and statistically significant in both Tables 4.3 and 4.4, implying that voters who thought tax was the most important issue in the 1996 election were significantly more likely to support Republicans. Of even greater importance, we again see the same type of gender differences in the weighting of the tax issue in the congressional election models that we saw in the presidential vote choice models. In the Senate vote model, while the tax issue is statistically significant in both equations, it is larger for women than for men. In the House vote model, furthermore, the tax issue is statistically significant only for women, for whom it is in fact strongly significant.

In the three different voter choice settings we examined from the 1996 presidential election we thus found systematic evidence for the role of tax as a motivating issue, and we also found that this impact varied by gender. As a matter of ranking, men were far more likely to count tax as the most important issue than were women. All voters who found tax to be the most important issue were significantly more likely to vote Republican than Democratic. Yet among the pool of voters who considered tax to be the most important issue, women were even more likely than men to vote Republican—were more likely, that is, to be affected by their attitudes on tax.

How much more heavily did women weight taxation than men? This is difficult to assess directly from the probit model. Probit estimates cannot be interpreted as easily as can simple regression estimates. Such estimates must be translated into probability terms, controlling for all of the other variables in the statistical model.

We present this type of analysis of the effects of the tax issue in Table 4.5. There we give the probability differences for our full sample, for men, and for women, in their voting decisions in each of the three national races. Holding all of the other variables at their sample modal or mean values, we compute the probability that the voter would support a Democratic candidate if she or he did not think of taxes as an important national issue, and then compute this same probability again assuming that they did think of taxes as an important issue. The difference between these two probability estimates gives us a measure of the estimated impact of this issue on voter choice.

Notice in Table 4.5 that the tax issue did have a reasonably large impact in the full sample. In the presidential case, if a voter thought of taxes as the most important issue, he or she was 15 percent less likely to vote Democratic. In the Senate, the same impact was slightly less, with a voter who believed taxes to be an important issue now 13 percent less likely to vote Democratic. The impact is even smaller in the House results, with the difference now only being an 11 percent reduction in the chances of casting a Democratic vote.

But notice the clear differences between men and women in how strong an impact the tax issue played in their voting decisions in the 1996 election. At the presidential level, the impact of taxes as an issue was 3 percent (in absolute numbers) greater for women than for men, 18 to 15 percent. The result is similar although a bit dampened in the Senate elections, with women again weighing the tax issue 3 percent

Table 4.5

Estimated Impact of Tax Issue for Men and Women

	Full sample	Men	Women
Presidential vote	−.15	−.15	−.18
Senate vote	−.13	−.11	−.14
House vote	−.11	−.07	−.15

more than men in their voting decisions, 14 to 11 percent. The difference is the most pronounced in the case of the House elections, where there is an 8 percent point difference between men and women, with women weighting the tax issue much more heavily than men by a 15 percent to 7 percent differential.

While we would again need much further and more nuanced research to pin this effect down, these results might suggest that men are more narrowly strategic in their voting behavior. It is widely thought that voters make decisions in local elections such as House ones looking to the effects on local spending, while deciding national elections such as the presidential contest looking to general tax and fiscal policy—a pattern leading to the phenomena of "ticket splitting" and divided government (see Alvarez and Schousen 1993; Jacobson 1990). Our finding suggests a possible gender dimension to this pattern. Men may be preferring a president who will cut their taxes and a congressperson who will "bring home the bacon," while women are evaluating all candidates by a consistent set of policy preferences. Once again, this would fit with the general theme of men as egocentric voters, and women as sociotropic ones.

Policy Analysis and Significance

Substantive Issues in Tax Reform

Why should we care? The controversy over men and women's possibly varying preferences in regard to matters of tax has thus far been largely academic, and it has centered on abstract propositions. This is evidenced by the Turnier study, which asked about attitudes toward "tax fairness" or progressivity in general. A gender gap in such matters would suggest that men and women differ in their fundamental con-

ceptions of self-interest, with men being more narrowly and traditionally self-interested, and with women being more altruistic or compassionate. This is consistent with the "different voice" school of
feminism (Gilligan 1982). A gender gap in such attitudes would also
suggest that as women began to assert more political power, broad
features of the institutional landscape—such as the general level of
taxation and the nature of the rate structure—might change. This possibility seemed to capture an early hope of the feminist movement.

Our central findings suggest that, just as men and women may not
differ too greatly in their attitudes toward broad questions of tax, so
too might they not differ in their self-interested orientation, once they
confront the same issues. But therein lies the rub: Men and women do
not always perceive the same issues as being equally important. A more
traditional interest group analysis of voting behavior, supplemented by
the critical dimension of salience, can thus help to explain the persistent gender-based dimensions of tax policy.

Large tax systems such as the United States has had since World
War II inevitably involve large choices, such as over filing units or the
deductibility of work-related expenses, that have impacts on family
structures and categories of persons sorted by marital and parental
status. As noted above, the U.S. tax system is in many fundamental
regards set up to favor more traditional, one-earner households, as opposed to more modern, two-earner ones. The type of detailed issues
leading to such biases differ from the broader ones typically discussed
in the survey literature. Measuring attitudes about progressivity in the
rate structure or the appropriate level of taxation captures general ideological orientation. Thus Turnier and colleagues find, not surprisingly,
that a liberal orientation is more important than gender in explaining
attitudes toward tax fairness. But it is a different matter to consider
more detailed questions of the appropriate filing unit, or the deductibility of child-care expenses, or exemption levels under Social Security.
Here gender might matter more.

A traditional interest group model of politics suggests that working
women should favor separate filing, increased child-care deductions,
and an exemption level under Social Security. The salience model suggests that, conditioned on paying attention to tax in the first place, men
and women are equally likely to be concerned with their self-interest.
But women are less likely to find tax issues salient. Our analysis suggests that, if they did, their self-interest might carry over to more spe-

cific issues. At the same time, a feedback loop is possible. Given that tax is less salient to women, candidates who are able to target their campaign advertisements or other means of appeal will not focus on women-oriented tax issues, which will continue to suppress their salience.

A Case Study: Marriage Tax Reform at the Millennium

Quite generally speaking, the United States had a system of separate filing for the income tax until 1948. Under separate filing, men and women file separate tax returns whether married or not, paying taxes on at least earned income under their own, individual rate schedule. A separate filing system, as most developed Western nations now have, is thus "marriage neutral"—marriage is more or less an irrelevance for tax purposes.

In 1948, as part of a large post–World War II "peace dividend," the United States adopted joint filing for married couples (McCaffery 1997; Jones 1988). The initial joint filing rate structure simply doubled the rate brackets in effect for single taxpayers so that the zero and all other rate brackets would extend twice as high for married couples as for single taxpayers. As a result, there were no "marriage penalties," only "marriage bonuses." A couple where each spouse earned the same amount of income would be indifferent to joint filing, since they were in essence doubling their rate brackets by filing separately. In contrast, a couple in which one earner was the dominant or exclusive wage earner would see their taxes go down because this dominant earner could take advantage of the wider lower-rate brackets.

The 1948 move to joint filing also created a secondary earner bias, however, since a potential second worker, at the margin of the household earning decision, would now enter the income tax rate structure in a rate bracket dictated by the primary earner's salary. This secondary earner bias is conceptually distinct from the question of the marriage penalty, and can be seen as discouraging women's paid work (Leuthold 1984). Indeed, there is evidence that this effect was intentional and that Congress was attracted to a policy that would generate incentives for women to return to the homes that they had left, at least briefly, during World War II (McCaffery 1997).

In 1969, in the face of protests against the "singles penalty," the precise converse of the marriage bonus (by forswearing a possible marriage bonus, high-earning singles could be seen as incurring a penalty), Congress lowered the rate brackets for joint filing by 20 percent. The resulting married-filing-jointly rate structure features two potentially offsetting effects. On one hand, married couples receive a benefit of implicit income-splitting, where each spouse is presumed to earn an equal amount, brought about by the fact of joint filing. On the other hand, married couples suffer the detriment of a less favorable rate structure, brought about by the 1969 change. (Because the married-filing-separately rate structure is set at one-half of the joint-filing rate structure, it contains only the detriment of the adverse rates without the benefits of the deemed income splitting. Separate filing under the current system is thus rarely a viable option, with more than 97 percent of married couples, quite rationally, filing jointly.) For roughly equal-earner couples, the harms outweigh the benefits, and these couples pay a "marriage penalty." For largely one-earner couples, the converse is true, and these couples continue to receive a benefit or marriage bonus.

By the late 1990s, approximately 50 percent of all married couples consisting of two earners were paying a marriage penalty. Approximately 40 percent of couples, typically consisting of a working man and a stay-at-home woman, were receiving marriage bonuses (Feenberg and Rosen 1995). The prevalence of marriage penalties was directly due to the increase in working married women. Following the inclusion of rather limited marriage penalty relief in the 1994 *Contract with America* and other events, the marriage penalty attained a high degree of political salience in the mid to late 1990s. Stories about the penalty ran on the front pages of major metropolitan newspapers, in leading popular magazines, and on television and talk radio shows across the country.

In this environment, Representatives David McIntosh and Jerry Weller, both Republicans, proposed a Marriage Tax Elimination Act in 1997 that would have given couples the option to file separately and singly, as if they were unmarried. Such "optional separate filing" would have eliminated the marriage penalties prevailing under present law while leaving the marriage bonuses unchanged. In other words, it would have helped the 50 percent or so of two-earner couples, who would elect to file separately, but do nothing for the 40 percent of one-earner couples benefiting from lower taxes under joint filing. McIntosh-Weller I, as it came to be known, was estimated to cost about $20 billion in foregone revenues each year. President Clinton and his fellow

Democrats failed to endorse the bill, preferring deficit reduction and social spending programs.

Meanwhile, socially conservative Republicans criticized McIntosh-Weller I as not helping one-earner families (see, for example, Schlafly 1998). Representatives McIntosh and Weller then proposed another Marriage Tax Elimination Act, McIntosh-Weller II. This would expand the marriage penalty relief to all married couples by doubling the rate brackets, that is, it would be a return to 1948-style rate brackets. McIntosh-Weller II differed from McIntosh-Weller I principally by increasing marriage bonuses for one-earner couples; equal-earner couples were treated the same under the two versions. Republicans thus responded to Democratic inertia on the first version of marriage penalty relief by upping the stakes; McIntosh-Weller II was estimated to cost $30 billion a year.

The saga of marriage penalty relief nicely illustrates the practical effects of the divergent salience of tax reduction for men and women. Whereas McIntosh-Weller I ought to have appealed to working women as lowering the secondary earner bias and the taxes facing two-earner couples, this traditionally Democratic constituency preferred using the money for general social spending. Left on their own to formulate tax-reduction plans, Republicans increased the stakes by widening their proposal to include all married couples, most notably including the more traditional, single-earner families at the center of the contemporary social conservative movement. Because taxes matter more to the core Republican constituency, the *form* of tax relief gets shaped by traditionally conservative preferences, even where the provisions at issue have deep impacts on traditionally liberal and feminist concerns and constituencies.

Prospects for Change

Our central thesis is that men and women do not differ significantly in their first order preferences toward tax or, presumably, in their self-interested orientation, once the same issue is joined. Men and women do seem to differ, however, in the second order weighting or ranking of their primary preferences, with men putting more emphasis on tax than women do. All of this plays out against a background fact of structural gender biases in the law.

If our analysis of political behavior is correct—we conclude by stressing the need for more research and analysis—the possibilities for effecting tax law change to help modern working women lie in two directions. One is through attaching greater salience of tax issues for women. In one way or another, women and feminists generally would have to pay more attention to tax—would have to weight the issues of tax more heavily in their political behavior. This change involves a reordering of private preferences.

A second possibility for change lies in reforming institutional mechanisms so that tax rules can be promulgated independent of other issues, for the pairing of tax with other issues can be seen to contribute to the gender bias of the law. Voting rules that allowed for separate input on discrete policy issues would make more manifest the underlying first order preferences of the voters. This change would not involve any change or reordering of private preferences; it would simply allow those preferences that already exist but can be hidden by a second order weighting procedure to come out.

Conclusions and Suggestions for Further Research

There is more research that needs to be undertaken to explore the basic findings presented in this chapter: one, men and women do not differ significantly in their primary preferences over matters of tax and, two, that they do differ in their secondary ranking of these preferences. Only by a much more thorough analysis of the ways in which tax issues play out in electoral politics in the United States can we better understand the persistence of significant gender biases in tax policy in recent decades. At this point in our research, we do know that these gender biases in tax policy exist and that women and men place different weight on tax issues when making candidate choices in national elections.

The next stages in this research agenda must take two different paths. The first is to explore more directly the relative salience of tax issues for men and women through additional studies of existing survey and public opinion data. Are the differences in opinions and decisions we have found a persistent attribute of American politics? Have men and women consistently in recent decades thought the same or differently about tax issues? There simply has been little research on this important question.

The second direction of research is to gain a better understanding of how tax issues are being raised and discussed by political leaders and elites. How are these leaders and politicians framing tax issues? Do they evoke different frames for men and women? Is this at least partially the source of gender differences in opinions about taxation? Can political elites and candidates produce "gender gaps" in opinions about tax policy? Again, there has been little research conducted on how politicians and elites politicize tax issues along gender lines. As in many other aspects of gender and politics and our understanding of their relationships, it is time for change.

Notes

1. There is a large literature on the gender gap in American national elections. See Chaney, Alvarez, and Nagler (1998) and Mattei and Mattei (1998) for helpful summaries.

2. McCaffery (1997) contains much of the relevant historical background. The principal features in the pattern of gender bias are the provision of spousal benefits under Social Security, put into law in 1939 (see chapter 4); joint filing under the income tax, put in effect in 1948 (chapter 3); and the refusal to systematically treat child-care expenses as tax-deductible business ones, beginning with a judicial decision in 1939 (chapter 5).

3. See Goldin (1990) and U.S. Department of Commerce (1998) for relevant statistics.

References

Alvarez, Michael, and Matthew Schousen. 1993. "Policy Moderation or Conflicting Expectations: Testing the Intentional Models of Split Ticket Voting." *American Politics Quarterly* 21(4): 410–438.

Chaney, Carol Kennedy, R. Michael Alvarez, and Jonathan Nagler. 1998. "Explaining the Gender Gap in U.S. Presidential Elections, 1980–1992." *Political Research Quarterly* 51(2): 311–340.

Feenberg, Daniel R., and Harvey S. Rosen. 1995. "Recent Developments in the Marriage Tax." *National Tax Journal* 48(1): 91–101.

Gilligan, Carol. 1982. *In a Different Voice: Psychological Theory and Women's Development.* Cambridge, MA: Harvard University Press.

Goldin, Claudia. 1990. *Understanding the Gender Gap: An Economic History of American Women.* Cambridge, MA: Harvard University Press.

Hanson, Sandra L., and Theodora Ooms. 1991. "The Economic Costs and Rewards of Two-Earner, Two-Parent Families." *Journal of Marriage and the Family* 53(3): 622–634.

Jacobson, Gary C. 1990. *The Electoral Origins of Divided Government: Competition in U.S. House Elections, 1946–1988.* Boulder, CO: Westview.

Jones, Carolyn C. 1988. "Split Income and Separate Spheres: Tax Law and Gender Roles in the 1940s." *Law and History Review* 6(Fall): 259–310.

Kahneman, Daniel, and Amos Tversky. 1979. "Prospect Theory: An Analysis of Decision Under Risk." *Econometrica* 47(2): 263–291.

Kornhauser, Marjorie E. 1997. "What Do Women Want? Feminism and the Progressive Income Tax." *American University Law Review* 47(1): 151–163.

———. 1987. "The Rhetoric of the Anti-Progressive Income Tax Movement: A Typical Male Reaction." *Michigan Law Review* 86(3): 465–523.

Leuthold, Jane H. 1984. "Income Splitting and Women's Labor-Force Participation." *Industrial and Labor Relations Review* 38(1): 98–105.

Mattei, Laura Winsky, and Franco Mattei. 1998. "If Men Stayed Home . . . The Gender Gap in Recent Congressional Elections." *Political Research Quarterly* 51(2): 411–436.

McCaffery, Edward J. 1997. *Taxing Women.* Chicago: University of Chicago Press.

Schlafly, Phyllis. 1998. "Watch Out for Marriage Tax Reform." Available from http://www.eagleforum.org. February 4, 1998 [cited November 1, 1998].

Turnier, William J., Pamela Johnston Conover, and David Lowery. 1996. "Redistributive Justice and Cultural Feminism." *American University Law Review* 45: 1275–1322.

U.S. Department of Commerce. U.S. Bureau of the Census. 1998. *Statistical Abstract of the United States, 118th Edition.* Washington, DC: U.S. Government Printing Office.

Welch, Susan, and John Hibbing. 1992. "Financial Conditions, Gender and Voting in American National Elections." *Journal of Politics* 54(1): 197–213.

5

Gendering Policy Debates
Job Training and Abortion Regulation

Dorothy McBride Stetson

Introduction

For over thirty years, organizations and individuals in the feminist movement in the United States have sought to influence government. What has been the impact of the movement on politics and policy-making?

There are various ways to try to assess the impact of social movements on government (Gamson 1975). One is to look at the *content* of laws passed. Another is to see if government leaders recognize and receive movement leaders as legitimate representatives of a constituency, a *procedural* response.

This chapter focuses on a third type of response which is an important link between movement demands on one hand and policy content and procedural responses on the other: *substantive representation* of movement demands in the policymaking process. Substantive representation is the inclusion of a group's policy preferences and issues in the agenda of government (Pitkin 1967). For the feminist movement, such representation involves more than just putting their issues on the agenda; it means the inclusion of their gender ideas in the framework of the debates on these issues.

This chapter is organized in three parts. First is a discussion of how the framing of policy debates may lead to substantive representation of feminist goals through gendering. A description follows of four policy debates in Congress, two on job training and two on abortion regulation.[1] Finally, there is an assessment of the effect of framing in these debates on policy content and procedural responses.

Substantive Representation and Framing Policy Debates

This research is based on a conception of the policymaking process in the American government as a conflict of ideas about what policy actions the government should take. In fact, conflict persists in regular patterns that develop around policy issues and become institutionalized. Policy actors—in Congress, the executive branch, interest groups, and the courts—participate in these structured patterns of controversy and are part of a policy community. Consideration of specific issues takes place in the context of a *frame* or mode of defining policy problems. The dominant frame of an issue is the accepted understanding in the policy community of what the conflict is about. For example, in considering a question of regulating pornography, whether on the street or the Internet, the problem is defined as a conflict over what the limits of government regulation of free speech should be. Although there are many points of view about problems raised by pornography other than free speech—for example, concerns about the exploitation of women, morality and decency, and literary merit—these are secondary topics that policy actors consider only as they pertain to the overall frame of the issue.

Knowing the frame of the debate is especially important to social movement activists and any others who are seeking to influence the content of policy. Gelb and Palley (1982) produced evidence of this in their study of the feminist movement's lobbying activities on a series of women's rights issues in the 1970s. They found that feminist activists had a better chance of success if they defined their demands in terms of achieving equality between the sexes—role equity—rather than in terms of recasting traditional roles of men and women—role change. Role change issues were considered to be too threatening and radical. In other words, they did not fit the dominant frame—the institutionalized definition of policy issues relating to gender.

The way debates are framed or defined also affects who gets access to public discussions, that is, the procedural aspect of policymaking. "To define an issue is to make an assertion about what is at stake and who is affected, and therefore, to define interests and the constitution of alliances" (Stone 1997, 231). The frame, therefore, sets forth which social interests should have a say when specific bills are considered by Congress. Issues defined as health concerns invite doctors and other health professionals into the political arena. Issues that are about role equity bring liberal feminist advocates to the congressional hearings. Of course, there are no formal regulations that bar others from trying to press their point of view. Getting the attention of the powerful, however, is problematic for those not considered to be affected by a particular policy discussion.

Taken together, the conceptual frameworks of all debates on public issues constitute a guide to what and who matter in a democracy. The public agenda consists of a set of issue conflicts that concern political leaders. There is a hierarchy of such conflicts: those at the top of the agenda, their dominant frames, and the people considered to be affected by them, are close to centers of power—they are *heard*. Those at the bottom are on the *margins* of the policy scope. And, conflicts not on the agenda and the people they affect are *unheard*. The vital conflict in policymaking in democracy, therefore, is over the conflicts themselves and the way they are framed (Schattschneider 1960; Przeworski 1991).

Feminist advocates seek to gender policy debates, that is, insert references to gender into the frame of the debate. *Gender* refers to ideas about men and women in relation to each other and ideas about women or men as groups distinct from each other. Gendering means policy actors explicitly and intentionally insert ideas about gender differences into a policy debate. But not just any gendering means feminist substantive representation. To be a success for the feminist movement, the gendered terms must coincide with feminist perspectives, usually in terms that advance the status of women in relation to men and that challenge gender hierarchies.[2] It is important to remember, at this point, that feminist activists do not always agree among themselves on precisely what actions will best accomplish this goal.

Until the first wave of the American women's movement in the 1800s, the main business of government did not pertain to citizens in their gender roles. Laws certainly affected women, especially married women, as a separate group, but policy conflicts about them were not high on the public agenda. And when issues were debated in gendered terms, these ideas reinforced traditional gender roles. The hierarchy of conflicts occupying policymakers did not place women as a significant part of the democratic polity. The great goal and success of that first movement was to convince politicians that policy areas relating to property, labor, and the franchise were issues that affected women. In other words they wanted to *gender* these issues in a particular way—

to frame them in terms that compared the rights of women to those of men—and then to campaign to achieve equitable policies.

By the early 1900s, the movement goal remained the same, but the advocates began to promote a different set of gender references, those that advanced arguments in terms of the effects of policies on women in their roles as mothers and social reformers. In the last thirty years, the contemporary women's movement, sometimes referred to as the third wave, has campaigned to bring private gender issues to public attention. Advocates promote matters such as reproductive rights, sexuality, sex crimes, and sexual harassment in ways that challenge the gender-based social hierarchies prevailing in intimate relationships. Although activists in these movements had different priorities and views of gender, they all had the same goal: to convince policymakers to incorporate gender ideas in terms they believed would improve the status of women into the framing of public issues. The stakes were high: the frame of the issue affected not only the content of laws, but also who would gain access to the centers of power.

Feminist activists, therefore, are concerned with more than simply presenting petitions relaying the demands and interests of their constituents in the hope that Congress will act. Their challenge is twofold: First is to push their priority conflicts higher on the agenda of government. Second is to influence the institutionalized frame of debate on important issues in feminist terms, so that the questions policymakers will consider concern whether or not to enact policy provisions that will improve the status of women in relation to men. If both steps are achieved, then they are in a position to present their list of demands and interests and call upon their political resources to promote them. Their long-term goal is to institutionalize their definition of the issue in the policy community. In short, women's rights activists want government to take women's situation into account and to make it and its relation to men's situation the business of government. Of course, it is not enough that policies be defined as gender questions; feminists want to see that the debate presents congressional representatives with one choice: whether to act for or against improving women's rights and status.

What do feminists hope to gain by such a strategy? They want legislation that advances the feminist agenda, in other words, success for their movement in influencing the content of policy. Then, as a matter of course, statutes enacted by Congress would include provisions to advance women's status in relation to men. But there are other rewards, possibly more important in the long run. By defining policy issues in terms of women and their status, feminists, as representatives of women's groups and as advocates for a particular agenda, would be considered important spokespeople for a particular constituency and experts in a policy area and become regular participants in the policy process. Thus, whenever a proposal arises within this—let's call it a feminist—frame, feminist organizations would be called upon to participate. And, their views would be taken into account.[3]

Goal and Approach

This chapter examines debates on job training and abortion regulation, two issue areas periodically before Congress. These policy areas were selected to represent two different types of gender issues in the public arena. Job training is a distributive policy question: conflicts pertain primarily to the assignment of public funds to various groups needing job training or are interested in operating programs for workers. Job training is also an issue that pertains to gender roles distributed between work and family responsibilities. Other issues in this area are child care, labor rights, education, and equal opportunity laws. Abortion policy is an example of an emotive-symbolic issue. Conflicts pertain primarily to basic values such as the beginning of life and fundamental human rights. Abortion regulation represents a group of issues that involve gender roles in reproduction. Other issues in this area include contraception, sterilization, and new reproductive technologies.

The two job training debates involve consideration of significant legislation affecting the federal government's role in job training: renewal of Comprehensive Employment and Training Act (CETA) in 1978 and the Job Training Partnership Act (JTPA) of 1982. The abortion regulations revolve around the debates over the Freedom of Choice Act (FOCA) in 1990–1993 and the Partial Birth Abortion Ban Act (PBAB) in 1995.

Both job training and abortion regulations are gender issues in that they affect men and women differently. But each can be discussed without reference to ideas about men and women. The task here is to find the gendered references, if any, and compare them to demands of feminist movement individuals and organizations. The policy debates for each of the bills studied in this chapter will be presented according to the following outline. First will be a description of the dominant frame of the debate and the positions of proponents and opponents in relation to it. Then there will be a discussion of the gendered ideas in the debate—images of women and men as presented by the proponents and opponents—including a judgment on the centrality of the gender debates to the overall frame of the debate on the bill. Finally, there will be a conclusion about the extent to which the gendering of the debate coincides with goals and demands of feminist organizations and the impact on policy content and procedures.

Job Training 1: CETA 1978

The 1973 Comprehensive Employment and Training Act (CETA) consolidated federal job training programs and accelerated public job creation to combat unemployment. Its renewal prompted Congress to convene hearings between 1976 and 1978. President Carter proposed to use CETA reauthorization to increase job creation as part of an economic stimulus package to cope with both cyclical unemployment of skilled workers, caused by recessions, and structural unemployment, associated with those who lacked necessary skills to find regular employment. The Carter plan also directed special funds toward training programs for disadvantaged groups, especially youth, older workers, the handicapped, migrants, and Indians. Another bill to include divorced and widowed middle-aged women—the Displaced Homemaker Act of 1977—was debated in public hearings as an amendment to the CETA proposal.

Controversy over the public jobs creation portion of the proposal became the dominant frame of the CETA debate. It was fueled by growing opposition to the expansion of federal programs spawned by the Great Society agenda of the 1960s. A related question involved evidence of fraud and abuse in local CETA programs. Conservatives favored job training over job creation, thus placing the two parts of the Act in opposition. Labor unions and Labor Department officials lobbied to retain financial support for creation of public jobs.

Because there were separate hearings on the Displaced Homemaker Bill, most of the gender ideas were introduced away from the CETA hearings. Displaced homemakers were depicted as a special group of women who, as life-long homemakers, were economically dependent with few skills or job experiences. When divorce or widowhood came upon them, they were disabled as workers. Their lot was depicted in bleak terms, painting a picture of devastated, disappointed middle-aged women, forcibly exiled from their homes and facing sex discrimination in seeking jobs. Both men and women can be unemployed, it was agreed, but men are more likely to lose their jobs because technology has replaced them. Women homemakers lose their jobs when their husbands leave them. Advocates blamed sex role stereotyping for the plight of displaced homemakers, leaving them without education, training or experience to cope with work responsibilities. Society urged women to become mothers and homemakers; now society had to step in, in the form of the federal government, to help them support themselves.

The Alliance for Displaced Homemakers was the chief women's advocacy group participating in the hearings. Their goal to get financial support for their group was fully supported by the National Organization for Women, the Women's Bureau of the Department of Labor, and many commissions on the status of women in the states. Thus the gendered depiction of this group of women, as a disadvantaged group in comparison to men, coincided with the dominant liberal feminist organization in the United States in the 1970s as well as federal and state women's policy agencies.

In the hearings on CETA itself, some attention to women workers appeared in two areas: efforts to train women into nontraditional jobs to overcome occupational segregation, and efforts to help women who were reentering the work force after raising a family. Participants in the debates referred to the inequalities women faced in job training programs and advocated affirmative action and better enforcement of equality laws in general. The growing recognition in the 1970s that poverty was primarily a women's condition also made its way into the hearings on CETA. Even though women participated in large numbers in CETA programs they were being trained for low paying jobs.

All these gendered themes were marginal to the debate on CETA itself; the dominant frame remained the issue of job creation versus job training. The separate hearings on displaced homemakers and active support of Representative Yvonne Burke gave the displaced homemaker approach a special boost. Thus it was the only gender theme included in the final version of the Act. Displaced homemakers were included as one of those groups of disadvantaged workers—migrants, veterans, youth—who were eligible for federal funds for job training. Otherwise there were no gender references in the Act. Therefore, despite this recognition, gender was marginal to the overall content of CETA policy.

The day President Carter signed CETA into effect, the Alliance for Displaced Homemakers reorganized as the Displaced Homemakers Network (DHN). It became the central source for coordinating all the job training and counseling programs supported by federal funds throughout the country. The DHN also became a regular representative of the interests of displaced homemakers in congressional hearings and with the Department of Labor for the next 15 years. Opening this policy door a crack also brought in another group, Wider Opportunities for Women (WOW). Both became regular if marginal participants in subsequent job training hearings.

Outcome

CETA passed both houses of Congress and was signed by President Carter in 1978. The renewed CETA focused the program more than the first version on the chronically unemployed and away from skilled workers who had lost jobs due to recession. Thus, public service employment went from serving primarily white males to providing help for low income minorities and women. This was in the absence of explicit gendering of the debate or the act. In 1980, however, Ronald Reagan was elected president along with a Republican majority in the Senate. Reagan and the Republicans brought new resources to those opposing big government jobs programs.

Job Training 2: JTPA 1982

CETA had been reauthorized for 4 years, but soon after Reagan took office the advocates of creating public jobs were in retreat, replaced by a bipartisan focus on job training. The proposed Job Training Partnership Act (JTPA) of 1982 reached the public arena based on the assumption that CETA 1973/1978 had been a dismal failure, fraught with abuses, fraud, and mismanagement. The dominant frame of the JTPA debate pertained to the role of the federal government in employment policy. The proposal was to change this role dramatically, by eliminating job creation provisions and shifting administration of job training activities to the private business sector and oversight to the states. The federal government would provide some funds, and retain its special projects for disadvantaged groups.

Feminist activists agreed that CETA was inadequate. But the JTPA proposal looked worse: it had no special provisions for women workers, no attention to nontraditional occupations, displaced homemakers, or to poor women. Their task was to insert gender into the debate, in the hopes of changing the provisions of the Act to help women workers improve their status. However, only one advocate for women, a representative of WOW, appeared at the main hearings on the bill. Feminists had to content themselves with special hearings on "Sex Discrimination in the Workplace" in the Senate, convened by Senator Edward Kennedy in a subcommittee in 1981 and 1982. Thus, gendering the policy debate over job training in 1981 and 1982 was again marginal to the dominant frame of the issue before Congress.

The gender ideas in the debate were similar to those of the CETA debate. Women were represented as a separate group deserving special attention: they were represented as poor, with inadequate information about jobs and training. Especially disadvantaged was the group known as displaced homemakers. Further, women held poorly paid, occupationally segregated positions. Advocates gave evidence that women and men were segregated in different jobs. Women were paid less than men and men had a higher status in the work force than women. Others argued that age affected women differently than it did men: women in their middle years are "over the hill" while men of the same age are in their prime. To blame for this situation were stereotyping of women and their abilities and family responsibilities, which push women into segregated jobs.

These gender ideas were presented in policy debates by leaders of organizations well recognized for their activities in promoting the status of women workers: the National Commission on Working Women; DHN; and WOW. Their views coincided with the goals of many feminists: for the most part, those actively interested in issues of work and training. They were confined, however, to a minuscule place in the public arena of debate on the job training issue in the early 1980s.

The content of the JTPA was disappointing to feminist advocates. While displaced homemakers were again included as one of the disadvantaged groups eligible for special federal job training funds, the

Act included little focus on affirmative action goals or the needs of other women workers for training. There also was little change in the procedural response to the movement. DHN and WOW remained recognized spokespeople for women on the job training issue.

Outcome

The JTPA passed both houses of Congress and was signed by President Reagan. With its emphasis on decentralization and private sector partnerships, it has remained the basic template for federal job training policy, with periodic review and amendments. Feminist advocates gained more attention for women in some of the subsequent amendments. For example, the Nontraditional Employment for Women (NEW) Act of 1991 urged governors to track and report on the number of women trained in nontraditional occupations under the JTPA funds. With the NEW Act, groups representing women in nontraditional occupations gained access to congressional hearings.

Abortion Regulation 1: Freedom of Choice Act of 1989/1990

The Freedom of Choice Act (FOCA) brought the issue of legalization of abortion directly into Congress for the first time since *Roe v. Wade* (410 U.S. 113 [1973]). In the 1970s and 1980s, opponents of restrictions on abortion had not been very successful in congressional encounters with antiabortion advocates. After 1976, when the Hyde Amendment restricted the use of Medicaid funds for abortion services, they failed in efforts to provide federal funds for abortion counseling or for international family planning. Abortion opponents were frequently successful in inserting the abortion restrictions into many bills including military appropriations, education policy, and health policy. Abortion-rights groups relied on the federal courts, not Congress, to maintain legalized abortion in the United States. In the late 1980s, however, there was evidence that the courts were beginning to waiver. Presidents Reagan and Bush had appointed justices who, they believed, opposed abortion. When the case of *Webster v. Reproductive Services* (57 U.S.L.W. 5023 [1989]) reached the Court in 1989, many feared there were enough votes to overturn *Roe*.

This threat stirred the congressional supporters of the *Roe* decision in Congress to action. They introduced FOCA, and debates took place in the wake of the *Webster* decision. While the case did not affect the legality of abortion, a plurality of the Supreme Court indicated their willingness to overturn the abortion rights guaranteed in *Roe v. Wade* in 1973 and invited state governments to pass restrictive legislation to provide test cases for the impending reversal. To avoid this prospect, FOCA was drafted explicitly to write the *Roe* guarantees into federal law: that abortion before viability of the fetus was legal.

The dominant frame of debate over FOCA involved the conflict between the woman's right to choose to seek abortion services against the right of the unborn to continue life. Proponents of the bill argued that the Act would guarantee the fundamental right of reproductive freedom. Opponents claimed that abortion was killing children and should be banned. There was a secondary debate over whether the bill was constitutional or an unwarranted and illegal grab of federal power. Opponents charged that the simple but absolute language of FOCA went far beyond the guarantees in *Roe* and was an unconstitutional power grab by the federal government over the states. It would, they charged, nullify state regulations on abortion that provided for informed consent, parental notification, and waiting periods, all upheld in the *Webster* decision.

Unlike the job training debates we have reviewed, the dominant frame of the debate over FOCA focused on the rights of a gendered group—women—against a nongendered entity: the unborn fetus. Ideas expressed included all women, although in practice only women of child-bearing age are directly affected. The opposing entity—the unborn fetus—may be male or female; it was ungendered in the debate. Images used by policy actors to describe legal abortion illustrate this pattern. Proponents of FOCA saw legal abortion as: fundamental freedom for women; women's self-determination; advancing women's health care; and a highly personal decision between a woman and her doctor. For opponents legal abortion was: child abuse; killing children; a destructive right; or termination of the unborn (U.S. Congress, House 1990; U.S. Congress, Senate 1992).

Both proponents and opponents used vivid imagery of women in their presentations. Proponents saw women as a group with special health concerns relating to their reproductive functions and thus the need for self-determination in seeking care. Women would take risks to end pregnancies if abortion became illegal. They depicted desperate women either self-aborting with coat hangers and knitting needles or seeking back street butchers. Proponents of FOCA also mentioned that some women—poor, young, pregnant because of rape or incest—are particularly vulnerable to mistreatment in the absence of accessible legal abortion services.

For the most part, opponents of FOCA focused on the rights of the unborn and other right-to-life arguments. However, to counter the freedom of choice arguments, opponents discussed their views of women who may be considering abortion. They were likely to choose abortion due to emotional distress or ignorance of fetal development ("until they view that little baby on the screen" said one). Opponents also spoke of those who are especially vulnerable to making the abortion decisions because they are "poor, minority, young, black" and do not know what abortion does, how it is performed, and the effects or complications. Opponents did not extend their discussion to all women; they focused on the pregnant woman only, claiming that this condition changed a woman's rights fundamentally. She is not alone, there are two individuals with rights. Her right then is to give birth, not to kill her unborn child. Interestingly, a few opponents of FOCA were the only ones to bring another gendered approach into the discussion: characteristics of men. It was not in a positive way, as they lamented the fact that too many males saw abortion, the pill, and the IUD as relieving them of responsibility for their sexual actions.

Gendered ideas were central to the debate over FOCA because the dominant conceptual framework defined the abortion issue as a conflict between the rights of women and the rights of the unborn fetus. In addition, the gendered references, for the most part, were consistent with demands of the mainstream feminist lobbies in Washington such as NOW and the National Abortion Rights Action League (NARAL) (Staggenborg 1991). The specific gender terms isolated women as a group without any reference to men and cast a woman's rights against those of the fetus and the states to regulate them. There was even some reference to the rights of physicians to assist patients in obtaining reproductive health options, which had been central to the actual decision in *Roe v. Wade*. As we will see in the next section, that was not the case with the next abortion debate to be covered.

Despite the central frame of the debate, no representatives of feminist groups testified at congressional hearings on FOCA. The feminist position in the debate was presented by members of Congress themselves, such as Representatives Patricia Schroeder and Don Edwards, and Senators Edward Kennedy and Christopher Dodd. There is no doubt that groups such as NOW and NARAL are recognized as legitimate representatives of the feminist movement. What it does indicate is that the frame of the debate was so embedded in the policy community surrounding the regulation of abortion, that members of Congress articulated the demands. With FOCA, however, the organizations representing the rights of the fetus, such as the National Right to Life Committee, did testify.

Outcome

Although FOCA fared well in congressional subcommittees, it was never brought to a vote by either the House of Representatives or the Senate. The bill enjoyed majority support in both houses, but not sufficient to withstand procedural tactics of opponents (*Congressional Quarterly* 1990). In 1992, the Supreme Court upheld the basic ruling of legalized abortion in *Planned Parenthood v. Casey* (112 SCt 2791[1992]) while sustaining states' efforts to erect administrative hurdles to services. That case, along with the election of Bill Clinton to the presidency in 1992, lessened the urgency that had motivated sponsors of FOCA. In one of his first acts as president, Clinton rescinded a series of antiabortion directives put in place by Reagan and Bush.

Abortion Regulation 2: Partial-Birth Abortion Ban Act of 1995

Much changed in Congress between the debates in 1989–91 on FOCA and the Partial Birth Abortion Ban (PBAB) Act of 1995. The Republican party gained majorities in both houses and many ardent opponents of legal abortion considered abortion regulation to be a high priority. Despite twenty years of campaigns, *Roe v. Wade* continued to be in force with no change in the dominant frame of abortion debates. Although administrative hurdles and declining services hampered many women seeking abortions, it was still legal. With the PBAB Act, the proponents of abortion regulation took a bold new tactic: to change the frame of the debate on abortion, making the issue the procedure itself.

The PBAB Act of 1995 proposed a nationwide ban on a procedure the proponents of the bill called "partial birth." They let their definition of this procedure stand as representative of the public policy problem they hoped to address: "An abortion in which the person performing the abortion partially vaginally delivers a living fetus before killing the fetus and completing the delivery." They offered both clinical and emotional elaborations of the procedure to complete their definition of the issue at hand: this procedure is gruesome. Because the fetus is killed while its head is still in the uterus, they claimed, it is "3 inches" away from a procedure that would be called murder.

Opponents of the ban sought to turn the discussion away from baby killing and the proponents' emotion-laden version of the procedure but they were not united in their definition of the issue. Some said that partial birth did not exist as named. A few assumed there was a medical procedure involved but wanted to make the issue the question of the federal government prohibiting a medical procedure, an unprecedented extension of federal power, they said. Another opposition argument pleaded for an exception to the ban to protect a woman's life and health. Some Senate Democrats confronted this bill as a tactic in the pro-life agenda to outlaw all abortions, and saw the bill, while not affecting many people who seek abortions, as an assault on the basic right to have an abortion. In this they hoped to return the debate to right-to-choose/right-to-life terms.

Despite such efforts, during the PBAB hearings Congress was arguing less over women's rights and more over physicians' rights to use a particular medical procedure. There were gendered ideas in the debate, to be sure, but they were not central to the conflict. In fact the fetus took center stage in the discussions as the "partial birth" procedure was characterized as an assault on human life: "This is a method that takes that life as the baby emerges from the mother's womb and while the baby is in the birth canal" (U.S. Congress. House. 1995, p. 1). In the depiction of the procedure there was no gender, except to the extent that body parts were representative of gender: the uterus (womb) and the vagina (birth canal). But these were part of the environment and important only in reference to the placement of the fetus during the procedure. When whole women were discussed, they were either as pregnant women, "the natural protector of her child in the womb" or, if a doctor performs an abortion on her, "her child's deadly adversary." One participant described women as victims of abortion, casting physicians in the role of villains and putting women on the margins of the issue.

Opponents of the ban sought to place gender—specifically the rights of women to seek medical care—in a more central position in the debate. They charged that the proponents were trying to cast women, along with doctors, as demons, even witches, by making the procedure sound so terrible. They tried to discuss women as responsible citizens seeking health care. The bill would interfere with a medical decision between a woman and her doctor, they claimed. Women must have the right to decide when and where to bear children and government should place no limits on the doctor's choices. Many also focused on the question of federal government power, trying to shift attention toward a question of federalism, and saying that the government should not tell the "women of America and their families" what medical procedures they should have.

The debate on the PBAB Act is noteworthy because it represents a change in the dominant frame of the abortion regulation issue which had been institutionalized since *Roe v. Wade*. This change degendered the conflict and put feminist advocates outside the policy process. The proponents of the ban were successful in shifting the frame away from the gendered issues of rights of women to make the issue under consideration a gruesomely depicted abortion procedure. Opponents of the ban tried, unsuccessfully, to bring gendered ideas of women's rights, self-determination, and health into the discussion. They made their points, but they were not successful in casting the proposal in gendered terms. These points were consistent, as before, with mainstream feminist organizations. So, a failure for them can be seen as a failure for the feminists regardless of whether the ban went into effect or not. Further, this new definition of the abortion issue undercuts the legitimacy of feminist groups, and their friends in Congress, jeopardizing their membership in the policy community.

Outcome

The PBAB Act passed both houses of Congress in 1995 but was vetoed by President Clinton. He maintained that the Act did not have adequate provisions in case the procedure was necessary to protect the life or health of the mother. In 1997, advocates again successfully pushed the bill through Congress followed by a presidential veto. Efforts to override the veto succeeded in the House of Representatives but failed by three votes, in 1998, in the Senate.

Conclusion

In this chapter we have been able to review two policy debates on two issues of interest to the feminist movement in the United States. These cases represent only a small number of many efforts by feminist activists to influence Congress. Yet, they show that encounters between the movement and the government are dynamic, and they reinforce the conclusion that assessing the impact of the feminist movement is a complex undertaking. This section describes two patterns of movement impact suggested by the analysis of congressional hearings.

The issue of job training is defined, primarily, in nongendered terms. The dominant frame of the debate has changed from a question of public jobs versus job training to concerns about the role of the federal government in job training programs. The feminists were successful in inserting gender into this frame by aligning displaced homemakers— women disadvantaged in the job market due to marriage and child rearing—as a group deserving of federal attention. Although efforts were made to introduce other gender ideas in relation, especially, to job training, only displaced homemakers gained official recognition. This niche in the frame of the debate was established during consideration of CETA, and remained through the enactment of JTPA. The content of job training policy included funds for training and counseling programs for displaced homemakers from 1978 until the early 1990s. At the same time, there were procedural successes for the feminists. Two feminist organizations, the DHN and WOW, appeared regularly at congressional hearings on job training; in 1991 they were able to secure additional funds for training women in nontraditional occupations. The story of the job training policy debates shows a modest success for feminist organizations in obtaining substantive representation, changes in policy content, and procedural access to the policymaking process.

The cases of debates on abortion regulation in the 1990s show a different pattern of interaction between the feminist movement and Congress. What we have seen in the two debates is a transition from movement success to failure. The feminists had been successful in the early seventies, aided by the Supreme Court's ruling in *Roe v. Wade* in inserting the idea of women's right to choose abortion into the dominant frame of the abortion issue. Evidence of the effects of this successful substantive representation for women was the debate on FOCA in 1989–1991. The debate focused directly on ways of advancing women's rights. The content of the Act put the basic rights of *Roe* into federal law, which, if enacted would have undermined restrictions found in many state laws. Procedural access for feminists was so complete that prominent congressional leaders represented their views at the congressional hearings.

From that pinnacle of success, the feminist movement failed to divert the successful efforts by proponents of abortion regulation to degender the dominant frame of the abortion debate. With the PBAB Act debate, the question for congressional action became whether doctors should be allowed to use a particular abortion procedure against a fetus in the second trimester of pregnancy. Women's rights and status were displaced to the margins of the debate. Content and procedural failures followed from this substantive de-representation. The law Congress enacted restricted an aspect of abortion rights for women, and in the "partial birth" debates, representatives of the feminist movement lost their status as insiders. Thus, the abortion regulation debates show the costs to feminist activists of losing in the conflict over the definition of policy issues.

The information in this chapter illustrates a way of using the concept of gender to study change in the policymaking process and the impact of social movements. The debates studied here demonstrate the significance of the use of language and ideas in securing access to power and resources. It is not just the provisions of policy proposals that matter—the meaning of these provisions to policy actors is just as important. To be successful, movement activists must recognize what is at stake and struggle to retain a place for their ideas in the dominant frame of policy issues high on the public agenda.

Notes

1. The sources of information on these debates are transcripts of congressional hearings: U.S. Congress, House: 1997, 1978, 1982, 1990, 1995. Senate: 1978, 1981, 1982, 1990, 1992, 1995. These are an excellent source of information about the range of debates because the practice is to include a variety of policy actors—members of Congress, bureaucrats, interest group spokespeople, experts, and personal testimony of individuals. Newspapers would be another source. Often these depend heavily on information found in the hearings.

2. For various studies of feminism, its origins and impact on politics see, for

example, Offen (1988), Ferree and Martin (1995), Gelb (1989), Katzenstein and Mueller (1987), and Ryan (1992).

3. Rochon and Mazmanian (1993) refer to these movement successes in terms of *process change*. They argue that process change may prove to have a more long lasting impact than changes in policy content.

References

Ferree, Myra Marx, and Patricia Yancey Martin, eds. 1995. *Feminist Organizations*. Philadelphia: Temple University Press.

Gamson, William A. 1975. *The Strategy of Social Protest*. Homewood, IL: The Dorsey Press.

Gelb, Joyce. 1989. *Feminism and Politics: A Comparative Perspective*. Berkeley: University of California Press.

Gelb, Joyce, and Marian Lief Palley. 1982. *Women and Public Policies*. Princeton: Princeton University Press.

"Hill Faces Trench Warfare Over Abortion Rights." 1990. *Congressional Quarterly* (25 August): 2713–2719.

Katzenstein, Mary Fainsod, and Carol Mueller, eds. 1987. *The Women's Movements of the United States and Western Europe*. Philadelphia: Temple University Press.

Offen, Karen. 1988. "Defining Feminism: A Comparative Historical Approach." *Signs* 17(1): 119–157.

Pitkin, Hanna Fenichel. 1967. *The Concept of Representation*. Berkeley: University of California Press.

Przeworski, Adam. 1991. *Democracy and the Market: Political and Economic Reforms in Eastern Europe and Latin America*. Cambridge: Cambridge University Press.

Rochon, Thomas R., and Daniel A. Mazmanian. 1993. "Social Movements and the Policy Process." *Annals of the American Academy of Political Social Science* 528(July): 75–87.

Ryan, Barbara. 1992. *Feminism and the Women's Movement: Dynamics of Change in Social Movement Ideology and Activism*. New York: Routledge.

Schattschneider, E.E. 1960. *The Semisovereign People: A Realist's View of Democracy in America*. New York: Holt, Rinehart & Winston.

Staggenborg, Suzanne. 1991. *The Pro-Choice Movement: Organization and Activism in the Abortion Conflict*. New York: Oxford University Press.

Stone, Deborah. 1997. *Policy Paradox: The Art of Decision Making*. New York: Norton.

U.S. Congress. House. 1977. Subcommittee on Employment Opportunities of the Committee on Education and Labor. "The Displaced Homemakers Act." July 14.

U.S. Congress. House. 1978. Subcommittee on Employment Opportunities of the Committee on Education and Labor. "Comprehensive Employment and Training Amendments of 1978." February, March, April.

U.S. Congress. House. 1982. Subcommittee on Employment Opportunities of the Committee on Education and Labor. "Hearing on Employment and Training Proposals." March.

U.S. Congress. House. 1990. Subcommittee on Civil and Constitutional Rights of the Committee on the Judiciary. "Freedom of Choice Act of 1989." October 2–3.

U.S. Congress. House. 1995. Subcommittee on the Constitution of the Committee on the Judiciary. "Partial Birth Abortion Ban Act of 1995." June 15.

U.S. Congress. Senate. 1978. Subcommittee on Employment Poverty, and Migratory Labor of the Committee on Human Resources. "Comprehensive Employment and Training Amendments of 1978." February, March.

U.S. Congress. Senate. 1981. Committee on Labor and Human Resources. "Sex Discrimination in the Workplace, 1981." January, April.

U.S. Congress. Senate. 1982. Subcommittee on Employment and Productivity of the Committee on Labor and Human Resources and Subcommittee on Employment Opportunities of the House Committee on Education and Labor. "Employment and Training Policy, 1982." March.

U.S. Congress. Senate. 1990. Committee on Labor and Human Resources. "Freedom of Choice Act of 1989." March 27, May 23.

U.S. Congress. Senate. 1992. Committee on Labor and Human Resources. "Freedom of Choice Act of 1991." May 13.

U.S. Congress. Senate. 1995. Committee on the Judiciary. "The Partial Birth Abortion Ban Act of 1995." November 17.

6

Gender and Social Policy

Jyl J. Josephson

Introduction

Scholars of public policy have long observed that much of the policy process, from agenda setting to policy implementation and evaluation, is not rational. Often, public policies are contradictory, have unclear goals, and bear little relation to the empirical findings of policy analysts (Stone 1997). As a result of this long-standing observation, scholars have been paying increasing attention to the nonrational aspects of policy formulation and implementation.

One aspect of this new arena in the study of public policy is the study of the interactions between policies and the groups to which public policies are targeted. As Schneider and Ingram have observed, policymakers target policy to specific groups (Ingram and Schneider 1991). Because of their ultimate goal of reelection, elected officials will target policy goals and benefits or costs in ways that will provide them with the greatest "political value: votes to be gained, co-optation of potential opponents, possible campaign contributions, and/or favorable press reactions" (Ingram and Schneider 1991, 340). In a subsequent essay, the same authors argue that the social construction of target populations will shape the nature of the policy process as well as the type of policy (Schneider and Ingram 1993). These arguments are developed more extensively in their recent book on the same subject (Schneider and Ingram 1997). Public policy scholars have found Schneider and Ingram's theoretical framework useful in application to a variety of policies (Donovan 1997; Goetz and Sidney 1997; Hogan 1997). Here, the theoretical framework will be extended by adding the role of gender in the social construction of target populations and by applying this framework to social policy.

Men's and women's actual gender roles, as well as perceptions about

133

appropriate gender roles for men and women, have played a significant role in the formation of social policy in the United States. Some programs, such as unemployment compensation, and worker's compensation, were designed primarily with male wage earners in mind; other policies, such as the Aid to Dependent Children (ADC)[1] program, were designed specifically for women who were single mothers (Nelson 1990). Scholarship on the formation of the welfare state in the United States has clearly outlined the role that gender played in the design of these and other social policies (Gordon 1990, 1994; Mink 1995; Orloff 1991). Contemporary social policy, however, is focused more on program retrenchment and termination than on the formation of new social policies and programs. Thus, this essay will examine the role that gender plays in the process of public policymaking involving program termination or restructuring. Because much of the focus of termination has been on moving those recipients of public benefits who are seen as capable of working for wages off of social programs, the gender analysis will focus especially on gender and wage labor, comparing the actual characteristics of target populations to the ways that they were depicted in the policy debates.

The Model

Schneider and Ingram provide a useful way to analyze the role that perceptions and descriptions of populations targeted by social policy play in policy formulation and implementation. They argue that both the relative power of groups who are the targets of specific public policies, and the positive or negative public perceptions of these groups affect the kind of policies that are implemented. As they put it,

> The social construction of target populations refers to the cultural characterizations of the persons or groups whose behavior and well-being are affected by public policy. These characterizations are normative and evaluative, portraying groups in positive or negative terms through symbolic language, metaphors, and stories. (Schneider and Ingram 1993, 334)

Schneider and Ingram argue that both agenda setting in public policy and the design of policies themselves are shaped by the social construction of the populations targeted. To explain how the public perception and the relative power of target groups shape public policy, they construct a simple two by two table, one dimension of which is the political power of the groups targeted by a public policy, and the other of which is the social construction of the population targeted. This typology provides four different groups into which target populations are categorized: the advantaged, contenders, dependents, and deviants.

In this model, public policies are seen as instruments that distribute both benefits and costs (or burdens) to the affected target population. Different categories of target populations will be treated in different ways through public policy. Groups constructed positively, and with relatively greater political power, such as the elderly, veterans, and business leaders and interests, are likely to be targeted by public policies that will be beneficial to them. Schneider and Ingram term this group the "advantaged." On the other hand, groups with relatively little political power who are perceived in negative terms are likely to be the objects of punitive public policies. Schneider and Ingram term this group "deviants," including such groups as drug addicts, communists, and flag burners. The group termed "contenders," who are negatively constructed but have political power, will have some control over the agenda-setting process, are likely to receive burdens that are more symbolic than actual, and are provided benefits in less visible ways than the advantaged groups. The group identified as "dependents" will have little control over the agenda-setting process, and will tend to receive more burdens than benefits, although they will receive more benefits than the "deviant" target populations. This categorization is summarized in Table 6.1.

Schneider and Ingram argue that elected officials will concentrate most of their efforts in the policymaking process toward two cells of this table: the "advantaged" and the "deviant." Such policies provide the greatest rewards in terms of public approval, and translate into benefits in the electoral process (Schneider and Ingram 1993, 337). Thus, advantaged groups will receive more benefits than would be warranted either by their size or on the basis of policy effectiveness considerations. Similarly, groups constructed as "deviants" will receive more burdens than would be warranted by their size or the scope of the perceived social problem that they represent.

Although they only briefly develop this point, Schneider and Ingram suggest that social policy is one arena in which it is particularly useful to examine the distinction between "dependents" and "deviants"

Table 6.1

Social Constructions of Target Populations

| Power | Constructions | |
	Positive	Negative
Strong	*Advantaged* Veterans The elderly	*Contenders* The wealthy Big unions
Weak	*Dependents* Children People with disabilities	*Deviants* Criminals Gangs Drug addicts

(Schneider and Ingram 1997, 124). They note in particular that the termination of AFDC results in part from the negative construction of its recipients as deviants, given

> increasingly negative constructions of the target groups as undisciplined persons unwilling to work or immoral mothers who have illegitimate children to garner the increase in their welfare checks. When dependent populations who have not done anything overtly deviant are, nevertheless, socially constructed in a negative manner, public officials want to enjoy the political benefits of appearing to be tough while avoiding the pitfalls of seeming to be mean. (1997, 124)

The "dependent" category is especially noteworthy because benefits provided to these groups must be justified, in part, by showing that those who receive benefits are deserving of them, and by carefully constructing the policies so as to separate the deserving from the undeserving (Schneider and Ingram 1997, 138–140). Thus, public officials are more likely to write legislation that requires strict eligibility determinations for social policies targeted toward dependent populations, to ensure that deviants, or the undeserving, do not receive these benefits. The policies examined below show a shift in the construction of target populations from dependent to deviant status.

Another way to see the importance of the social construction of a target population for the nature of the public policies targeted toward them is in terms of what scholars who study the media call "framing." According to Nelson, Clawson, and Oxley, "frames act like plot or story lines, lending coherence to otherwise discrete pieces of information. . . . Frames organize the presentation of facts and opinion within a newspaper article or television news story" (1997, 568). Such framing has been especially important in the recent devolutions and terminations of social programs, especially in the two social programs discussed below. The "story line" or "plot" of program termination is that the program creates and sustains the deviancy of the recipients. Thus, the story goes, to treat the deviant target population in a way that is appropriate through public policy, the program must be terminated. In the policies examined below, the framing of these target populations was pervasive in the statements of public officials justifying policy termination, as well as in media reports on the policy areas involved. In addition, as Daniels argues and as will be illustrated below, gender plays an important role in the framing of target populations (Daniels 1997). We now turn to an application of the Schneider and Ingram model to policymaking in the social policy arena.

The Social Construction of Social Policy Target Populations

Social policy in the United States consists of two types of programs: social insurance programs and public assistance programs. Social insurance programs, such as Old Age Survivors and Disability Insurance (commonly known as Social Security), Medicare, and unemployment and workers compensation, provide benefits for recipients based upon payments made into the program by the beneficiary or on his or her behalf. For example, both employers and employees pay Social Security taxes; recipients of Social Security are eligible for benefits upon retirement (or on the basis of a disabling condition) based upon these payments. On the other hand, public assistance programs, such as Temporary Assistance to Needy Families (TANF) (formerly AFDC), Medicaid, food stamps, and General Assistance (GA), are funded through general tax revenues.

Because of this difference in the funding mechanism for these two types of programs, the recipients of social insurance have generally been viewed very differently from the recipients of public assistance (Mettler 1998; Nelson 1990). People who receive social insurance benefits such as unemployment compensation or Medicare are seen as deserving of assistance, and are relatively powerful politically among groups targeted by social policies. People receiving food stamps or

TANF, on the other hand, are perceived as undeserving. Thus, the structure of the programs themselves provides the basis for very different levels of political power and influence among the target populations of these two types of programs. People who receive public assistance benefits consequently have very little political power, and are constructed at best as dependents, and at worst as deviants. These differences in political power are reflected in Table 6.2, which provides a typology of political power and social construction of target populations in the arena of social policy.

However, it is not only the type of benefits that target populations receive that determines their placement in the Schneider and Ingram schematic; gender also plays a significant role. Feminist scholars have argued that gender roles are socially constructed through a variety of mechanisms, including the socialization of children in families and by society, the structure of economic and political institutions, and the deployment of symbols (Scott 1986). Through these many mechanisms, children learn very early on what types of behavior are considered appropriate for their gender. Gender roles, in turn, have historically shaped social policy in significant ways: social policies intended primarily for women have historically focused on women in their gender role as mothers, whereas social policies designed primarily for men have focused on their attachment to wage labor through social insurance, unemployment, and pension programs (Abramovitz 1988; Gordon 1990, 1994; Mettler 1998; Mink 1995).

Social policy takes gender into account by providing services in different forms for different gender roles. Programs intended to address men in their gender-appropriate roles generally relate benefits to working for wages, and do not consider any family-related responsibilities that a worker may have. For example, to collect unemployment, leaving employment for such reasons as conflicts with child care, or caring for a sick or disabled child are not considered allowable, since these reasons are considered a matter of personal choice. On the other hand, the program now known as TANF was originally called Aid to Dependent Children (ADC) and was designed for single-mother families with minor children—that is, for women in their traditional gender roles. The program was designed to provide support for mothers to care for children without working for wages, though the benefits were always so low that families generally could not survive on the benefits alone.

Table 6.2

Social Constructions and Political Power in Social Policy

Power	Constructions	
	Positive	Negative

Strong
Social
insurance
	Advantaged
	Elderly
	  Social Security recipients
	  Medicare
	  Medicaid—Long Term
	    Care
	  Widows (Survivor's benefits)
		Contenders
		Work-based beneficiaries
		  Worker's Compensation
		  Unemployment Insurance

Weak
Public
assistance
	Dependents
	Children
	  School lunch
	  Medicaid/health care
	  Food stamps
	  Widows (under ADC)
	  Persons with Disabilities
		Deviants
		Drug addicts
		"Welfare" mothers
		Teenage mothers
		Jobless adults
		Racial/ethnic minorities

Indeed, there is some evidence that, as a result of the type of unemployment compensation rules noted, many women have utilized AFDC/TANF as a form of unemployment compensation (Mettler 1998, 150–157). Even before the 1996 welfare law more than 40 percent of women receiving AFDC had earnings from wages during the same year as they received benefits (Spalter-Roth et al. 1995). Further evidence for this claim is supported by another study, which found that, of those women receiving AFDC who had substantial work hours, only 11 percent worked in jobs that were covered by unemployment insurance (Spalter-Roth, Burr, and Hartman 1994; see also Williams 1999). Of course, since the adoption of civil rights laws, men who are single parents and are otherwise eligible for AFDC/TANF do qualify and receive benefits; women who work for wages and are otherwise eligible receive unemployment insurance and Social Security on the same basis as eligible men. The point is that the structure of these programs was designed with assumptions about gender roles in mind.

In the social construction of gender-appropriate roles, race and class are important factors. For example, behavior that is perceived as gender-appropriate for white middle-class men will not be the same as behavior that is perceived as gender-appropriate for black working-class men. Social policies that are intended to target specific groups will be targeted based on these perceptions about appropriate gender, race, and class roles. For example, it has been fairly clearly established that the exclusion of agricultural and domestic workers from eligibility for Social Security was intended to, and resulted in, the exclusion of most African American workers, especially in the South, from eligibility for Social Security benefits (Quadagno 1988).

In times of policy devolution and termination, it is the contention here that public officials will construct target populations who are seen as failing to comply with appropriate gender/race/class roles as deviants, and consequently that policy decisions will place greater burdens on these groups. Groups that are already marginalized in terms of political power, and who are constructed as dependents through public assistance programs, may move from that category to the category of deviants, if the target population can be successfully depicted as deviant by policymakers. Thus, previously positive social constructions of politically powerless groups will be transformed in public discourse, in media presentations, and in agenda setting and policy formulation, into negative constructions of these groups as deviants who deserve whatever burdens are placed upon them. These social constructions, in turn, will serve as justification for program termination. Such was the case in both of the policy changes examined here: the termination of GA programs in Michigan in 1991, and, at the federal level, the end of the AFDC program in 1996.

Social construction can occur through many mechanisms. For present purposes, we will consider the social construction of target populations through depictions of the population by political leaders, and through analysis of the deployment of cultural stereotypes regarding these populations in the form that the policy itself takes, as contrasted with empirical data regarding the actual demographic and other characteristics of the target population.

Ending General Assistance in Michigan

Background

Prior to the New Deal, assistance was provided to impoverished people through state and local governments. One of the reasons that federal social programs were created during the New Deal was that state and local governments could not address the burden of providing assistance when unemployment rates skyrocketed during the Great Depression. But, despite the programs created during the New Deal period, and the expansion of social assistance through the Great Society programs of the 1960s, some impoverished people are not covered by federally funded programs. Many state and local governments thus continue to provide assistance to people who are not eligible for federal aid through programs termed General Assistance. Generally, GA programs provide assistance for impoverished adults who do not have minor children living with them. These programs vary a great deal from state to state; in some states they are completely locally administered, whereas in others it is the state that administers the program. The type of assistance also varies greatly from one state or local program to the next: some provide only in-kind assistance or emergency aid, while others provide ongoing monthly cash assistance based on eligibility.

Although a number of states were making major changes to their GA programs in the late 1980s and early 1990s, Michigan was the only state to completely terminate its program in that period (Begala and Bethel 1992). This is what makes it a useful case for present purposes. In Michigan, the state-level GA program was created in the late 1970s, replacing previous county-level programs. The program provided cash assistance. Most persons eligible for this program were also eligible for other forms of assistance, such as food stamps and housing assistance. At the time that the program was terminated in 1991, GA required recipients to earn less than $262 monthly, to have total assets of less than $250, and if the recipient owned a vehicle, its value could be no more than $1,500. Total expenditures by the state for this program increased steadily from its inception until 1985, when an improving economy led to decreasing numbers of recipients and thus declining expenditures (Thompson 1995, 82).

Opposition to the GA program in Michigan grew during the 1980s, and Republican representatives and senators made repeated attempts to both curtail and eliminate the program (Thompson 1995, 85). In the 1980s, the Democratic Party controlled both the house and the governorship, but this changed with the 1990 election of John Engler as governor. Engler's determination to end the program, and the political failings of his Democratic predecessor, Jim Blanchard, were important components of the demise of GA. Another important factor was the fiscal crisis facing Michigan in the 1990–1991 budget cycle. The termination of GA was part of an effort to reduce expenditures, given that the state had a budget shortfall. But the choice of termination of this particular program, rather than other possible solutions such as across-the-board budget cuts, was related to the relative ease with which program termination could be justified for GA. This in turn is related to the social construction of the population targeted by this program: they were depicted by public officials as able-bodied minority men who were unwilling to work—that is, as "deviants."

Crucial to termination of the program was not only the reality of who received GA in Michigan, but the public rhetoric that moved this group from the category of dependent, and thus deserving of minimal support, to the category of deviant. The realities of business cycles and capital mobility in capitalist economies mean that there will be cycles of unemployment, and that when capital exits a geographic area, workers will be displaced. This is the justification for programs such as unemployment insurance. GA was also a program that provided assistance to persons displaced by these cyclical functions of a capitalist economy: many Michigan GA recipients had received unemployment benefits in the past but were no longer eligible. A program such as GA that is perceived as providing temporary support for workers displaced through no fault of their own constructs the target population in sympathetic terms, although they are relatively politically powerless. Therefore, at the time that the program was created, GA recipients were originally constructed as "dependents" in Schneider and Ingram's typology.

Over the course of the 1980s, however, Michigan's economy was changing. Deindustrialization, especially cutbacks in the auto industry, meant that unemployment rates remained very high throughout the 1980s in the state, and even higher in Detroit, where most of the GA recipients lived. In addition, real incomes were falling in Michigan in the 1980s, as they were in the rest of the country (Thompson 1995, 86). As a result, though many GA recipients worked for wages, many others were chronically unemployed.

Gender and the Justification for Policy Termination

The justification for termination of the GA program involved, in part, constructing GA recipients as deviants. The demographic characteristics of recipients highlighted ways that the target population could be characterized in this way. In March of 1991, prior to the termination of the program, the Michigan Department of Social Services profiled the characteristics of recipients. Recipients were majority male (59 percent), predominantly African American (56 percent), and nearly half (49 percent) of the recipients lived in Detroit (Wayne County). Since the majority were also between the ages of sixteen and forty (60 percent), recipients were generally seen as able-bodied minority men who were able to work (Thompson 1995, 84). Those opposed to continuation of the program pictured recipients as "slackers" who were capable of working, but were not doing so because of an overly-generous public program. Because men's appropriate gender role is to work for wages, and because urban minority men especially are seen as workers who should take any available job, it was fairly easy to depict GA recipients as deviants rather than dependents.

This perception was heightened by the way that GA was terminated. Prior to termination, Governor Engler initiated the creation of two new programs to address the needs of sub-groups of GA recipients who were still pictured as "dependents": families with children, who constituted 11.5 percent of recipients in March 1991, and recipients who were elderly or disabled, who constituted about 1 percent of recipients. These new programs were created with the intention of serving the "deserving" recipients of GA. This isolation of the deserving recipients of GA made it possible to depict those who would lose their GA benefits as "deviants." Moved from being seen as temporarily out of work (and therefore deserving dependents) to being seen as chronically unemployed despite being able-bodied adult men and capable of work, GA recipients could be depicted as deserving of the policy burden of benefits termination. Indeed, public officials argued that former recipients would be forced into the work force through policy termination, and that they would thus benefit from termination of the program.

Through Engler's strategizing on budget cuts, the GA program was also set off and compared to other programs. In the spring of 1991, a stand-off developed between the governor and the Democratically controlled house. Engler wanted to terminate GA to save costs; the Democrats favored other approaches to cost savings. As the stand-off continued, the governor invoked the seldom-used State Administrative Board and transferred funds from the GA program to other social services programs. Legislators immediately filed suit, claiming that the funds transfer exceeded the authority of the Board, given that budget allocations are legislative, not executive, functions.[2] While the legislators eventually won in court, a legislative solution ultimately was reached. Engler essentially presented the legislature with the choice of accepting across-the-board budget cuts to all social service programs, including Medicaid, or accepting the termination of GA (Thompson 1995). Thus, Engler provided legislators with explicit trade-offs between funding GA and funding other social services programs. Required to choose between target populations which had successfully been depicted as "deviants" and those still in the "dependent" category, the choice was simple. Enough Democrats crossed party lines to secure a vote for the termination of GA, which was terminated in October of 1991.

Empirical Evidence Regarding the Target Population

How did this characterization of GA recipients as able-bodied male slackers, or deviants, compare with their actual ability to work? The Michigan Department of Social Services study conducted in 1991 indicated that only half of the recipients had a high school diploma, limiting the job opportunities available to them. Further, given that studies of GA programs indicate that receipt rates generally correspond with the unemployment rate, as unemployment rates go up, so does GA receipt (Halter 1996). It is significant that most recipients lived in Wayne County, with the highest rates of unemployment, and of minority poverty, in the state of Michigan (Danziger and Kossoudji 1994). In a survey conducted two years after the policy was terminated, researchers found that large numbers of former recipients had health problems that interfered with their ability to work (Danziger and Kossoudji 1994). In this study, 58 percent of all former recipients (all of whom had been classified as able-bodied by the state) reported chronic health problems that required medical attention. Of those respondents over forty, 77 percent had chronic health problems. By June of 1993, 15 percent of those studied were enrolled in a state or federal disability program—an indication that they were not able-bodied, given the stringency of disability program requirements (Danziger and Kossoudji 1994).

This study also indicated that most former GA recipients did not find permanent employment; although 38 percent had some work in

1992, only 5 percent worked in all four quarters of that year. Those who did find work did not earn enough to become self-sufficient; average wages were $650 per month. Only 12 percent had health insurance. Generally, the jobs and benefits that recipients had were worse than those that they had held while they received GA (Danziger and Kossoudji 1994).

The studies also indicate that public costs for providing assistance to this target population may not have been reduced, but rather shifted to different entities. For example, 25 percent of former GA recipients reported experiencing homelessness within seven months after the program was terminated. In addition, utilization of emergency rooms for medical services increased significantly after the end of GA. Since local public hospitals are required to provide services regardless of ability to pay, costs for the medical care provided to these former recipients were simply shifted to a different public entity (Hauser 1994, 1458–1459). As Hauser puts it:

> . . . it is unclear whether costs are saved in the long run or are simply shifted to different agencies or arms of government, such as publicly funded shelters, public hospitals, other publicly funded service providers, and the criminal justice system. (1994, 1459)

There is little evidence that GA recipients belong to a subculture that does not share mainstream American values regarding work. For example, respondents in a study by Kathleen Kost all indicated that they would prefer working for wages to receiving GA. This sentiment is made clear by the quote that forms the title of her study, from a statement made by one of the respondents: "A man without a job is a dead man." All of the recipients in this study had been employed, most in many different short-term jobs, and all indicated that they preferred working to receiving GA; most indicated that they had used it only as a last resort (Kost 1996).

Thus, the depiction of GA recipients as deviants, able-bodied but unwilling to work, and likely to find employment if forced off of public assistance does not accord with the empirical evidence. In this instance, it would seem that policymaking was driven more by budget constraints and the social construction of the target population than by empirical reality.

The 1996 Welfare Law: Ending Entitlement to Assistance

Background

When the program originally known as Aid to Dependent Children (ADC) was included in the Social Security Act of 1935, it was as the result of vigorous lobbying by women's groups which had been involved in the development of the state-based programs on which ADC was modeled. These programs, termed "mothers' pensions," were intended to provide financial assistance to women who were single mothers. At the state level, these programs were adopted beginning in 1911; by 1920, most states had such programs, although they were small in comparison to the need, and were intended not only to support children, but also to supervise women who were single mothers (Gordon 1994, 37–64). The ADC program was based on these mothers' pensions, and was added to the Social Security Act in a last minute compromise (Gordon 1994, 253–285).

Crucial to the adoption of ADC was the framing of recipients in the category of deserving dependents by picturing the single mother families that would benefit from the program as those of widows. The reformers who advocated for ADC knew that many who might benefit from the program had become single mothers as a result of desertion or divorce, but chose not to emphasize this fact, fearing that this would erode support for the program (Gordon 1994, 281). Thus, ADC was depicted as a program that benefited the children of widows, and the legacy of moral supervision by social workers under the mothers' pensions was implicitly endorsed in the enactment of ADC. However, just four years after the adoption of the program, Old Age Survivors and Disability Insurance (commonly known as Social Security) was expanded so that widows and their children were eligible for survivors benefits if the deceased spouse was an eligible worker (Orloff 1991, 272–273). These benefits were much more generous, and were offered through a national program, not the state-based discretionary programs of ADC. Thus, since 1939, most widows and their dependent children apply for and receive Social Security benefits.

As Gordon shows, the women reformers who drafted ADC legislation intended it to be a small and temporary program, hoping for more universal programs that never materialized for families with children (Gordon 1994, 253–285). What happened instead was that this program was altered and expanded, until by the 1960s it had become one of the principal programs for children available in the partial, decentralized social welfare programs of the U.S. welfare state. As a result, instead of expanding social supports for all families with children, the programs developed in the New Deal divided citizens along gender lines and according to family structure, offering expansive benefits for beneficiaries of social insurance programs while limiting and restricting the inclusion of public assistance recipients as citizens (Mettler 1998). Despite the establishment of ADC as an entitlement program, meaning that all families who were eligible were entitled to receive benefits, it was still a state and locally implemented program, which meant that states were provided a great deal of discretion regarding whether and to what extent to implement the program. States utilized a variety of means, including moral supervision through the so-called "man in the house" rules, as well as administrative exclusions, to keep the program relatively small in relation to the level of need.

Changes to the AFDC Program

The limited availability of ADC, now renamed Aid to Families with Dependent Children (AFDC), began to change in the 1960s, due to several court decisions, as well as the advocacy of the welfare rights movement. The National Welfare Rights Organization (NWRO) was a grassroots movement in the late 1960s and early 1970s of poor women advocating for the rights of women receiving welfare. Among other things, the NWRO advocated for the enforcement of the entitlement status of welfare, insisting that everyone who requested an application for benefits had a right to apply, and that eligibility rules must be made clear to applicants. The NWRO also conducted public information campaigns, ensuring that people who might be eligible for public assistance benefits were aware of the programs. In part as a result of the work of the NWRO, the number of people receiving AFDC benefits expanded rapidly in the late 1960s and early 1970s (Amott 1990, 288–89).

As a result of this expansion of participation in the program, Congress enacted a series of changes to federal AFDC policy beginning in the 1960s. These changes increasingly encouraged participation in work and education programs, and introduced a number of cost-saving or cost-recovery measures, including the implementation of a program to collect child support from absent parents as a reimbursement for AFDC payments (Josephson 1997). States also were permitted to let their benefit levels fall in relation to inflation, so that the value of benefits decreased markedly from the early 1970s through 1996. The most extensive change prior to the 1996 law was the Family Support Act of 1988, a bipartisan effort which reformed a number of aspects of the AFDC program, and created Job Opportunities and Basic Skills Training Program (JOBS), which was intended to provide support for recipients seeking work, as well as work training through postsecondary education. JOBS provided assistance with expenses such as child care and transportation for recipients who were working or were in school, as well as transitional assistance (such as continued health benefits) for those recipients who obtained paid employment. The services provided by JOBS were very popular with recipients, and many states had long waiting lists of those eligible for these services, which were chronically underfunded in most instances.

The effort to reform welfare in the 1990s began with President Clinton's campaign promise to "end welfare as we know it." The rhetoric called for extensive changes, including time limits and work requirements, despite the fact that in 1992, many provisions of the 1988 Family Support Act were only beginning to be implemented by the states. Upon election, Clinton promised to reform health care first, and only introduced his welfare reform proposal in the summer of 1994, after his health care proposal had died a very public death. The proposal, though watered down from the original proposal of Clinton's Domestic Policy Council, would have provided *more* funding for the JOBS program, expanding the number of recipients who would be eligible, with the intention of providing them a path to education and training, and then to jobs that would offer wages that would support their families. The Domestic Policy Council argued that this was the only way to have effective welfare reform that would lead to self-sufficiency for former recipients. However, the proposed legislation died in committee in both houses.

Campaigning in the 1994 election based on the *Contract with America*, the Republican Party came to power in the House and the Senate promising, in part, to reform the welfare system. One of the ten items in the contract was the Personal Responsibility Act (PRA), introduced as H.R. 4. This legislation, which was eventually passed by Congress but vetoed by the president in January of 1996, had many provisions that ended up in the Personal Responsibility and Work Opportunity Reconciliation Act (PRWORA) of 1996, which the president did sign. However, as originally introduced, it also would have changed entitlement and funding for the school lunch program and supplemental security income for disabled children, which provided part of the justification for Clinton's veto (Edelman 1997; U.S. House of Representatives 1996).

Perhaps most significant among the changes enacted with the elimination of AFDC and the creation of TANF through the 1996 law is the end of the entitlement status of AFDC through the creation of a block grant system of providing TANF benefits. Under an entitlement program, persons who are eligible for benefits are entitled to receive them, regardless of how many other people are receiving benefits. Entitlement programs are responsive to cyclical fluctuations in the economy: when there is an economic downturn, more persons will be eligible to receive benefits. In times of economic prosperity, on the other hand, more people will have earned income in amounts that make them ineligible for benefits, which are means-tested. With the new block grant system, the federal government provides a block grant to the states, but states may choose to limit the amount that they spend on the program, as long as they maintain at least 80 percent of their historic expenditures. Thus, persons otherwise eligible for benefits may be denied them on the basis of the state's limitations on the amount it will spend on the program, making the program less responsive to both individual circumstances and economic fluctuations.

More familiar changes in the 1996 law are the addition of work requirements and lifetime limits. Many states had such provisions in their AFDC programs prior to the 1996 law, and states were given the option of continuing to follow their preexisting programs. However, the federal law requires states to require all recipients to work after two years of receipt of benefits, and to require community service work of beneficiaries after two months of assistance. The law also changes what is defined as work or work-related activity. Under previous law, recipients could participate in postsecondary education, including two- and four-year degree programs; such activities were defined as training, given that they were more likely to lead to higher wage jobs and the ability to be self-sufficient in supporting one's family. The 1996 law eliminated postsecondary education as a work-related activity, limiting eligible training programs to those lasting twelve months or less, thus providing states with incentives to emphasize work first, regardless of the recipients' education or skill level. Recipients not meeting the work requirement may be sanctioned and/or terminated from the program. The time limits include a lifetime sixty-month (five-year) limit on receipt of benefits for any family including an adult recipient. Benefits will be terminated for all family members after five years' total time receiving benefits. States are permitted to grant limited exemptions to the time limits.

These provisions are based on a set of perceptions of the target population of AFDC that see recipients as capable of working, but unwilling to do so. The incentives of time limits, work requirements, and the end of entitlement are based on the idea that recipients do not work for wages (which, as we will see below, is not accurate) and that they simply need the incentive to work and they will do so. The provisions also assume that recipients will be better off working for wages, regardless of their employment skills or educational backgrounds, than they would be receiving public benefits. As we will see, these perceptions differ in rather significant ways from both the actual characteristics and work experiences and opportunities of women receiving AFDC. However, first we will examine the role that the perception of women on AFDC as deviants played in the justification for the termination of this program.

It is important to note as well that the strategy of isolating the target population constructed as deviant occurred in the case of federal welfare reform as it did in the termination of GA in Michigan. As noted, the original welfare legislation, the PRA of 1995, called for block grants for the school lunch program and for supplemental security income. However, the school lunch program proved difficult to terminate, given that this program is targeted at all school-age children and benefits middle-class children as well, since the federal aid provided through the program supplements the provision of hot lunches to all schoolchildren. It is difficult to construct all school-age children in a negative light, and this proposal did not survive the legislative process. The early versions of PRWORA also included block grants for the Medicaid program (Edelman 1997). However, President Clinton indicated early on that he would veto any effort to create block grants for the Medicaid program. This program actually benefits middle- and working-class voters, since most Medicaid expenditures go to long-term care recipients, especially elderly persons in nursing home care, because Medicare does not pay for long-term care. These beneficiaries are, for the most part, the parents and elderly relatives of middle- and working-class voters, and a block grant program that might have reduced these benefits would have been particularly unpopular with these groups (Edelman 1997, 46). The removal of block grant programs for Medicaid and for school lunches left AFDC as the primary program targeted for termination. Thus, AFDC recipients were isolated from other beneficiaries of social programs, constructed as deviant, and therefore deserving of policy burdens, regardless of the empirical evidence regarding this population.[3]

Gender and the Justification of Policy Termination

Negative constructions of recipients of AFDC were not new to the welfare debates of the 1990s. Indeed, when the first work requirements were added to the AFDC program in 1967, the debate focused on a characterization of AFDC recipients as "unmarried illiterate women with a massive number of children and a lack of appropriate parenting skills" (Williams 1997, 5). Racial imagery was prominent in the depictions of AFDC recipients as bad mothers, such as in New York Senator Jacob Javits's statement that the children whose families received AFDC were "from Harlem. That is what creates the problem. Forty-six percent of the people in Harlem are from broken homes" (Williams 1997, note 101). Members of Congress, in 1967 and in 1996, argued that women who were single parents should be in the work force, and that they were using their children as an excuse not to work. Williams points out the contrast drawn during the debates between these irresponsible mothers on AFDC and responsible mothers who, if they are single parents, work for wages, or who are properly married to husbands who earn wages high enough that they are able to stay home and care for their children.

One significant factor in the changing perceptions of women on AFDC beginning in the 1960s is the changes that have occurred in women's roles, so that, by the 1990s, most women with young children work for wages. These changes with respect to women's gender roles in relation to wage labor have been especially significant for middle-class white women: while 33.6 percent of white women participated in the labor force in 1960, 56.4 percent did so in 1988 (Ortiz 1994).

African American women and Asian American women had higher rates of labor force participation than did white women in 1960, and continued to participate in the labor force at slightly higher rates in 1988. Latina women's labor force participation rates for this same period were relatively comparable to the labor force participation rates of white women, although this varies by subgroup (Ortiz 1994). As women's roles with respect to employment have changed, there has in turn been a change in perceptions of appropriate roles for women receiving AFDC. While the dominant perception of women's proper roles in 1935 when the legislation was first passed was that women, even single mothers, should stay at home with their children, by the 1990s, most women were working for wages, either full- or part-time. These changes in gender roles have been reflected in legislation regarding AFDC since the 1967 legislation noted above, as work requirements were increasingly added to the program until its termination in 1996.

As a result of these changes in gender roles in relation to work, as well as negative depictions of women who received AFDC in the media, by public officials, and by opponents of AFDC, the target population of AFDC moved from being seen as widows or single mothers through no fault of their own, who should be provided with public support to stay home and care for their children—that is, in terms of Schneider and Ingram's typology, from deserving dependents requiring support—to being seen as bad mothers, taking advantage of society through the AFDC program, passing their status as welfare recipients on to their children. Thus, despite being able-bodied and capable of work, these women refuse to do so. Public officials thus characterized recipients as able-bodied; capable of work, and therefore lazy; urban, minority, and sexually deviant females; addicted to public benefits and to their dependent status; and bad mothers, passing their dependency status on to their children. All of these characteristics added up to "deviant" status, since minority women's appropriate gender role is seen as being obligated to work for wages, not staying home and caring for their own children (Dill 1994).

The negative depictions of women on AFDC were particularly clear in the debates over the PRA of 1995. During floor debates in the House, Florida Republican John L. Mica compared welfare recipients to alligators, noting signs posted in Florida that read: "Do Not Feed the Alligators." He stated:

... we post these warnings because unnatural feeding and artificial care creates dependency. When dependency sets in, these otherwise able-bodied alligators can no longer survive on their own. Now, I know that people are not alligators, but I submit to you that with our current handout, nonwork welfare system, we have upset the natural order.... We have created a system of dependency. (141 Congressional Record H3766)

In a similar vein, Representative Barbara Cubin of Wyoming compared welfare recipients to wolves:

Recently the Federal Government introduced wolves into the state of Wyoming, and they put them in pens and they brought elk and venison to them every day. This is what I call the wolf welfare program. The Federal Government introduced them and they have since then provided shelter and they have provided food, they have provided everything that the wolves need for their existence. Guess what? They opened the gate to let the wolves out and now the wolves will not go. They are cutting the fence down to make the wolves go out and the wolves will not go. What has happened with the wolves, just like what happens with human beings, when you take away their incentives, when you take away their freedom, when you take away their dignity, they have to be provided for.... Just like any animal in the species, any mammal, when you take away their freedom and their dignity and their ability, they cannot provide for themselves.... (141 Congressional Record H3772)

Other members objected to the characterization, and these references were widely reported in the press. Although clearly all members of Congress did not agree with these depictions, the fact that some members felt free to characterize welfare recipients as animals on the floor of the House makes very clear that the target population of AFDC was being characterized as deviant in Schneider and Ingram's typology. The justification for terminating AFDC, and for the policy burdens of lifetime time limits for both parents and children, work requirements even for mothers with very young children, and the elimination of funding for educational programs, was based on this construction of AFDC recipients as deviant single mothers who are able-bodied and simply unwilling to work.

Empirical Evidence Regarding the Target Population

How did the characterization described above compare to actual characteristics of recipients? First, it is crucial to note that the above depictions focus almost exclusively on adult recipients of AFDC, although two-thirds of recipients in 1996 were children (under eighteen), and half of those children were under the age of six. In addition, the characterization of AFDC recipients as unwilling to work is an inaccurate depiction of their actual behavior, as has been documented in numerous scholarly studies. For example, in a study of a nationally representative sample utilizing data from the Survey of Income and Program Participation, Spalter-Roth and colleagues found that 43 percent of the women in their sample worked either while they were receiving AFDC, or cycled from work to AFDC and back to work (Spalter-Roth et al. 1995). They also found that more than half of those who did not work spent substantial amounts of time looking for work. Thus, most of the women (about 70 percent) in this study demonstrated their willingness to work either by working or by looking for work. This does not accord with the image presented of women unwilling to work for wages. However, most of the women in the sample worked in jobs at or near the minimum wage, and often were not able to obtain full-time employment. Thus, they were unable to lift their families out of poverty through their work, despite their willingness to work.

Another study by Kathryn Edin and Laura Lein involved interviews with women on welfare and women in low-wage work in four U.S. cities. The study found that, because the benefits that they received through AFDC and food stamps were simply not enough to cover their families' basic needs, most AFDC recipients supplemented benefits with other income from wages, contributions from family members, or from other sources. In addition, about half of all the welfare recipients in this study had worked in the formal economy during the previous year (Edin and Lein 1997, 221). Sixty percent of the wage-reliant women in the study had used AFDC recently. Therefore, Edin and Lein argue, women in low-wage jobs and women receiving welfare should be seen as "two overlapping populations on a single continuum" (Edin and Lein 1997, 220). In general, they found that women in low-wage jobs were often worse off than their counterparts on welfare, given the added expenditures for childcare, medical care, and transportation that go with working for wages.

Edin and Lein also utilized their study to test the thesis that women who receive AFDC are part of a deviant "culture of poverty." They looked at differences among the women based on welfare status, marital status, family background, neighborhood, and race and ethnicity to see what effect these factors had on their abilities to manage their meager funds, whether they engaged in work, what kinds of social networks they utilized to obtain additional economic support, and whether they utilized the assistance of charitable agencies to supplement their resources. They found that women on welfare were actually more frugal and more capable of managing their resources than were the women who worked for wages. They found that African American and Mexican American mothers spent significantly less, on average, than did white mothers. They found that the vast majority of the women in their sample wanted to work for wages, and had fairly realistic ideas about the amount that they would need to earn (at least eight dollars an hour) to provide minimal support for their families. Overall, their data contradicted in many ways the thesis that women on AFDC are somehow part of a "deviant" subgroup, with values different than those of the mainstream culture (Edin and Lein 1997, 192–217).

Perhaps most significantly, the Edin and Lein study, which involved repeated in-depth interviews with 379 women, found that the consistent theme of these mothers, whether wage-reliant or welfare-reliant, was that they were trying to provide the economic support necessary to ensure their children's well-being. The series of economic choices that these women made, based on the fact that their monthly expenditures for basic needs exceeded their monthly income whether from wages or AFDC or a combination thereof, were based on their efforts to protect and provide for their children. As the authors put it,

> . . . our data . . . strongly suggest that most women usually behaved in ways that reflected reasoned calculations of which alternatives would be likely to expose their children to the least harm. (Edin and Lein 1997, 221)

The contrast between the empirical evidence regarding women receiving AFDC in 1996 and the description offered by political leaders and policy entrepreneurs provides compelling evidence of the way in which the target population of public policy is socially constructed in a way very different from the reality of actual policy targets. Once again, policymaking was driven by the social construction of a dehumanized, deviant female subject rather than by empirical evidence regarding the characteristics of the target population and the means by which their poverty might be alleviated.

Conclusion

As noted at the outset of this chapter, much policymaking is not about rational choices based on empirical evidence, but rather is the result of a series of political calculations regarding the populations targeted by public policies. This chapter has argued that, in times of austerity, when social programs are being cut, target populations are constructed as deviant by policymakers through a use of their perceived compliance with appropriate gender-, race-, and class-based social roles, irrespective of empirical evidence regarding the characteristics of target populations. In the two programs examined, these depictions differed by gender: although both AFDC and GA recipients were characterized as deviant for not having earnings from wage labor (despite the fact that, as noted, many in both populations actually did have such earnings), women on AFDC were also characterized as deviant for being "bad mothers." Their deviancy derived from the circumstances that made them eligible for the program itself: their status as single mothers. In these two cases, both groups were characterized as deviant for failing to comply with gender role expectations. These evaluations were used by policymakers to construct the target population as deviant, and therefore deserving of public policy burdens through termination of public programs. These negative constructions were in turn used to justify policy terminations to the public, and to those opposed to policy termination.

Budget shortfalls and political ideology help explain why program termination was on the agenda. However, the model utilized here helps explain why programs with politically weaker target populations were proposed for termination. It also helps to explain why the programs that were actually terminated were those whose target population was successfully constructed by policymakers as deviant. And, as I have shown, this "deviancy" had much to do with the perceived failure of the target population to conform with the role expectations suited to their gender, race, and class status.

Notes

1. Aid to Dependent Children (ADC) was later renamed Aid to Families with Dependent Children (AFDC) and was terminated in 1996. The program will be referred to as "ADC" for the period 1935 through 1962, and "AFDC" for the period 1962 through 1996.

2. See *Dodak et al. v. Miller et al.* 191 Mich. App. 689; 479 N.W.2d 361 [1991].

3. It should be noted that this same legislation imposed policy burdens on immigrants as well, which is beyond the scope of this chapter, but could be subjected to a similar analysis.

References

Abramovitz, Mimi. 1988. *Regulating the Lives of Women: Social Welfare Policy from Colonial Times to the Present.* Boston: South End Press.

Amott, Teresa L. 1990. "Black Women and AFDC: Making Entitlement Out of Necessity." In *Women, the State, and Welfare,* ed. Linda Gordon, pp. 280–298. Madison: University of Wisconsin Press.

Begala, John A., and Carol Bethel. 1992. "A Transformation Within the Welfare State." *Journal of State Government* 65 (January): 25–30.

Daniels, Cynthia. 1997. "Between Fathers and Fetuses: The Social Consruction of Male Reproduction and the Politics of Fetal Harm," *Signs* 22 (3): 579–616.

Danziger, Sandra K., and Sherrie A. Kossoudji. 1994/5. "What Happened to General Assistance Recipients in Michigan?" *Focus* 16 (Winter): 2

Dill, Bonnie Thornton. 1994. "Fictive Kin, Paper Sons, and *Compadrazgo:* Women of Color and the Struggle for Family Survival." In *Women of Color in U.S. Society,* ed. Bonnie Thornton Dill and Maxine Baca Zinn, pp. 149–169. Philadelphia: Temple University Press.

Donovan, Mark C. 1997. "The Problem with Making AIDS Comfortable: Federal Policy Making and the Rhetoric of Innocence." *Journal of Homosexuality* 32(3–4): 115–144.

Edelman, Peter. 1997. "The Worst Thing Bill Clinton Has Done." *The Atlantic Monthly* 279(3): 43–58.

Edin, Kathryn, and Laura Lein. 1997. *Making Ends Meet: How Single Mothers Survive Welfare and Low-Wage Work.* New York: Russell Sage Foundation.

Goetz, Edward G., and Mara S. Sidney. 1997. "Local Policy Subsystems and Issue Definition: An Analysis of Community Development Policy Change." *Urban Affairs Review* 32 (March): 490–512.

Gordon, Linda. 1990. "The New Feminist Scholarship on the Welfare State." In *Women, the State, and Welfare,* ed. Linda Gordon, pp. 9–35. Madison: University of Wisconsin Press.

———. 1994. *Pitied But Not Entitled: Single Mothers and the History of Welfare.* New York: The Free Press.

Halter, Anthony P. 1996. "State Welfare Reform for Employable General Assistance Recipients: The Facts Behind the Assumptions." *Social Work* 41 (January): 106–110.

Hauser, Sandra. 1994. "Jobless, Penniless, Often Homeless: State General Assistance Cuts Leave 'Employables' Struggling for Survival." *Clearinghouse Review* 27 (April): 1456–1459.

Hogan, Nancy Lynne. 1997. "The Social Construction of Target Populations and the Transformation of Prison-Based AIDS Policy: A Descriptive Case Study." *Journal of Homosexuality* 32(3–4): 77–114.

Ingram, Helen, and Anne Schneider. 1991. "The Choice of Target Populations." *Administration & Society* 23(3): 333–356.

Josephson, Jyl J. 1997. *Gender, Families, and State: Child Support Policy in the United States*. Lanham, MD: Rowman & Littlefield.

Kost, Kathleen A. 1996. "'A Man Without a Job Is a Dead Man': The Meaning of Work and Welfare in the Lives of Young Men." Discussion paper no. 1112–96. Madison, WI: Institute for Research on Poverty.

Mettler, Suzanne. 1998. *Dividing Citizens: Gender and Federalism in New Deal Public Policy*. Ithaca, NY: Cornell University Press.

Mink, Gwendolyn. 1995. *The Wages of Motherhood: Inequality in the Welfare State, 1917–1942*. Ithaca, NY: Cornell University Press.

Nelson, Barbara J. 1990. "The Origins of the Two-Channel Welfare State: Workmen's Compensation and Mothers' Aid." In *Women, the State and Welfare*, ed. Linda Gordon, pp. 123–151. Madison: University of Wisconsin Press.

Nelson, Thomas E., Rosalee A. Clawson, and Zoe M. Oxley. 1997. "Media Framing of a Civil Liberties Conflict and Its Effect on Tolerance." *American Political Science Review* 91(3): 567–598.

Orloff, Ann Shola. 1991. "Gender in Early U.S. Social Policy." *Journal of Policy History* 3(2): 249–281.

Ortiz, Vilma. 1994. "Women of Color: A Demographic Overview." In *Women of Color in U.S. Society*, ed. Maxine Baca Zinn and Bonnie Thornton Dill, pp. 13–40. Philadelphia: Temple University Press.

Quadagno, Jill. 1988. "From Old-Age Assistance to Supplemental Security Income: The Political Economy of Relief in the South, 1935–1972." In *The Politics of Social Policy in the United States*, ed. Margaret Weir, Ann Shola Orloff, and Theda Skocpol, pp. 235–263. Princeton: Princeton University Press.

Schneider, Anne, and Helen Ingram. 1993. "Social Construction of Target Populations: Implications for Politics and Policy." *American Political Science Review* 87(2): 334–347.

———. 1997. *Policy Design for Democracy*. Lawrence: University Press of Kansas.

Scott, Joan. 1986. "Gender: A Useful Category for Historical Analysis." *American Historical Review* 91(5): 1053–1075.

Spalter-Roth, Robert, Beverly Burr, and Heidi Hartman. 1994. *Income Insecurity: The Failure of Unemployment Insurance to Reach Working AFDC Mothers*. Washington, DC: Institute for Women's Policy Research.

Spalter-Roth, Robert, Beverly Burr, Heidi Hartman, and Lois Shaw. 1995. "Welfare that Works: The Working Lives of AFDC Recipients." *Focus* 17 (Fall/Winter): 10–12.

Stone, Deborah. 1997. *Policy Paradox*. New York: W.W. Norton.

Thompson, Lyke. 1995. "The Death of General Assistance in Michigan." In *The Politics of Welfare Reform*, ed. Donald F. Norris and Lyke Thompson, pp. 79–108. Thousand Oaks, CA: Sage.

U.S. Congress. House. 1996. Personal Responsibility and Work Opportunity Act of 1995: Veto Message from the President of the United States, House document no.104–164, p. H342.

Williams, Lucy. 1997. "Decades of Distortion: The Right's 30-Year Assault on Welfare." Somerville, MA: Political Research Associates.

———. 1999. "Unemployment Insurance and Low-Wage Work." In *Hard Labor: Women and Work in the Post-Welfare Era*, ed. Joel F. Handler and Lucie White, pp. 158–174. Armonk, NY: M.E. Sharpe.

7

"Women Get Sicker; Men Die Quicker"

Gender, Health Politics, and Health Policy

Sue Tolleson-Rinehart

Introduction: The Practice of Medicine and Gender Ideology

For most of human history, and in most human cultures, the practice
of medicine has been a matter of tradition, the passing down of knowledge from one generation to the next. Most of this knowledge was the
accumulation of anecdotal experience that was experimental in spirit,
but essentially the result of individual attempts to link cause and effect
through case-by-case observations. Today, much of what physicians,
surgeons, nurses, pharmacists, and other caregivers do is still the result
of the same kind of iterative process. These practitioners administer
treatments or use techniques that they have learned from their own
teachers and textbooks, or that they judge to be effective based on
observations of the health outcomes of patients in their care. Great
scientific and public health breakthroughs like the discovery of essential anatomical functions, or the germ theory of disease, the ability to
conduct surgery on patients who stood a chance of surviving the operation, or the discovery of antibiotics, have been the exception rather
than the rule of accumulated medical knowledge. Such a system of
knowledge accumulation, like that of any other human cognitive activity, has not been immune to the beliefs and values of the culture in
which it occurs.

In the second half of the twentieth century, the paradigms of the
scientific method and a desire to raise our understanding from the level
of the individual to the level of whole populations, increased their hold

on health care. Two powerful developments in particular have relevance for the changing context of the politics of gender and health policy. The first development emerges directly from the value Americans accord to scientific research. The conception of medical practice, like other endeavors, has changed to embrace notions that it should be more rational, experimental, and rigorous. The "best practice" of care should be science-based, and emerge from intense, objective, and systematic reviews of the evidence. Today, these orientations are known collectively as "evidence-based medicine" or "evidence-based practice," and they are increasingly treated as benchmarks for the making of health policy, as well as the delivery of health care.

Evidence-based practice and its emphasis on "best" practice moves in tandem with another enormously important development in American health care: the emphasis on improving what is known as "quality of care." Quality of care was defined by the Institute of Medicine as "the extent to which health services for individuals and populations increase the likelihood of desired health outcomes and are consistent with current professional knowledge" (Lohr 1990). In theory, quality of care is measured at three levels: the structure of the delivery system (the organizations and institutions that provide care), the processes by which care is delivered (whether, and how, segments of the population have received a particular treatment or service), and the outcome of that care, including clinical results as well as the "outcome" for the patient, in terms of her ability to function in everyday life, her well-being, and her satisfaction with her care (Gonen 1998).

In the best of all possible worlds, according to the evidence-based medicine and quality of care paradigms, a particular medical condition has been widely and carefully researched; the results of that research have been published in scientific journals; and the combined evidence of this published research can be searched systematically, measured, and evaluated. The result of the evaluation, it is to be hoped, is a clear picture of what the "best practice" in treating the condition should be. We make this standard of best practice known to health care practitioners, enabling all who suffer from the condition to receive superior health care. We know that the care is superior, because we have measured the structure, processes, and outcomes of care for that condition, and we can say where and how the best care ought to occur. At the highest level, these emphases on best practice and quality of care also guide the formulation and implementation of health policy, as is currently the case when Congress tries to develop policy regarding basic preventive health services, or when the Health Care Financing Administration demands that health care systems provide evidence of quality indicators as a condition of receiving federal Medicare and Medicaid funds. Health policymakers in Congress and elsewhere, indeed, speak of wanting to make "evidence-based policy."

In practice, though, we seldom find ourselves in this best of all possible worlds. Serious problems of access to and economic resources for medical care prevent millions of people from obtaining care of any kind, without regard for its quality. Not all practitioners or systems of care are equally competent, and those who wish to demonstrate the quality of the care they give are drowning under the paperwork associated with documenting it. People may be unable or unwilling to follow directions or otherwise participate in their own care, reducing the likelihood that they will achieve the best health outcomes. The measurement of quality itself is extraordinarily problematic: the things that are easiest to define and measure may tell us little about the quality of care in any comprehensive sense, while the things that may tell us most are the hardest, and most expensive, to define and measure. These problems, though grave, are not the central focus of this chapter. Instead, we will focus on the influence of gender ideologies on health policy, a prime example of the potent influence of gender politics even on something as ostensibly "scientific" as medical care.

Even today, most of the health care we receive is not undergirded by a mass of scientific evidence, making "evidence-based medicine" a difficult if not impossible standard of care (Lohr 1998). Research takes time and a great deal of money, and not every question attracts the interest or resources of researchers. Many other questions, though demanding answers, do not easily lend themselves to controlled research studies, whether for reasons of ethics, feasibility, or the limits of our knowledge. Even with the best intentions, practitioners cannot base their care on evidence that is not there. When evidence does exist, it is likely to be conflicting and inconclusive, and, in the nature of science, always subject to change as new investigators undertake further explorations. If clinicians and policymakers are frustrated, the public is in an even greater quandary, when it sees news reports saying eggs or coffee are bad for us, soon replaced by reports that, on the contrary, eggs and coffee are good.

In such a climate of uncertain information, it should be no surprise that cultural preferences and political ideology can play just as large a role in this "age of science in medicine" as they ever did in medicine's more traditional past. Nowhere is this cultural and political framing effect (Kinder and Berinsky 1999) more evident, and more challenging, than in the case of gender, health politics, and health policy.

Breast Cancer and Standards of Care

To take one contemporary example, for most of 1996, scientists, physicians, and surgeons met in what is called a "consensus conference" sponsored by the National Institutes of Health (NIH) to try to resolve when and how mammography screening should be used to reduce mortality from breast cancer, in the hope of setting a science-based standard to be used in breast cancer care and policy. This group, the NIH Consensus Development Conference on Breast Cancer Screening for Women Ages 40 to 49, volunteered to search for and review the scientific literature on the effects of breast cancer screening for the purpose of determining whether such early screening saved lives. On the afternoon of January 23, 1997, the conference panel met to announce its conclusion that "There is insufficient evidence to make an informed decision regarding efficacy of screening as measured by reduction in breast cancer mortality in women aged 40–49 years" (Fletcher 1997, 1180). That is to say, the extant scientific evidence simply could not say "yea" or "nay" to the question of whether or not regular breast cancer screenings of women in the forties detected enough curable cancers to outweigh the various costs (economic and otherwise) of screening this entire population. Should all women in their forties be having regular mammograms, or should they wait? The consensus conference found that the balance of the scientific literature did not favor either view. In this case, as in so many others, the evidence cannot dictate what "best practice" should be. This indeterminate conclusion was not what anyone, on either side of the issue, had been hoping for.

The outrage greeting this conclusion astonished many, but it might have been foreseen: breast cancer screening has become as much a political subject as a scientific one. Breast cancer screening has all the hallmarks of the most bitterly contested political issues. It has become enormously visible. It is *politicized* because it addresses a problem that has come to be seen as a *public* problem, no longer judged to be a personal or private responsibility, a prerogative of experts, or an inevitable consequence of the free market (definition from Disch 1996). This public problem particularly engages certain expert or elite segments of the policy domain, the traditional stakeholders, but it is also a problem that affects or could affect a huge proportion of the population. The prospect of breast cancer frightens women, and that fear stimulates women to take action by organizing into new advocacy groups as "stake challengers" (as defined by Peterson 1993), enter the political arena, and demand policy solutions. The size of the potential population that could be visited by breast cancer, and the fear that it induces, causes the policy to burst the bounds of low conflict, insider/ expert policymaking and engage the public consciousness.

Many groups' interests come into opposition: women whose breast cancer may or may not be detected early by regular screening define one set of interests. Radiologists and mammography clinics, whose income is partly or wholly derived from interpreting mammography films, define another set of interests. What may be called the "Cancer Lobby" of research and advocacy organizations has yet another stake. And the managed health care industry, which is driven to reduce the costs of medical care, defines an interest of its own. There are many other stakeholders and stake-challengers, including those for whom there may *seem* to be no stake in this issue, but who believe they have one nonetheless. This is thought to be the case with Senator Arlen Specter, who may have condemned the consensus conference report as a tool to repair his image with women voters, still in tatters after his questioning of Anita Hill six years before during the Clarence Thomas confirmation hearings. The director of the NIH himself condemned his own committee's report, perhaps fearing repercussions from women's health interests in Congress and the public.

The features surrounding the breast cancer screening report—the perception that something has become a public problem, high visibility and conflict surrounding the problem, potential consequences for large numbers of people, and a broad range of interested parties with high stakes in and different frames for the issue—describe the rise onto the policy agenda of *any* difficult political question. When one adds our culture's ambivalence about gender, as breast cancer screening and so many other issues do, the mixture becomes dangerously volatile. The medical profession itself has been all too apt to leave the scientific method behind when it comes to thinking about men and women and the nature of gender roles. But the breast cancer screening issue illustrates something else that is new: the solid placement on the public agenda of something called "women's health."

Gendering Public Policy

In this chapter, it is my intent to elucidate the ways in which the larger context of the politics of gender affects health policymaking. *Sex* differences are biological, stemming from differences in reproductive function. But *gender* differences are contextual; they are the social constructions built upon sex differences, and the "context" of gender can become so important that they may obscure the relevance, or even the difference, of the sex differences on which they are erected. Perception, so very real a quality in a representative democracy, takes on the force of fact. Varying perceptions compete for attention in our pluralist, interest-based system with its almost endless points of access. In this system, it is easier to see something grind to a halt than it is to see it proceed, and "policy windows"—those spaces where the political terrain is configured in ways that favor the conversion of "issues" into policy—do not stay open for long (Kingdon 1995).

Making things even more challenging, policy emerges from a system in which citizens are increasingly disengaged by politics, perhaps in great part because the politics of adversary democracy is *not* conducted in informed civil debate, in which members of the polis come to understand their preferences through exchange of information. Rather, it is conducted in sound bites, slogans, and attacks on opposing points of view, and these techniques are put to use in mass media, not in citizen forums (Disch 1996). In these circumstances, information is difficult and costly to obtain, and almost impossible to exchange with other citizens. Information about science, medicine, and health is particularly difficult for the public, and even policymakers, to acquire and digest; nor is it immune to the colorations of ideology.

In the broadest strokes, certain enduring beliefs in an individual vested with inalienable rights and freedoms, a most important one of which is participation in a free (more or less) capitalist system, wherein the individual may contract and may reap the benefits of individual economic initiative, have restrained the range of policy alternatives that the system could consider. This has been especially evident in the case of health policy, as this past decade's debates over health insurance and "patients' bills of rights" demonstrate. To say that politics is more important than economics sounds extraordinary, but the fact is that we make political choices about our resources. The United States, for instance, *could* simply choose to devote a larger share of its vast resources to health care. We could decide to tax ourselves more, or spend less in other policy domains. The fact that we do not make this choice is not because we don't have the resources, but because we have decided that we don't have them for health care.

Finally, we see that the individual whose rights and freedoms are at the very center of the system's justification is a man, or has almost always been one. In fact, as Virginia Sapiro argues:

> If we consider the subjects of policy not in the apparently gender-neutral terms (such as individual, worker, family) usually used, but in the explicit terms of male and female, we find that the dominant ideology underlying social-policy thinking and action has never stressed individualism pure and simple. . . . Instead, it has supported individualism, independence, and self-reliance for some people (primarily men) and dependence and reliance on paternalism for others (primarily women). This is largely because individuals have been viewed in terms of functional roles depending upon gender. (1986, 227)

While these functional gender roles do, of course, arise from the biological roles of reproduction, the biological foundation has been made to support astonishingly durable social and political edifices, no more so than in the paradoxical, often irrational history of providing health care for men and women. That male individual to which Sapiro refers has been the human being to which medicine has directed its attention. The paradox is found in the widespread ideology that has treated *all* health as "men's health," meaning that although it seems that "women get sicker, but men die quicker," there has been no need to study women's health or sex differences in health. In fact, studying sex differences is tedious, expensive, and unproductive, so we can confidently study men and then apply the findings to women. In other words, we have not needed to study women because their "medical interests" are "represented" by men, just as English Common Law tradition held that women had no separable political interests.

This is true *except* in the case of reproduction, where women, otherwise treated as indistinguishable from men, are reduced solely to their reproductive functions and therefore seen as utterly alien. A leading obstetrical textbook says that *"women are physiologically ill-adapted to spend the greater part of their reproductive lives in the nonpregnant state. . . .* Menstruation, therefore, is indisputable evidence of fertility failure, whether purposefully chosen or naturally occurring" (Cunningham et al. 1993, 13–14; italics in the original). This is not a textbook of the nineteenth century, claiming that education would wither women's wombs. On the contrary, it presents itself as advocating strongly for the health and well-being of women. Yet even this book, in its earliest pages, has reduced women to their endocrine systems.

Serving State Interests by Privatizing Women

From the beginning, our political system, like most others, has sought its own interests in its treatment of women. Privatizing women, or deliberately regarding them as outside the public arena and restricted to a private domain, has been an effective control strategy. The strategy of control benefited from two ancient Anglo-American traditions. First, there is the doctrine of *femme couverte* or, in English Common Law terms, the legal principle (so-called) that a woman need not represent her own interests because her father or her husband represents them for her. This doctrine effectively guaranteed that women would be unable to own property or participate in public life in their own right. Second was a steadfast belief in a prohibition on governmental interference in private contractual arrangements between employers and employees. This deep reverence for the right of contract, so important to other civil rights, effectively barred women from exercising many if not all of their rights as workers and economic actors. The combined influence of these two traditions, overlaid on a system that simply could not see the extension of political rights to women as a pressing, or even serious, question, left women in a position of legal and economic dependency, without the political or financial resources to challenge the *status quo*.

Only in this century have women gained the political rights that citizens have, and only in the last three decades have they gained the kind of liberty that the Supreme Court so eloquently defined in *Meyer v. Nebraska* 262 U.S. 390, 399 (1923) as the freedom to "engage in any of the common occupations of life." It is easy to overlook the magnitude of the political and social revolution that women's "engag[ing] in . . . the common occupations of life" has wrought.

But at the same time that states have put embargoes on women's citizenship, all states have historically had an intense interest in women's reproductive behavior. Every nation-state has had pronatalist policies; every state has sought to induce women to reproduce the next generation of citizens or subjects. The state of South Carolina was established in no small part by single women who were given grants of land and cash in the new colony *providing* they married within a year of arriving there. The British West India Company and the British Government were certain that the fastest way to create a stable, profitable colony was to get women to it, women who would marry, "tame" men, and create stable communities (Spruill [1938] 1972). But the woman who was unwilling or unable to marry within the year, of course, forfeited both land and money. She was a producer and reproducer for the state, not one of its citizens. A similar ideology helped a young United States pioneer its Western territories.

Pronatalist policies, however, have never meant a state's unambiguous celebration of women's reproduction. Pregnancy has always been seen in highly ambivalent ways; it has been seen as the source of future generations on one hand, but as evidence of women's sexuality on the other (Tolleson-Rinehart 1987). Thus pronatalist policies have gone hand in hand with sweeping state controls on women's reproduction. The notorious *Buck v. Bell*, 274 U.S. 200 (1927), sanctioning sterilization of the unfit, could be seen as no different from policies that prevented "fit" women's use of contraception or voluntary sterilization. In both cases, a woman's reproductive life was not her own, and thirty-one states enacted such selective combinations of eugenics and pronatalism into law. In the teens and 1920s, the Comstock Laws were "health policy" with particularly harmful consequences for women, since it was by this device (the prohibition on sending obscene materials through the mails) that the spread of information about contraception was effectively limited. *Griswold v. Connecticut*, 381 U.S. 479 (1965) opened the door to women's reproductive freedom and, most would say, to the legalization of abortion. Today, abortion issues are still very much with us, as Dorothy Stetson's analysis in this volume of partial-birth abortion legislation makes clear.

Pronatalist policies are also reflected in three policies that had a devastating effect on increasing research on women's health questions. These policies are the Federal Policy for the Protection of Human Subjects, made law in 1974 (45 CFR 46), in 1960 amendments to the Food and Drug Act, and in the Food and Drug Administration's (FDA) 1977 guidelines, *General Considerations for the Clinical Evaluation of Drugs* (HEW/FDA-77-3040), and industry interpretations of them. Each of these federal policies had the effect of excluding women from almost all biomedical research. In each case, the limiting factor on conducting research with women subjects became that of protection of the fetus. This was an understandable, if not entirely rational, reaction to congenital malformations in babies born to mothers who had taken diethylstilbestrol (DES) or thalidomide, and to the horrifying "research" abuses committed by Nazis in World War II and by Americans in the infamous Tuskegee experiments. The intent of these policies was to *protect* human subjects from the unchecked power of science. But the immediate and continuing problem they caused was that a paternalistic, unreflective culture interpreted the protections so broadly that women *capable* of becoming pregnant, including celibate, sterile, lesbian, or perimenopausal women, were simply eliminated from research pools. And if one is to eliminate such a huge proportion of women, one might as well eliminate them all. Hence women were "protected" out of virtually all systematic, controlled research into their health (Johnson and Fee 1997b; Baird 1999).

Women as autonomous individuals, capable of understanding risks to the fetus, and capable of providing informed consent, were nowhere to be found in these policies, or in the attitudes of the research community. In recent years, this severance of "woman as citizen" from "woman as reproductive system" is represented in the excruciating conflict engendered by the newly identified public problem of "fetal rights," the proposed solutions for which most often involve incarcerating or otherwise controlling women, even to the extent of invading women's bodies to perform state-sanctioned medical procedures on the fetus (Daniels 1993). As with drug and other biomedical research, these solutions have also involved attempting to deny *all* women of childbearing age the right to work in certain occupations. While that policy initiative was stopped by the Supreme Court, which ruled it unconstitutional in *Automobile Workers v. Johnson Controls*, 499 U.S. 187 (1991), the question of fetal rights makes clear how terribly difficult it has been to think beyond women's reproductive functions. It might also be noted that fetal rights arguments are not advanced in terms of men's health behavior (Schroedel and Peretz 1994).

Decent people could not trivialize the idea of doing deliberate harm to fetuses. Nevertheless, this issue shows once again how deeply contradictory women's relation to the state remains. Indeed, women's health advocates themselves made deliberate choices in the early 1990s to take the first steps on the road to a women's health agenda by eschewing reproductive health. Florence Hazeltine, then director of the Center for Population Health at the NIH, and other high-ranking women in the federal health bureaucracy, proposed a major study of menopause for the first NIH-funded Women's Health Initiative in the early 1990s not only because so much about it was unknown—meaning that evidence-based practice would not be possible until more research was conducted—but precisely because it was free of any taint of the politics of abortion (Hazeltine 1997).

Many serious people of good conscience can be harrowingly divided over questions of reproductive freedom and "fetal rights" versus women's rights. But feminists are particularly concerned about the conflicts because of their awareness of the long, and often disingenuous, history of using the language of morality or patriotism to control women, just as they are aware of the state's history of privatizing women—of keeping women and their needs from being a part of our civic conversation. An underlying understanding of this profoundly difficult history contributes to the current debates over the definition of "women's health" (Weisman 1997). In the past, a state ideology that favored controlling and privatizing women was not an ideology that could be considered to promote women's health. That ideology has by no means disappeared, as Dorothy Stetson's and Jyl Josephson's chapters in this volume make clear. The war of ideologies—those of feminism and privatization—also affects the debate over the most effective definition of women's health. As Dr. Hazeltine said:

There has always been a vital tie between a woman's freedom over her sexual rights and her ability to control whether and when she will become pregnant. That is why it was so crucial to sever the link between women's sexual functioning and the new and important women's health research issues that were trying to emerge. Once that was accomplished, it became much more difficult to try and reconnect the two. (1997, xv)

While some feminist advocates deplore this severance of the link, its significance as a political strategy is obvious. In any case, the severance is hardly complete.

Changing the Policy Agenda

After more than a century of struggle for women's rights, women have now achieved sufficient power that they can make their own definition of their interests and that of the state seem more synonymous. As the Women's Movement produced durable political interest groups, and women policymakers' numbers increased in both the elective and bureaucratic arenas, they began to have meaningful opportunities to reframe "women's health." The breast cancer lobby achieved the first success, by getting the National Cancer Institute to devote 300 percent more money to breast cancer research over the 1980s and early 1990s. Congresswoman Patricia Schroeder used her position on the House Armed Services Committee for the ingenious purpose of adding money to the defense budget for even more breast cancer research (and the success of this lobby was to create an unexpected political problem for the Mammography Screening Consensus Conference, as illustrated above).

But women's health is more than an absence of breast cancer, as important as that is. There was the whole question of medical research on, about, and for women to address. By the mid-1980s, the consequence of excluding women from most biomedical research was attracting growing attention. Massive research on cardiovascular health such as the Harvard Physicians Health Study or the Multiple Risk Factor Intervention Trials (MR. FIT) drew results from studies on a combined 37,000 research subjects, including not one woman. Heart disease is the leading cause of death in women, but could we apply any of the findings of these studies to them? Similarly, although "men die quicker," the Baltimore Longitudinal Study on Aging, begun in 1958, included no women for its first 20 years, thereby sacrificing opportunities to understand aging in the population that achieves the longest average life expectancies. By 1986, the NIH issued a statement encouraging, but not requiring, the inclusion of women in clinical research trials. By 1990, the General Accounting Office (GAO) published a report saying that little progress had been made and, in fact, it could not even be determined how much of the total NIH budget had been spent on research questions relevant to women's health (Johnson and Fee 1997a; Baird 1999; Weisman 1997).

By the early 1990s, women in Congress and at the higher levels of the federal bureaucracy were poised to use the GAO report for action. Major research efforts were authorized; the 1993 NIH Revitalization Act both created the NIH Office of Research on Women's Health and moved to a *requirement* that women be included as subjects in federally funded research unless there is scientific justification for excluding them, legislation drafted in part by the Congressional Caucus for Women's Issues. In 1993, the FDA issued new guidelines "strongly encouraging" the inclusion of women in clinical trials of new drugs (Johnson and Fee 1997b; Baird 1999).

At the same time, the rapidly growing network of women scholars, bureaucrats, and politicians set themselves the task of reconceptualizing women's health. At the most basic level, one can focus on diseases found only in women—those that stem from reproductive roles. Next, we can consider diseases that "present" differently in women, that have a higher incidence in women, or exhibit different symptoms, or that have different risk factors for women (Hazeltine 1997; this is also the 1993 NIH definition). But it can also be argued that definitions devolving too tightly on women's reproductive roles, or focusing too much on disease rather than health, or using men as the standard, hark back to the status quo that women's health advocates have tried to change; hence the "biopsychosocial" model of women's health now so frequently propounded. The biopsychosocial model reconceptualizes women's health "in terms of the totality of women's experiences throughout the life span," including their social, economic, cultural, and psychological roles, and the environments in which they live (Weisman 1997, 182).

This is a marked departure from the NIH's 1993 "biomedical" definition, and represents a genuine paradigm shift, but no paradigm occurs in a vacuum, and the definition is not without its critics. While the principles of sex and gender in the biopsychosocial model certainly can be applied to men's health also, it may place too much emphasis on social change, hampering more direct efforts to improve health. While recognizing that our health is influenced by the culture in which we live, more modest but helpful political opportunities may be lost in too grand a vision.

While this discussion continues, an explosion of activity in women's health is taking place. Women are still, of course, a minority of public officials, clinicians, and researchers. But through the 1980s and especially the 1990s, political women have achieved a higher visibility than ever before. Women are perceived to be powerful political actors, and recall that in the political arena, perception matters. Thus women, though only 12 percent of the Congress, have succeeded in passing legislation that benefits women, often (especially in recent years) by acting as a bipartisan bloc. Because women gave President Clinton the margin of victory in both of his campaigns for the presidency, "women's issues" also have more credibility in the White House than ever before.

The general change in orientation and activity, in both politics and research, can be seen in Table 7.1. That women's health has come to be seen as a matter of public concern is illustrated by recent congressional activities. The first row of the table shows *all* introductions using the phrases "women's health" or "men's health," including resolutions and private bills, in the past three Congresses. The second row shows the policy used to structure scientific information. The final two rows reveal contemporary academic behavior, in that scarce space in academic journals is an indicator of where the research money and interest is going.

With regard to the congressional introductions, it should be noted that less than 5 percent of introduced bills, in their original form, go on to become law, and many introductions are actually re-introductions of legislation, sometimes unmodified and sometimes only slightly changed. Congressional activity in the form of bill introduction, however, does provide a partial sketch of what Congress considers to be on the public agenda.

Clearly, women's health has captured the attention of researchers and agenda-setters in a way that a phrase like "men's health" certainly has not. There is no medical subject heading for men's health, and no articles have been published using "men's health" as a key word phrase. The three men's health bills introduced into Congress all concerned the health of veterans in the Persian Gulf War (introduced in the 104th Congress). This heightened interest in women's health reflects a very broad range of issues in women's health care, from health care coverage under Medicaid, to changes in preventive services, to authorizations for studies on osteoporosis.

Table 7.1

Uses of Women's Health and Men's Health Terminology

	Key word: Women's Health	Key word: Men's Health
Bills introduced in Congress, 104th–106th	227	3
National Library of Medicine Medical Subject Heading (MeSH)	N01.400.900	none
Scholarly articles using the key word, 1995–1999	1,707	0
Scholarly journals	3	none

Source: For congressional introductions, THOMAS, Legislative Information on the Internet. The Library of Congress, http://thomas.loc.gov/home/thomas/html. Key word search of all introductions (bills, resolutions, and private bills) into the House and Senate in each of the past three Congresses, as of June 1999. MeSH from search of National Library of Medicine headings and verification with health affairs librarians. Articles and journals from key word search of journals listed in *Medline* using the key word (journals) or MeSH (articles) from 1995 to August 1999.

Medline is the National Library of Medicine medical literature database (journals identified were *Women's Health*; *Women's Health Issues*; and *Women and Health*, all having begun publication in the 1990s). All searches performed by the author. Of all scholarly articles cataloged as "women's health," 325, or 19 percent, were published in the women's health journals.

The interest, especially in Congress, is certainly not entirely benign. Numerous other introductions denoted "women's health" in each of the past three Congresses include attempts to limit women's access to contraceptives, perhaps questionable demands that all women receive screening mammograms after age 40 (recall the controversy surrounding the Consensus Conference!), attempts to deny citizenship to U.S.-born children whose mothers are not citizens, and numerous attacks on the legality of abortion.

But recent public policy also has included reauthorizations of the NIH's Office of Research on Women's Health (ORWH), the Department of Health and Human Services' Office of Women's Health, and other such federal centers for health policy generation. The ORWH was, as we have seen, a necessary response to unacceptable status quo of excluding women from biomedical research. Other agencies, such as the FDA and the Health Resources and Services Administration (HRSA) have also established women's health offices. Interestingly, both the FDA and HRSA women's health offices treat women as gatekeepers of family health, and target education and outreach programs to women—and especially to women in vulnerable populations—in the expectation that this is the most efficient way to benefit public health generally (see the FDA and HRSA women's health web sites at www.fda.gov/womens/default.htm and www.hrsa.gov/WomensHealth/, respectively). This would seem to represent a synthesis of older gender ideologies with newer ones; women are still seen as the primary care-takers of the family, but the policy arena is reaching out to them in the expectation that they are significant actors. Other notable policy efforts that seem to reflect the new sense of women as an observant and active political force include efforts to permit women to designate obstetrician-gynecologists as their primary care providers in managed care systems. While this hardly seems like the kind of inflammatory issue that abortion is, it is nonetheless a direct consequence of the reframing of gendered health questions.

If the table and foregoing discussion make one thing clear, though, it is this: women are still singular, viewed as different from a male standard. At one time women were singularly excluded from public policy, when they were not being controlled or limited by it. Now, women are singular in the interest they generate among policymakers. Perhaps the most dramatic change of all is that so many of the poli-cymakers now also are women. But is this new, fashionable singularity entirely good? The fact that the National Library of Medicine formed a medical subject heading for women's health makes the job of iden-tifying scientific research on women's health much, much easier, but it also says that there is "health" and then there is "women's health." In other words, all health is "men's health" *unless* denoted otherwise, and women are the "otherwise." Similarly, the rise of three scholarly journals devoted to women's health offers researchers a place to pub-lish their work, and clinicians and consumers a place to read it. But is the showcase also a marginalization?

The debate on appropriate gender roles is not over, as reflected in current debates over the best definition of women's health. Should women's health care providers and advocates be trying to solve soci-ety's problems? Do socioeconomic and/or psychological definitions of women's health also not risk marginalizing women, and making them seem only to be something contrary, something "not men," and, per-haps, as passive victims of the culture, rather than autonomous sub-jects? We have not finished weaving the tapestry. The debates over definitions of women's health are likely to continue, and must necessarily be influenced by political and policy considerations.

The Treatment of Preterm Labor

These debates are fought even among different women's health advocates, as one further example demonstrates. Preterm labor, or the onset of labor before the pregnancy has reached thirty-seven weeks (close enough to full term to mean a better outcome for the baby), is the single most significant cause of perinatal and neonatal mortality and morbidity (the stillbirth, death, or resulting major illness or disability of newborns). At the same time that preterm labor is a massive, tragic, and costly public health problem, it is also poorly understood. There is as yet no "best practice" treatment guideline for preterm labor (Berkowitz and Papiernik 1993). For this reason, physicians use a wide range of drugs and other techniques to try to stop preterm labor, in the hope that, if pregnancy can continue longer, the fetus might have a better chance of surviving. The FDA has approved only one drug, ritodrine, for the specific purpose of interrupting preterm labor. Every other drug that physicians use in preterm labor is "off label"—neither specifically tested, nor approved, for use in preterm labor. One drug labeled for the treatment of asthma, terbutaline sulfate, is widely put to such "off label" use. In 1996, the National Women's Health Network (NWHN) petitioned the FDA to issue a statement urging physicians *not* to use terbutaline in a particular form known as an infusion pump (this is a device that pumps a continuous low dose of the drug just under the skin) for treatment of preterm labor, after two women reportedly died during such treatment (NWHN Petition to the Food and Drug Administration, Docket No. 96P-0258, 1996).

After conducting its own investigation, the FDA granted the central point of the NWHN petition, and, through its MedWatch program, issued a so-called "dear colleague" letter in November of 1977. "Dear Colleague" letters are meant to warn the clinical community of potential dangers in drug use. In this case, the letter warned physicians that the use of terbutaline in an infusion pump had not been tested for safety and efficacy in the treatment of preterm labor, and was potentially dangerous. The letter said in part:

It appears that women receiving continuous subcutaneous terbutaline sulfate infusions experience side-effects and complications similar to those experienced by women receiving terbutaline and other beta-sympathomimetics intravenously. Complications include chest pain, tachycardia, dyspnea, and pulmonary edema. At least one maternal death occurred during outpatient use of a continuous infusion of terbutaline sulfate by subcutaneous pump. The impact of long-term use on maternal glucose metabolism and the risks of prolonged exposure of the fetus are largely unknown. (FDA Dear Colleague letter, 1997)

Some of the most impassioned critics of the NWHN petition were *other women*—specifically, members of multiple-gestation advocacy groups (groups representing women who are or have been pregnant with twins, triplets, or larger numbers of fetuses)—and the obstetricians who treat them. Preterm labor is one of the greatest dangers to the survival of fetuses in a multigestational pregnancy, and these advocacy groups give preterm labor treatments their highest priority, from the perspective that virtually any risk is worth it if there is any increased chance to continue the pregnancy long enough to deliver live, healthy babies. While the salience of this issue for multiple gestation groups is certainly understandable, as is their hope that terbutaline is an effective treatment (although the literature does not unequivocally demonstrate this), their rhetoric was telling. They accused the NWHN of *not* being advocates of women's health, and of having suspect motives; they questioned why NWHN would "not reveal" its sponsors (it has none; it is solely supported by individual member dues) and called its action a "scare tactic" (Sidelines National Support Network 1997; Newman 1997).

For multigestation advocacy groups, beliefs about women's health appear to be in largest part framed by women's reproductive roles, while the NWHN appears to be addressing gender and health policy from the framework of evidence-based medicine, or, in this case, the *lack* of clear evidence. Both groups are concerned about quality of care, but they may define quality very differently. One group argues in terms of "best practice" grounded in the preponderance of evidence, and thus demands that the evidence be gathered. The other group's first priority is to interrupt preterm labor with medical action (even though the preponderance of evidence continues to leave us in doubt about whether the action is effective), and satisfaction with the degree to which medical action is taken is the framework within which this group measures quality of care. The FDA has called for the kinds of studies of terbutaline in the treatment of preterm labor that will offer more definitive answers but, as Baird (1999) points out, the FDA's regulatory powers are limited and it does not, as does the NIH, affect policy through the direct funding of such research (although the FDA Office of Women's Health has funded basic science projects as well as education and outreach programs; and it has proposed regulations requiring the inclusion of women in clinical trials of new drugs [FDA 1999]).

Finally, the preterm labor case reminds us once again how difficult it is to extricate "women's health" from women's reproductive roles, even, or especially, among women themselves.

Conclusion: Thinking Contextually About Gender

In contemporary American culture, the differences between sex and gender are seldom noted. Today, "gender" is the term we most frequently encounter, even when the context obviously calls for sex, as in "What gender [sic] are you? Male or female?" The quandaries of health politics and health policy should remind us of the differences between sex and gender—and remind us to ask whether *either* construct is masking a perhaps more medically useful difference. A simple illustration of this latter point comes from recent breakthroughs in repairing aneurysms (or ruptures) of the gastric aorta (the body's largest artery). Surgeons have recently announced progress toward a much better, safer, less invasive way to repair such very dangerous aneurysms—but the method is more applicable to men. Why? Because, at present, it can only be attempted in patients whose arteries are quite large and, on average, those patients are more likely to be men. Sex is not the limiting factor: size is. Men with small arteries could not have this procedure; women with large ones can. Most of the patients with larger arteries are men, but certainly not all are. If we assign this treatment using sex as the discriminating variable, rather than gastric aorta size, we will not give it to some women who could benefit from it, and we will try to give it to some men for whom it is not appropriate. In both cases, we will not have been able to apply a best practices standard, or assure the best quality of care, to a measurable portion of patients.

In other cases, sex is an obviously limiting factor. Almost no men get breast cancer (those who do are given medical treatments similar to those used for women with the disease). Men are far less likely to be disabled by osteoporosis, while it is the biggest source of disability among women over seventy-five years of age (HRSA 1999). Of course, no women get cancer of the prostate or testicles. And in the biggest case of sex as the limiting variable, the difference that started it all, only females can become pregnant.

Finally, sometimes it seems to be gender that makes the difference: because the sexes are socialized differently, their life circumstances are often dramatically different, as can be their access to economic and other resources. Adolescent girls and adult women are more likely to suffer from depression, while men are more likely to suffer substance abuse and violent death. Girls and women are more likely to attempt suicide, but men are more likely to succeed in the attempt, because women are more likely to call for help, and men are more likely to use guns as the method of suicide. More women are uninsured now than were at the beginning of the 1990s, probably a result of welfare reform and the erosion of employer-sponsored health insurance. Female-headed households continue to be poorer than are male-headed households, and poverty is strongly associated with poor health and poor access to quality health care (cf. Collins et al. 1999; Meyer et al. 1999; HRSA 1999). These meaningful health status differences are not organic or physiological but, rather, are the direct or secondary results of differential gender role socialization and gender ideology at large in the political culture.

Recall that Dr. Suzanne Fletcher, the chairwoman of the Mammography Screening Consensus Conference, was understandably dismayed that, after she and her colleagues presented their very carefully, deliberately formulated conclusions, she was greeted by a political firestorm. At this moment, the policy window for women's health remains open, and the issues are framed in such a way that it is politically advantageous to support any and all women's health initiatives (of course, many people do so with sincerity). But in the case of the reaction to the breast cancer screening consensus conference, politics and beliefs trumped the apparent weight of the evidence. One simply cannot envision the same intense reaction greeting a recommendation about prostate cancer screening, for now, anyway. This unprecedented interest in women's health is not the result of scientific or medical breakthroughs. If anything, we have more questions now than we did before, when it seemed enough to believe that "men die quicker and women get sicker," and that women were their reproductive systems. The interest, instead, is a result of the successful emergence of a new political interest.

Dr. Fletcher, in her *New England Journal of Medicine* editorial, proposed several new steps for producing health policy recommendations. First, she says that medical leaders should recognize that consensus-development conferences and other conferences that air all sides of a scientific controversy rarely resolve strong disagreements by issuing reports. Second, she says, NIH directors may want to develop an approach to panel reports with which they disagree. Third, she argues that the consensus-development process should be reexamined in terms of its appropriateness in issuing recommendations in matters of broad health policy. She notes that such recommendations also require a thorough evaluation of cost and cost effectiveness, as well as careful consideration of medicolegal, ethical, and economic implications. Finally, she says, it may be time to move to a "multilevel approach," with consideration of scientific evidence at the first level, and the deliberations of many concerned actors in the political arena and the public at the second (1997, 1182–83).

I regard Dr. Fletcher's suggestions as very welcome evidence that health care professionals are perhaps more willing today to recognize the very political nature of what they do. But this represents another opportunity to think carefully about the context of sex and gender differences, and the ways those differences frame our perceptions of health policy. A broad, deep, and inquiring recognition of when sex matters to health, when gender does, and when *neither* might matter, will produce more coherent health policymaking for women and men. It also will assist us in making sense of health politics. Men don't have to die quicker, and women don't have to get sicker. The political system's goal of better health outcomes, and superior quality of care, for everyone, is widely shared. We will not reach that goal without continuing to question the gender frames we have placed around it.

References

Automobile Workers v. Johnson Controls, 499 U.S. 187(1991).
Baird, Karen L. 1999. "The New NIH and FDA Medical Research Policies: Targeting Gender, Promoting Justice." *Journal of Health Politics, Policy and Law* 24 (3): 531–565.

Berkowitz, Gertrude S., and Emile Papiernik. 1993. "The Epidemiology of Preterm Birth." *Epidemiologic Reviews* 15(2): 414–443.

Buck v. Bell, 274 U.S. 200 (1927).

Collins, Karen Scott, Cathy Schoen, Susan Joseph, Lisa Duchon, Elizabeth Simantov, and Michelle Yellowitz. 1999. *Health Concerns Across a Woman's Lifespan: The Commonwealth Fund 1998 Survey of Women's Health*. New York: The Commonwealth Fund.

Cunningham, F.G., P.C. Macdonald, N.F. Gant, K.J. Leveno, and L.C. Gilstrap. 1993. *Williams Obstetrics*. 19th ed. Norwalk, CT: Appleton & Lange.

Daniels, Cynthia R. 1993. *At Women's Expense: State Power and the Politics of Fetal Rights*. Cambridge: Harvard University Press.

Disch, Lisa. 1996. "Publicity-Stunt Participation and Sound Bite Polemics: The Health Care Debate, 1993–94." *Journal of Health Politics, Policy and Law* 21 (Spring): 3–33.

Fletcher, Suzanne W. 1997. "Whither Scientific Deliberation in Health Policy Recommendations? Alice in the Wonderland of Breast-Cancer Screening." *New England Journal of Medicine* 336(16): 1180–1183.

Food and Drug Administration. 1997. "Dear Colleague" letter warning on terbutaline infusion pump as treatment for preterm labor. http://www.fda.gov/medwatch/safety/1997/terbut.htm.

Food and Drug Administration. 1999. FDA Office of Women's Health, U.S. Food and Drug Administration. http://www.fda/gov/womens/programs.html.

Gonen, Julianna S. 1998. "Quality in Women's Health: Taking the Measure of Managed Care." *Insights* 8 (July). Washington, DC: Jacobs Institute of Women's Health. http://www.jiwh.org/insights/july98no8.htm.

Griswold v. Connecticut, 381 U.S. 479 (1965).

Hazeltine, Florence P. 1997. "Foreword." In *Women's Health Research: A Medical and Policy Primer*, ed. Florence P. Hazeltine and Beverly Greenberg Jacobson. Washington, DC: Health Press International.

Health Resources and Services Administration. 1999. Women's Health: A Lifespan Issue. http://www.hrsa.gov/WomensHealth/wh__fact.htm.

Johnson, Tracy L., and Elizabeth Fee. 1997a. "Women's Health Research: An Introduction." In *Women's Health Research: A Medical and Policy Primer*, ed. Florence P. Hazeltine and Beverly Greenberg Jacobson. Washington, DC: Health Press International.

———.1997b. "Women's Health Research: A Historical Perspective." In *Women's Health Research: A Medical and Policy Primer*, ed. Florence P. Hazeltine and Beverly Greenberg Jacobson. Washington, DC: Health Press International.

Kinder, Donald, and Adam Berinsky. 1999. "Making Sense of Issues Through Frames." *The Political Psychologist* 4: 2 (The newsletter of the American Political Science Association, Political Psychology Section; Feldman, Huddy, and Lodge, eds, State University of New York at Stony Brook.)

Kingdon, John W. 1995. *Agendas, Alternatives, and Public Policies*. 2nd ed. New York: HarperCollins College Publishers.

Lohr, Kathleen N., ed. 1990. *Medicare: A Strategy for Quality Assurance, Vol. 1*. Washington, DC: National Academy Press.

———. 1998. "Clinical Practice Guidelines: Historical Perspectives." In *Guidelines for Clinical Practice: The International Challenge*, ed. Nancy Mattison and Hugh Tilson. London: Pharmaceutical Partners for Better Healthcare.

Meyer v. Nebraska 262 U.S. 390, 399 (1923).

Meyer, Jane E., Joan M. Leiman, Nina Rothschild, with Marilyn Falik. 1999.

Improving the Health of Adolescent Girls: Policy Report of The Commonwealth Fund Commission on Women's Health. New York: The Commonwealth Fund.

National Women's Health Network Petition to the Food and Drug Administration, Docket no. 96P-0258/CP1 filed July 19, 1996 and FDA Response dated November 7, 1997 (copies of documents supplied to the author by the National Women's Health Network).

Newman, Roger B. 1997. "Subcutaneous Terbutaline Pump Therapy: The Triplet Connection." http://www.tripletconnection.org/subcutan.html. See also a statement by the president of the Triplet Connection at the same site.

Peterson, Mark A. 1993. "Political Influence in the 1990s: From Iron Triangles to Policy Networks." *Journal of Health Politics, Policy and Law* 18 (Summer): 395–438.

Sapiro, Virginia. 1986. "The Gender Basis of American Social Policy." *Political Science Quarterly* 101(2): 221–238.

Schroedel, Jean Reith, and Paul Peretz. 1994. "A Gender Analysis of Policy Formation: The Case of Fetal Abuse." *Journal of Health Politics, Policy and Law* 19 (Summer): 335–360.

Sidelines National Support Network. 1997. "Volunteer Organization for High-Risk Pregnant Women Questions Motives of National Women's Health Network." Press release supplied to the author by a researcher at the University of North Carolina at Chapel Hill. Sidelines web site at http://www.sidelines.org/.

Spruill, Julia Cherry. [1938] 1972. *Women's Life and Work in the Southern Colonies.* With an introduction to the Norton Library ed. by Anne Firor Scott. New York: Norton.

Tolleson-Rinehart, Sue. 1987. "Maternal Health Care Policy: Britain and the United States." *Comparative Politics* 19 (January): 193–211.

Weisman, Carol S. 1997. "Changing Definitions of Women's Health: Implications for Health Care and Policy." *Maternal and Child Health Journal* 1(3): 179–189.

Part Three
Institutions

8

Gender, Politics, and Change in the United States Cabinet
The Madeleine Korbel Albright and Janet Reno Appointments

MaryAnne Borrelli

As the executives of their departments and as presidential appointees, cabinet secretaries are representatives to and from the Oval Office, the Congress, their departments, and their departments' constituents. Recognizing the power that flows from relationship and communication—definitive functions of representation—political scientists have engaged in a protracted debate about which alliance decisively affects the secretaries' performance. The result has been a thoughtful conversation, encompassing the dilemmas of practicing politics in a system of separated powers, where no branch is monolithic and where political complexities constantly multiply. In other words, study of the president's cabinet has provided a window into theories, behaviors, and developments in U.S. politics. However, this inclusiveness notwithstanding, cabinet research generally has been blind to the workings of gender.

With few and noteworthy exceptions, scholars have failed to consider how the societal construction of women's and men's identities have affected decision making about and in the cabinet. Indeed, gender studies are just beginning to influence the research agenda for presidency studies. Though some seek to dismiss the applicability of gender studies by noting that a woman has not yet been elected president, the appointment of women to elite positions and the increasing salience of so-called women's issues argues for a wider perspective. After all, presidency scholars have never confined themselves to the Oval Office. Yet gender analysis is useful in understanding more than the comparatively recent personnel and policy developments. Gender studies, specifically, give us the insight and the tools to ask what it means that the presidency has been built and predominantly staffed by white males.

This chapter will address the politics that surround and accompany the inclusion of women—a previously marginalized group—into elite decision making. As women are now nominated to politically and governmentally influential posts, questions need to be asked about their selection, appointment, and confirmation. Because representation is the constitutive function of a cabinet officer, research can best be organized in terms of its various facets.

- Formal representation: In what ways do women's appointments change previously established appointment and confirmation procedures?
- Descriptive representation: How does the inclusion of women in the cabinet alter the demographic profile of that institution? What are the implications for the political ambitions of prospective secretaries, presidents, and departmental clients/networks?
- Substantive representation: What effect does the inclusion of women have upon the cabinet's policy agenda?
- Symbolic representation: What are the ideological implications of numbering women among the president's cabinet secretaries? How does this practice affect the wider development of U.S. political institutions?

This chapter focuses on the questions associated with descriptive and symbolic representation. Any enquiry will touch upon formal representation, because appointments are made in a formal context of legislative-executive relations. Substantive representation, in its turn, is largely the product of descriptive and symbolic representation. The personal, political, and professional profile of the cabinet (descriptive representation) conveys messages about whose, which, and what perspectives are legitimate. It reveals the president's constituents, which is to say that it reveals who an administration deems "politically relevant" (symbolic representation).[1] Who is present in decision-making circles will then determine whose concerns become policy priorities.

Research investigating women as representatives in the cabinet and the consequent changes in executive branch politics necessarily proceeds through the following steps. First, past standards for these officeholders are identified. These are requirements devised by and applied to white males; they are also standards that excluded women until comparatively recently. Second, therefore, the relevance of these standards to the women appointees is assessed. This will determine whether and how cabinet members' professional qualifications and political ideologies are changing. In this context, ideology extends beyond mere partisan affiliations to encompass a nominee's understandings of human nature, government, and politics. Senate confirmation hearings often examine these very points. A nominee's credibility is determined in significant part by her (or his) acceptance of and facility in a Madisonian system of self-interested and highly competitive negotiation. Thus we come to symbolic representation, as the endorsement of one particular political vision becomes a condition for officeholding (Borrelli 1997).

It may seem that this enterprise is about sex differences rather than gender analysis—that women and men are being compared with individuals assigned to one or another exclusive category on the basis of their physiological appearance. The research presented in this chapter is unquestionably indebted to pioneering studies of sex differences among officeholders. Yet this study also recognizes that institutions and ideologies of power are highly gendered. One cannot study how gender and the cabinet intersect, as if the two were once separate. Each infuses the other and it is impossible to speak of one in isolation from the other. As a socially constructed identity, gender is consistently influenced by politics as the "authoritative allocation of values." When studying the politics that surround cabinet appointments, therefore, there are questions to be asked about the relationship between nominees' credentials and credibility. In terms of ideologies of power, one can also query the presumptions that surround standards of fitness and achievement. Because men have historically been the political leaders, it is reasonable to suggest that masculine attributes will be deemed essential to political success (Duerst-Lahti and Kelly 1995).

This chapter, to summarize, argues three points. First, it is maintained that studying the appointment of women to the president's cabinet provides us with important insights on the United States political system. Advancing from that claim, the second argument holds that gender analysis provides us with the intellectual tools for a sharply focused investigation of the cabinet. Third, and finally, it argues that investigating descriptive and symbolic representation, through consideration of cabinet members' professional qualifications and political ideologies, will facilitate assessing women's incorporation into the ranks of executive branch elites. But which cabinet, and which secretaries, should be studied?

The baseline for this work is provided by the seven presidential administrations that have numbered at least one woman among their cabinet secretaries. This yields a population of almost 200 secretaries, of whom seventeen are women.[2] Within this population, the focus will be on the cabinet appointments of Madeleine Korbel Albright and Janet Reno. The first women to serve in the inner cabinet, these cabinet members are fascinating case studies in descriptive and symbolic representation. Are they reflective of enduring trends in cabinet appointments and/or in women's inclusion in elite decision making? Or does their appointment to higher office signal change? This chapter will argue in favor of the latter, though the changes may well be subtle and contradictory.

Madeleine Albright, in particular, has contributed to foreign policy deliberations for well over thirty years. Her connections throughout the foreign policy community were far more extensive than were those of the president who appointed her, first as permanent U.S. representative to the United Nations (1993) and then as secretary of state (1997). The implications of her career, and its divergence with some longstanding patterns, may signal that future women secretaries will have more varied careers and, consequently, more diversified roles in the cabinet.

In its turn, the selection and service of Janet Reno suggests that masculinist political ideologies may be challenged (and even displaced) as definitive of secretarial credibility. Throughout her tenure as attorney general, Reno has persistently articulated a vision of justice premised upon other-directedness and relationship. She also resists self-interest as the defining characteristic of political exchange, insisting that credit claiming is not necessary to the formulation of good policy. More, she argues, in terms that are intensely pragmatic, that Lockean rights-based priorities should make way for policies that value and enhance care.[3] Reno's rhetoric, it will be shown, has consistently advanced a feminine and feminist political ideology. In so doing, she has begun to challenge accepted masculinist standards of symbolic representation.

The following sections provide a more detailed examination of descriptive and symbolic representation in the cabinet through study of Madeleine Albright and Janet Reno. In so doing, they explore the ways in which the appointment of these women signals significant changes in cabinet appointments specifically and in the processes of representation generally.

Descriptive Representation and Presidential Dependence

The vast majority of presidential advisors have been descriptive representatives of the president. In association with this staffing practice, Georgia Duerst-Lahti has argued that comity in the White House is a highly gendered practice. Since medieval times, and doubtless earlier, leaders have depended upon a small group of advisors (the *comitatus*) for wisdom. In building these relationships, trust (i.e., comity) has most readily been achieved in homosociable environments. Male leaders generate male leadership structures. Support and advice move upward through these hierarchies, while mentoring and guidance flow downward. Men help men to succeed, proving that there literally are powerful benefits to being the same sex as the leader (Duerst-Lahti 1997).

By this same reasoning, there are powerful costs to being a different sex. As organizational analysts have long noted, tokens attract more attention precisely because they are in the extreme numerical minority. Their contributions are likely to be scrutinized more closely, even as they are isolated from the support networks that facilitate majority members' success (Kanter 1977). A woman's entry into the comitatus is unlikely because her presence alters the gendered presumptions implicit in this advisory body. If the comitatus experiences a gendered integration by women, its longstanding members must either divorce the institution from its roots in warfare or must accept women as loyal soldiers. Perhaps not surprisingly, women are rarely accepted into the comitatus. One study of presidential advisors has concluded that (some) first ladies are the only women who have been included in this inner circle (Burrell 1997).

Foreign policy has been a particularly masculine preserve. Traditional gender roles and institutional practices have reinforced one another, as when the Defense Department prohibited women from combat and then made combat duty a condition for certain promotions. At the State Department, deliberately discriminatory practices removed women from policymaking positions. More recent presidential administrations have sometimes advocated more equitable promotion standards, doing so under the compulsion of court orders and the threat of further litigation. However, it remains a continuing truth that women are more readily appointed to high-level foreign policy offices than they are promoted through the foreign services (McGlen and Sarkees 1993, 1997).

The comitatus and the president, representation, and presidential advisors, brings us to the work of Nelson Polsby. Having examined the careers of cabinet secretaries, and having considered the circumstances of their presidential appointments, Polsby proposed a tripartite classification schema. First are the specialists, professionally trained in their policy areas and loyal to their professions' canons. These secretaries are reminders of the sociopolitical circumstances that led to a department's founding. As such, they are also reminders of the original legislative-executive mandate that inaugurated the department. Second in the list are the liaisons, whose expertise lies in their mastery of the department's client relationships and issue networks. Liaisons remind the president that checks and balances may be both constitutional and extra-constitutional, as with interest groups. Third, though most definitely not the least in importance or number, are the generalists. These secretaries have acquired their political experience through service in Washington law firms and as political consultants. Their political alliances and thus their loyalties are wholly focused upon the president (Polsby 1978). Alone among the secretaries, the generalists do not check and will instead expand presidential power.

Polsby notes that the appointment of specialists and liaisons constitutes an explicit acknowledgment by the appointing president-elect or president that the legitimacy of his office is determined in part by actors he cannot control. In the case of specialists, there is an acknowledgment of the historic strength of a legislative-executive agreement. Liaisons, similarly, are proof of the power of interest groups, issue networks, and departmental clients. Specialist and liaison secretaries therefore find themselves in a curiously dualistic role. On one hand, they implicitly hold the president hostage (to use the popular phrase) to interests outside the Oval Office. On the other hand, they explicitly serve as the president's emissaries (note the possessive) to those same interests. When this classification schema is placed in the gendered context of the comitatus, the representative task of these secretaries is revealed in all its fine complexity.

As already discussed, the members of the comitatus are routinely the president's descriptive representatives, a shared identity facilitating the judgment that advisors are trustworthy and dependable. The influence of generalist secretaries, who are dependent upon the president, is a function of the similarity between their priorities and those of the chief executive. Specialist and liaison secretaries, however, are appointed—at least in part—to check the president. Their power is contingent upon perceptions that they are, literally and successfully, the president's loyal opposition. However, the chief executive will want any checks upon his office to be exercised cautiously and respectfully.[4] In simple terms, when a president is potentially vulnerable to—or, one might say, must depend upon—a cabinet member, the president will set higher standards for the cabinet member's dependability.

We would therefore expect to see a stronger comitatus emerging in policy areas where the secretary represented interests outside the Oval Office. By the same reasoning, less attention and correspondingly less scrutiny would occur in policy areas where secretaries were generalists and the president was free from such external checks. Given the linkages between the comitatus and descriptive representation, this theory would lead one to expect white men to be the specialist and liaison secretaries. Women and other "diversity" appointees would be generalists.[5] Further, white men would presumptively be nominated to the more important inner cabinet posts, "diversity" appointees to those in the outer cabinet. This expectation is verified by a survey of cabinet appointments across the seven presidential administrations. Women (and other diversity appointees, as well) have routinely been generalist secretaries in the outer cabinet. This practice has minimized presidential dependence upon the women cabinet secretaries, even as it has allowed the president to provide women voters with descriptive representation. In terms of symbolic representation, these circumstances have enabled the presidency to continue to function as an institution of white male exclusivity.

Madeleine Korbel Albright as Departmental Liaison

Still, there is Madeleine Korbel Albright, a woman who is a liaison secretary and secretary of state. As such, she stands as an acknowledgment of President Clinton's ignorance of foreign affairs, an issue area that is viewed as essential to national identity and fortunes. That a governor-become-president would need to appoint a liaison secretary to lead the State Department is predictable. That a woman would be the liaison is not, given the gendered dynamics at work within this policy network. Albright could, of course, be the exception that proves the rule. This author, however, believes that her appointment signals the next stage of women's incorporation as elite decision makers in the executive branch. If this is true, her career path offers a constructive example for women who share her ambitions.

Four lessons can be drawn from Albright's career, in regard to gender and political ambition for cabinet office. First, Albright does not challenge all of the informal standards for cabinet office. Like the other secretaries, she is in her early sixties, white, and possessed of an extensive education obtained at elite academic institutions. (Albright earned her undergraduate degree at Wellesley College, her doctorate at Columbia University.) She is divorced, with three grown daughters and two grandchildren. Like the majority of inner cabinet secretaries, she has served in a lower post within her department: Albright was appointed permanent representative of the United States to the United Nations in 1993. At that time, she was also accorded the status of plenipotentiary ambassador extraordinaire, cabinet rank, and National Security Council membership. Observers quickly concluded that the posting was Albright's "audition" for higher office (Martin 1985, 1988; Sciolino 1996).

Second, like virtually every other woman secretary, Albright was well known to the president who appointed her. During the Reagan–Bush administrations, while she was teaching at Georgetown, Albright's home became an informal center for conversation and consultation among Democratic Party activists. It was in this context that a good friend and party leader introduced Albright to Bill Clinton. She subsequently served as a policy advisor for his 1992 presidential campaign, volunteering expertise she had previously gained in campaigning for Walter Mondale and Michael Dukakis (Blood 1997, 45–51). Though women are not (yet) descriptive representatives of the president, Albright's example suggests that length of service may be accepted as evidence of women's loyalty and dependability.

Third, Albright's career developed largely outside the State Department and with the guidance of powerful mentors. The daughter of an exiled Czech diplomat, Albright's own political career began with campaign fundraising for then-Senator Edmund S. Muskie. She subsequently earned her doctorate in political science, studying with Zbigniew Brzezinski. Both men gave her extraordinary professional opportunities and both profited from her analytic abilities. Albright was a member of Muskie's Washington staff from 1976 to 1978, and a congressional liaison officer for Brzezinski's National Security Council from 1978 to 1981. When Muskie was appointed secretary of state and exchanges between the two men became progressively more difficult, Albright remained loyal to Brzezinski while sustaining a constructive relationship with Muskie.

Pushed out of the White House by Carter's defeat in the 1980 election, Albright became even more entrepreneurial. Initially a Woodrow Wilson Fellow, she subsequently secured a teaching post at the Georgetown School of Foreign Service. She remained in close contact with her Washington networks even as she educated the next generation of foreign policymakers. She directed two foundations, one bipartisan and one Democratic. She was a policy advisor in every Democratic presidential campaign. By the time she was appointed representative to the United Nations, she had served in every possible foreign policy context outside the State Department (Miller Center; Blood 1997, 41–73). In so doing, she had established relationships with departmental personnel that took the sting out of what might otherwise have been perceived as an end run.

Albright's career has unquestionably, routinely involved confrontations with the structural barriers of sex discrimination. She has acknowledged that her age and gender led to some difficulties during her congressional staff service, the senator initially being uncertain of her abilities. (Not to mention her fortitude—Muskie's temper was legendary.) Still, her career is less about confrontation than it is about momentum and about developing relationships that facilitate success. That is the fourth lesson of her career: Albright has a proven ability to serve as a lightening rod for contentiousness *and* as a mediator for peaceful accord. Most important, she usually has been able to balance these inclinations to good effect.

As U.N. representative and as secretary of state, Albright has become well known for her sound bites. Some would even suggest that she has become infamous (Blood 1997; Marcus 1997; Sciolino 1996). When two civilian planes were shot down in international space by the Cuban air force and the Cuban pilots proceeded to gloat over this accomplishment, Albright issued her oft-repeated declaration, "Frankly, this is not *cojones*, this is cowardice!" In negotiating Bosnian peace accords, Albright squared off with Colin Powell, then chair of the Joint Chiefs of Staff, concerning the use of the military in foreign policy. Albright insisted that U.S. troops should be used to buttress peace efforts.

> The fact is, Colin Powell has a different approach to the use of power. I mean, of course you can use power when the earth is flat and you have six months to prepare and you're facing a crazy dictator with nuclear weapons and someone else is paying for it. But that is not always the situation. (Quoted in Blood 1997, 163)

Munich analogies run throughout her arguments, a perspective that has been attributed to her early experiences as a political refugee. Notably, however, public opinion polls of women in the electorate and surveys of women in the State Department suggest that there are few gendered differences on the use of the military "to preserve world order." (This is distinct from attitudinal measures regarding the use of force and the fear of war, where there are enduring and decided gender differences [McGlen and Sarkees 1993, 187–215].) Albright is not effecting an ideological change in State Department policy. And yet, while her willingness to exercise force appears masculine, she nonetheless is providing women with substantive representation.

It is Albright's peacemaking within the government that has seemed the most remarkable of her skills. Certainly it has distinguished her as a departmental liaison. Most notable has been her constructive relationship with Jesse Helms, chair of the Senate Foreign Relations Committee and enduring opponent of Albright's predecessor, Clinton Secretary of State Warren M. Christopher. In a profoundly symbolic statement of reconciliation, Albright dispensed with Senate tradition and asked that Christopher present her credentials to the committee at her 1997 confirmation hearing. This task is usually undertaken by the appointee's home-state Senator, who provides a personal endorsement legitimizing the secretary-designate. To ask a disfavored retiring secretary to perform this task, before the committee and committee chair that had contributed to diminishing his reputation, was to signal support for the cabinet officer and confidence in the committee's pending vote. No doubt of Albright's style, abilities, or priorities surfaced during the hearing (U.S. Congress, 105th, January 22, 1997).

Cumulatively, then, Albright's career suggests ways in which women secretaries may prove themselves as representatives who will value rather than exploit a president's dependence. In so doing, Albright's career opens another way for women to enter the elite ranks of the executive branch. After all, notwithstanding competition with the National Security Advisor and others, the secretary of state cannot be easily excluded from foreign policy councils. Nor can presidents safely neglect foreign policymaking responsibilities, a point well demonstrated by the events of Clinton's first term. But Albright's career also suggests that the gendered nature of the presidency will change incrementally. Individuals gain little from directly challenging structures of privilege. End runs can be excused as exceptional. The vision of power that presumptively questions women's credibility as warriors, and sees leadership as an undertaking that requires the defenses of the comitatus, endures. Or perhaps it is slightly shaken by the presence of two women in an inner cabinet of four secretaries.

Symbolic Representation and Presidential Politics: Janet Reno as Attorney General

The first woman appointed to the inner cabinet, Janet Reno ended four months of controversy with her nomination. Shortly after the November 1992 elections, President-elect Clinton indicated interest in appointing a woman attorney general. His statement was both logical and surprising. Logical because, of the professions and networks from which inner cabinet secretaries have emerged and by which they have been judged, women have made the furthest inroads into the law. It was therefore understandable that the first woman to enter the inner cabinet would do so as attorney general. The more notable and imposing eligibility requirement for an attorney general was a close and longstanding relationship with the president. Though the "Bobby Kennedy law" precludes appointment of a relative, presidents have repeatedly nominated campaign managers and close friends to this office. With the exception of some first ladies, however, no woman has been able to claim such an influential role in a presidential campaign or career. To appoint a woman attorney general, therefore, was to decisively change the prevailing, if informal, requirements and standards for the office. Here was the first way in which the Clinton attorney general appointment altered the symbolic representation provided by this cabinet officer.

One withdrawn nomination (Zoe E. Baird) and one aborted nomination (Kimba Wood) later, Clinton appointed Florida's Dade County

State Attorney Janet Reno. Few attorney generals had come so immediately from state-level elected office, though this Democrat's ability to carry a Republican district (five times) was an encouraging indicator of her political abilities (Rohter 1993; Berke 1993; Marcus 1993; Davidson 1993; "Case for Politicians" 1993). Reno also seemed to promise objectivity and impartiality, which were desperately needed in the attorney general's office (U.S. Congress, 103rd, 1993, 46). In the years following her confirmation, questions have been raised about her influence with the president and her ability to effectively lead the Justice Department. Every investigative ruling, particularly in regard to the Branch Davidian/Waco crisis and the appointments of independent counsel, has been closely scrutinized. Though many expected her to be gone after the 1996 election, she is still in office three years later, as this book goes to press. What messages do her appointment and tenure as attorney general send?

Reno's career does evidence some similarities to Albright's. Like the secretary of state, the attorney general satisfies many of the expectations for cabinet officers. Reno was in her mid-fifties at the time of her appointment; she is white and has received an elite education. (She earned her undergraduate degree at Cornell, her law degree at Harvard.) Reno, however, has never married, a circumstance that has caused political opponents to campaign against her as a lesbian. Forced to counter these attacks while preparing for her confirmation, Reno defiantly countered one stereotype with another, describing herself as "an old maid who prefers men." During the Senate floor debate and confirmation vote, none other than Jesse Helms defended her insistence upon privacy (*Congressional Record* 1993).

Reno resembles Albright, and other women secretaries, in that male mentors provided support at crucial moments in her career. Most notably, her predecessor in the state attorney office retired before completing his term, having arranged for Reno's interim appointment to the office. This opportunity provided Reno with a significant electoral advantage. During her five terms in office, she endured urban riots and controversial court rulings, earning widespread support throughout Miami and its suburbs. She also acquired a reputation as a reformer who linked legal initiatives to social programs (Anderson 1994; Isikoff and Booth 1993).

Reno also resembles the majority of women secretaries, though contrasting with Albright, in her status as a policy generalist. She is not a policy specialist: at the time of her appointment, she did not have the reputation of being a legal scholar and her legal experience had been comparatively narrow. Nor is she a departmental liaison: prior to her appointment, Reno had never worked in the federal legal community, a circumstance that initially led Clinton to reject her for the cabinet post (President's News Conference 1992). Reno's vulnerability as a generalist has undoubtedly been magnified by her lack of a prior professional relationship with the president. Though her loyalty and dependence upon the president therefore appeared an unchangeable and institutional fact, the president's support was an unknown. Arguably, she was appointed with none and without the expectation of any—the typical circumstance of a generalist cabinet secretary. Notably, her independence from the president has subsequently been subject to praise and to ridicule.

What is typical for most generalists, however, is not typical for an attorney general, even though many attorney generals have been generalists. As campaign loyalists and as close friends of the president, attorney generals have had a prior relationship that muted their dependence upon the president. For these generalists, there is a sense in which the president is actually dependent upon their fortunes and therefore needs to facilitate their success. Reno lacked all such connections and resources.

This inventory of similarities and differences can be fairly summarized by stating that Reno is similar in important respects to other cabinet officers, particularly the women, but she is highly distinctive among the attorney generals. The events of the Clinton presidency, moreover, suggest that future presidents will have a renewed appreciation for the utility of a partisan loyalist in this post. Presidents-elect and presidents may recruit their attorney generals from an even more select group within the comitatus, effectively excluding women from consideration for some time. In regard to this aspect of her symbolic representation, therefore, Reno may give presidents cause to be more exclusive in their inner cabinet appointments. Reno's political ideology, however, may have the potential to shift policy agendas toward greater inclusiveness.

Reno's concern for rights is therefore consistent, unequivocal, and multifaceted. She is an attorney general whose political vision is based as much upon care as it is upon rights, upon transformation as much as justice. In reference to criminal acts, for example, she speaks about the perpetrator, the victim, and *both* of their families. She perceives crime as a societal problem and as a challenge to the community. Consensual crimes such as drug use are even more emphatically presented in these terms, Reno drawing attention to the plight of crack babies and abandoned children. Once crime is presented as an abuse of relationship—even strangers share a society and a community—then care becomes a central concern. For Reno, it is not enough that each person be protected against governmental intrusion, as Locke promised. There also must be an appreciation of what each human being owes to each other human being, so that every person can live a good and constructive life.

Reno advances her concerns through an insistence upon the importance of family and a protected childhood. Noting that illegal behavior has its roots early in an individual's life experience, and acknowledging that later rehabilitative efforts have had mixed success, the attorney general has argued forcefully for social programs centered upon early intervention:

> You develop a conscience by being loved, by having guidance, by having limits laid down, by being punished when you don't comply with the limits, but being punished fairly and consistently with the crime. But as importantly, because I remember being punished as I grew up, after you got punished, after you got sent to your room, after you got spanked, after your mother got furious with you, you knew that she was going to be there to love you and carry on. What we have got to do is give families and children the chance to grow in a strong and constructive way. Now your question is going to be, to me, is how can government do it? Government can do a lot more to preserve families, to protect them, to give them a chance to grow as strong and constructive human beings by providing care and attention and prevention up front instead of waiting until the crisis occurs. (Quoted in Moyers 1993)

Similar assertions at her confirmation hearing led *Washington Post* syndicated columnist Mary McGrory (1993) to dub Reno the "Nanny with a Nightstick" while the more reserved *Wall Street Journal* commented upon an appointee who was "Attorney General and Social Worker" (Eastland 1993). Reno, for her part, acknowledged that she had consulted and would continue to consult Health and Human Services Secretary Donna E. Shalala in regard to a number of her programmatic initiatives (see also: Reno 1996a, Reno 1997).

What is notable about Reno's statements, of course, is her interweaving of personal history, societal commentary, and old-fashioned (even Rooseveltian) Democratic principles. Each policy statement or speech is accompanied by an experiential reference, which constitutes an implicit rejection of criticisms that her goals are too idealistic. There is a constant insistence that government is obliged to safeguard and cultivate each individual's abilities (see: Reno 1998c, Reno 1996b).

As state attorney in Dade County, Florida, Reno advanced a number of institutional reforms. In each undertaking, her concern was to reserve prison as a last recourse (see, for example: Reno 1998a). An opponent of the death penalty, she insists upon the state's responsibility to foster reform and rehabilitation:

> I think it is imperative that we go after the dangerous criminal; that we prosecute them as vigorously as possible; that we get them put away and kept away; and that we focus on other offenders and think of what we can do better. To give you an example, what we face in Florida now is someone sentenced to 3 years, if the average sentence being served is 20 to 30 percent of the sentence, they're probably going to get out almost as soon as they get in, because Florida doesn't have enough prison cells. I would prefer to focus on those people and send them to jail, but let them know that, under judicial supervision, they could carefully work their way back out into the community. If they have a drug problem, get them into drug treatment in the jail, get them detoxed, stabilized, and then when people think they are ready, move them into nonsecure residential, then into day treatment. They are coming back to the community anyway, and they are coming back sooner, rather than later. Far better that for these short-term offenders, we get them back in an integrated coherent way that will give them a chance to serve as constructive citizens in that community, rather than repeat offenders almost immediately. (U.S. Congress 1993, 103rd, 82)

Here again the reference is to relationship, to a redemption that is both personal and societal. In this instance, as in so many others, government performs functions that Reno has elsewhere identified with good parenting: government instills a conscience in the lawbreaker through punishment and rehabilitation; it reminds those who uphold the law of the importance of supporting and forgiving others; and it instills in society a commitment to justice and to mercy. Reno never abandons Locke's commitment to rights, but she most definitely nuances liberalism's individualistic stresses (see, for example: Reno 1998b).

One could object that Reno's innovations have been more rhetorical than programmatic. Such a criticism could then assess Reno's influence by reference to her White House connections, noting that she has always been slightly (and sometimes more than slightly) outside the presidential loop. Alternatively, one could examine Reno's role as a more independent actor within the Clinton administration. Her conduct of and response to numerous investigations, including the appointment of independent counsel, has been a matter of considerable concern to the administration.

These are important considerations. However, behavioral investigations should not substitute for attentiveness to decision-makers' ideologies. After all, those more theoretical conceptions influence the decision-makers' behaviors and direct long-term institutional developments.

Reno's insistence that rights and care be interwoven constitutes a significant reform in the Lockean conceptions that are at the foundation of United States law and politics. The Madisonian system of separated powers is premised upon competitive self-interest. In similar fashion, rights preserve the autonomy of the average citizen. Care, however, preserves relationship by allowing one person to have need of another. More, it values a compassionate sensitivity, dictating that one should respond to the needs of another.

To suggest that care be valued, therefore, is to profoundly alter the gender of politics. Autonomy has traditionally been viewed as a masculine quality; it is no accident that the first rights-bearing citizens were men, the franchise being only gradually expanded. As a class, men have been viewed as capable of conducting the business of the public sphere because their gendered nature was perceived as congruent with the demands of politics. To argue that politics is an exercise in autonomy *and* in other-directedness—a contradiction that in itself dictates reflection—is to argue that new attributes are necessary to political discourse and action. Care has been an attribute ascribed and often abdicated to femininity. It has also been the distinguishing function of the private sector, which has been women's traditional realm.

So, Reno's theory of justice is one that draws feminine traits and private sphere abilities into politics, the public sphere. As the quotation above indicates, the attorney general views good mothering as priceless, within the family and the polity, because it models the wisdom and the behavior that constitute the best kind of citizenship. In making this judgment, Reno dictates a new definition of integrity, initiating a profound change in the content of political self-understanding and consequently in the content of our symbolic representation.

Conclusion

This chapter has weighed the implications of the Albright and Reno appointments from a gendered perspective, assessing the ways in which these women endorse or modify enduring standards of descriptive and substantive representation. As a liaison secretary, Albright is a cabinet member upon whom the president is dependent. She is only the third woman secretary to be other than a policy generalist. Her appointment is the achievement of a career which has avoided undue confrontations with structural barriers to a woman's advancement and which has implicitly accepted many of the prevailing (if informal) standards for credibility. Albright has succeeded in "playing the game" and is remarkable for her skill in doing so. Her appointment is indicative of change in that the system is recognizing and rewarding her skills. Thus an appointee's sex is rendered less relevant to decision making, and the standards surrounding the descriptive representation of the president are accordingly revised. Insofar as Albright's appointment also signals that women are becoming accepted as loyal soldiers in the presidential comitatus, symbolic representation also changes to encompass a less constricted vision of women's gender.

In contrast to Albright, Reno's career and subsequent nomination appear supportive of traditional patterns of gender politics in cabinet appointments. Like the vast majority of women secretaries, Reno is a policy generalist. Though one can object that generalists have routinely been appointed to the office of the attorney general, those individuals have had strong friendships and professional relationships with the president. Reno's resemblance to other women secretaries is thus a measure of her uniqueness among attorney generals, and an indicator of why future attorney generals will most likely not resemble Reno in their professional and political profiles. Reno's tenure in office, given the circumstances prevailing throughout the Clinton presidency, may have the effect, at least in the short term, of moving the symbolic representation afforded by the attorney general toward greater exclusivity.

To conclude that Reno is of interest primarily as a "negative example," however, is to miss a significant piece of this cabinet member's contribution. As noted at the outset of this chapter, cabinet members need to be considered in terms of their credentials *and* in terms of their ideologies. Through her policy statements and commentaries, this attorney general has consistently and forcefully articulated a political vision that seeks to incorporate presumptively feminine, private sphere values into prevailing masculine, public sphere standards. To have the repeated, public articulation of a political ideology that incorporates care is a significant development, particularly when the cabinet member whose jurisdiction is traditionally rights-centered is effecting that development.

This chapter therefore offers contrasting, though not paradoxical, findings. On one hand, Albright has expanded women's opportunities by serving as an exemplar of their political abilities. She demonstrates that women and men share many of the same attributes, and thus broadens the boundaries of women's gender to include traditionally masculine traits. Reno has indicated the need of an Albright role model. Women as policy generalists, lacking claims to presidential loyalty, will remain unlikely candidates for the most influential posts in the executive branch. On the other hand, Reno has also insisted upon valuing the feminine for its contribution to the public sphere, identifying care as a constitutive element of citizenship. So while Albright has added breadth to women's gender role, Reno has drawn the gender more fully into the public sphere. Albright has effected change by altering traditional conceptions of women and Reno has concurrently sought change by recognizing the political importance of those same conceptions. Which development will have the greater impact can only be determined in the future.

Notes

1. This definition of constituency is taken from Melissa Williams' 1998 work, *Voice, Trust and Memory: Marginalized Groups and the Failings of Liberal Representation.*

2. Here, the cabinet is being defined in exacting terms, including only departmental secretaries and excluding cabinet officers who merely hold "cabinet rank." The latter is granted at the discretion of each president, introducing a lack of standardization to the workings of formal representation. The inner cabinet, then,

is composed of the departments of state, treasury, defense, and justice. All other departments fall in the outer cabinet.

3. The political theories of Carol Gilligan (1982) and Joan Tronto (1993) significantly parallel Reno's views.

4. The masculine possessive pronoun in this sentence is dictated by sentence structure and by the conclusion that the associated theory of power is strongly masculine in content.

5. "Diversity" is placed in quotations because, taken as a group, white women and people of color constitute a majority of the population. These are "diversity" appointees in regards to the Washington community, but not in reference to the wider society.

References

Anderson, Paul. 1994. *Janet Reno: Doing the Right Thing.* New York: John Wiley.

Berke, Richard L. 1993. "Clinton Picks Miami Woman, Veteran State Prosecutor, to Be His Attorney General." *New York Times* (12 February): 1, A22.

Blood, Thomas. 1997. *Madam Secretary: A Biography of Madeleine Albright.* New York: St. Martin's Press.

Borrelli, MaryAnne. 1997. "Gender, Credibility, and Politics: The Senate Nomination Hearings of Cabinet Secretaries-Designate, 1975 to 1993." *Political Research Quarterly* 50 (1): 171–197.

Burrell, Barbara C. 1997. "The Office of First Lady and Public Policy Making." In *The Other Elites: Women, Politics, and Power in the Executive Branch,* ed. MaryAnne Borrelli and Janet M. Martin. Boulder, CO: Lynne Rienner.

"A Case for Politicians." 1993. *Washington Post* (12 March): A22.

Clinton, William J. 1993. "The President's News Conference with Attorney-General-Designate Janet Reno, February 11, 1992." *The Papers of the President, The Administration of William J. Clinton, 1993.*

Congressional Record. 1993. 103rd Congress, 1st session, 11 March.

Davidson, Joe. 1993. "Miami Prosecutor Janet Reno Is Picked by President to Be Attorney General." *Wall Street Journal* (12 February): A3–A4.

Duerst-Lahti, Georgia. 1997. "Reconceiving Theories of Power: Consequences of Masculinism in the Executive Branch." In *The Other Elites: Women, Politics, and Power in the Executive Branch,* ed. MaryAnne Borrelli and Janet M. Martin, pp. 11–32. Boulder, CO: Lynne Rienner.

Duerst-Lahti, Georgia, and Rita Mae Kelly. 1995. "On Governance, Leadership, and Gender." In *Gender Power, Leadership, and Governance,* pp. 11–37. Ann Arbor: The University of Michigan Press.

Eastland, Terry. 1993. "Attorney General and Social Worker." *Wall Street Journal* (10 March): A15.

Gilligan, Carol. 1982. *In a Different Voice.* Cambridge, MA: Harvard University Press.

Isikoff, Michael, and William Booth. 1993. "Miami 'Drug Court' Demonstrates Reno's Unorthodox Approach." *Washington Post* (20 February): 1, A8.

Kanter, Rosabeth Moss. 1977. *Men and Women of the Corporation.* New York: Basic Books.

Marcus, David L. 1997. "The New Diplomacy." *The Boston Globe Magazine* (1 June): 16–17.

Marcus, Ruth. 1993. "Clinton Nominates Reno at Justice." *Washington Post* (12 February): 1, A23.

Martin, Janet M. 1985 "Cabinet Secretaries from Truman to Johnson: An Examination of Theoretical Frameworks for Cabinet Studies." Ph.D. dissertation, The
Ohio State University.

———. 1988. "Frameworks for Cabinet Studies," *Presidential Studies Quarterly*
18(4): 803–814.

McGlen, Nancy E., and Meredith Reid Sarkees. 1993. *Women in Foreign Policy:
The Insiders.* New York: Routledge.

———. 1997. "Style Does Matter: The Impact of Presidential Leadership on
Women in Foreign Policy." In *The Other Elites: Women, Politics, and Power
in the Executive Branch*, ed. MaryAnne Borrelli and Janet M. Martin, pp. 107–
125. Boulder, CO: Lynne Rienner.

McGrory, Mary. 1993. "Nanny with a Nightstick." *Washington Post* (11 March): A2.

Miller Center. Oral History Interview with Zbigniew Brzezinski and National Security Council Staff Members [including Congressional Liaison Officer Madeleine Albright]. Jimmy Carter Library, February 18, 1982.

Moyers, Bill. 1993. *A Conversation with the Attorney General, Janet Reno, 1993.*
Videotaped presentation.

Polsby, Nelson. 1978. "Presidential Cabinet Making: Lessons for the Political
System." *Political Science Quarterly* 93 (1): 15–25.

Reno, Janet. 1996a. Address Before the Bar Association of the District of Columbia, 125th Anniversary.

———. 1996b. Presentation Before the First National Interfaith Breakfast: A Call
to End Violence Against Women, Washington, DC, October 11, 1996.

———. 1997. Address to the National Sheriffs' Association Meeting, Atlanta, GA,
October 23, 1997.

———. 1998a. Address to the American Bar Association, Toronto, Ontario, Can-
ada, August 3, 1998.

———. 1998b. Closing Keynote Address at Harvard University, Cambridge, MA,
May 9, 1998.

———. 1998c. Keynote Address to the 1998 Radcliffe College Alumnae Association, Cambridge, MA, June 5, 1998.

Rohter, Larry. 1993. "Tough 'Front-Line Warrior,' Janet Reno." *New York Times*,
(12 February): 1, A22.

Sciolino, Elaine. 1996. "Madeleine Albright's Audition." *New York Times Magazine.* (22 September): 63–67.

Tronto, Joan. 1993. *Moral Boundaries: A Political Argument for an Ethic of Care.*
New York: Routledge.

U.S. House. 1993. Committee on the Judiciary. *Events Surrounding the Branch
Davidian Cult Standoff in Waco, Texas.* 103rd Congress, 1st session.

U.S. House. 1995. Joint Hearing of the Crime Subcommittee of the Committee
on the Judiciary and the National Security International Affairs and Criminal
Justice Subcommittee of the Government Reform and Oversight Committee.
Review of Siege of Branch Davidians' Compound in Waco, Texas. 104th Congress, 1st session.

U.S. Senate. 1997. Committee on Foreign Relations. *Nomination of Secretary of
State.* 105th Congress, 1st session.

U.S. Senate. 1993. Committee on the Judiciary. *Nomination of Janet Reno to Be
Attorney General of the United States.* 103rd Congress, 1st session.

Williams, Melissa. 1998. *Voice, Trust and Memory: Marginalized Groups and the
Failings of Liberal Representation.* Princeton: Princeton University Press.

9

Gender and the Federal Judiciary

Susan Gluck Mezey

Only two presidents, Ronald Reagan and Bill Clinton, have had the distinction of appointing women to the Supreme Court of the United States. Although Supreme Court nominations are always newsworthy, the selection of Sandra Day O'Connor and Ruth Bader Ginsburg, replacing Justices Potter Stewart and Byron White respectively, appeared to attract more attention than usual from legal scholars, politicians, special interest groups, and the public. As the first and second women to serve on the high court, their nominations were accompanied by speculation about how they would vote on issues coming before the Court. More specifically, there was widespread interest in how they would vote on claims involving reproductive rights. The assumption that gender affects votes largely fueled the preoccupation with the nominations of these two justices; observers believed that because they were women, they would behave differently from their brethren.

O'Connor and Ginsburg are, of course, the most visible women on the federal bench, but the appointment of women to the lower federal courts is typically accompanied by questions, concerns, and assumptions similar to those surrounding the appointment of the two women to the high court.

The Impact of Gender Differences on the Courts

This chapter explores the effect of gender on the federal courts in several ways. After presenting data on judicial appointments to the federal bench, the analysis focuses on the impact of gender on judicial behavior, ending with a brief look at the two women who serve on the highest court of the land.

Representation Theory

Scholarly investigations of the effect of gender in public office typically ask whether women in office "act for" women and also "stand for" them; that is, when compared with men, are women more inclined to initiate and support women's policy goals? This debate over whether women serve as "descriptive" or "substantive" representatives can be traced to Hannah Pitkin's (1967) classification of two types of representation. According to Pitkin, "descriptive representation," or "standing for," is accomplished simply by a member of a group occupying a seat of power without advocating the group's policy interests. Being defined on the basis of what "he or she is like rather than what he or she does" (Perry 1991, 10), a descriptive representative may serve as a role model for the group, but is not necessarily committed to achieving its policy goals. On the other hand, a substantive representative is a public official who "acts for" the group by seeking to accomplish goals that purport to benefit the group's members. While women judges as descriptive representatives might have an impact on the legal environment, the major concern of this chapter is whether, and to what extent, women judges are also substantive representatives of women in society.

Gender Effects in Legislatures

For more than three decades, scholars have examined the extent to which women in public office differ from their male counterparts. They have asked whether women voice more concern than men about so-called women's, or feminist, issues; whether women exert greater efforts than men to enact laws and policies that differentially affect women; and whether they serve as role models for other women. Most of this research has focused on state public officials, although scholars have paid some attention to examining congressional behavior.

The results of this research have been mixed. Taken together, the studies showed that attitudes and voting behavior of politicians were in part attributable to gender differences but that gender *alone* probably did not account for differences in political behavior, with ideology and party also playing a role (see Mezey 1978; 1994). Studies by Welch (1985), Saint-Germain (1989), Thomas and Welch (1991), Reingold (1992), and Dolan and Ford (1995) found that women expressed more concern for women's issues and accorded a higher priority to them; women were also more inclined than men to translate these concerns into action by introducing legislation to promote greater equality for women and improve the status of women. Women were also more attentive to legislation that revolved around women's traditional interests, such as children, education, family, and health. Additionally, many women legislators felt they had a special responsibility to represent their women constituents and were more likely to consider their support important.

The research on gender and legislative behavior thus suggests that many women officeholders are committed to "acting for" women in society; they perceive themselves as more likely to support issues benefitting women and their families and to pursue women's policy goals than their male colleagues.

Gender Effects in Courts

Federal court judges differ from other political actors in several ways. As lifetime appointees, they do not represent a constituency and are not subject to recall or defeat at the polls. Perhaps most important, however, their decisions must adhere to legal rules and principles rather than reflect their backgrounds or values. Thus, while it may be appropriate (and fruitful) to discuss the effect of gender on legislative decision making, it may not be fitting to ask what role gender plays in judicial decision making.

Despite the importance of legal principles in judicial decision making, judicial scholars have long been concerned with the role of extralegal influences, such as political party, gender, region, religion, and age, on the decisions of federal court judges from lower district court to Supreme Court (see, for example, Goldman 1975; Rowland and Carp 1980; Tate 1981; Carp and Rowland 1983; Songer and Davis 1990). Their studies reflected the belief that social background characteristics affect the way in which judges decide cases and are useful in explaining and/or predicting their votes.

In exploring the premise that gender affects a judge's goals, priorities, and, ultimately, behavior on the bench, Gottschall (1983); Walker and Barrow (1985); and Songer, Davis, and Haire (1994) focused on the votes of lower federal court judges. Similarly, Gryski, Main, and Dixon (1986); Gryski and Main (1986); and Allen and Wall (1987;

1993) looked at the effect of gender on voting by state supreme court judges. At the local level, Kritzer and Uhlman (1977) and Gruhl, Spohn, and Welch (1981) examined differences in the sentencing behavior of men and women urban trial court judges.

"Different Voices" Theory

Carol Gilligan's (1982) path-breaking work on moral development and her discovery that women and men exhibit differences in morality and reasoning, although criticized from several perspectives (see, for example, Baer 1991), produced a veritable cottage industry of literature on gender differences in legal analysis.

Sherry (1986) classified a type of jurisprudence, emanating from classical Republican (Jeffersonian) thought and exemplified by the opinions of Justice O'Connor, as a "feminine" rather than "feminist" voice. Drawing on Gilligan's analysis of gender differences, Sherry (1986, 582) noted that women emphasized "connection, subjectivity, and responsibility," while men valued "autonomy, objectivity, and rights." Sherry examined O'Connor's opinions in equal protection and religion cases in particular, and compared her votes to those of her ideologically compatible brother, Chief Justice William Rehnquist; she found that O'Connor valued membership in the community and exhibited a preference for communitarian values over individual rights. Sherry believed that the "pattern of disagreement [between O'Connor and Rehnquist] is highly suggestive of the operation of a uniquely feminine perspective" (Sherry 1986, 592). Although she suggested this perspective could have "a revolutionary effect . . . on jurisprudence," she noted that O'Connor voted with the conservatives on most issues (p. 613). Sherry's work implied that the opinions of women judges might differ from those of men in a predictable way, although, as O'Connor's votes show, not necessarily tending in a more liberal direction.

Also deriving their approach from Gilligan and Martha Minow's (1990, 15) "social relations" analysis, Sullivan and Goldzwig (1992) identified another type of judicial decision making. They cited a "female-associated approach" manifested in O'Connor's opinions in abortion cases. Asserting that O'Connor's moral decision making in abortion cases is derived from "female-identified values," they claimed that, among other things, her approach refrained from simple line drawing and sought to accommodate law to the lives of real people—in this case, women (Sullivan and Goldzwig 1992, 35). They noted as well that O'Connor's approach to decision making was not a feminist one and could not be conveniently categorized on the basis of an ideological perspective.

In an explicit test of Gilligan's theory, Davis (1992–1993) compared the votes of the five women on the Ninth Circuit to seven comparable men. To highlight the gender difference, she matched women with men appointed by the same president, and, as far as possible, by legal education, previous occupation, and previous prosecutorial or judicial experience.

She examined the reasoning of these judges in cases presenting equal protection and Title VII issues, as well as those alleging a deprivation of rights under the federal statute, 42 U.S.C. 1983. Basing her analysis on the theories expounded by Gilligan and Sherry, she looked for evidence that women spoke in different voices in three distinct categories: (1) "equality as connection v. equality as autonomy" (p.157); (2) "the duty to protect v. freedom from abuse" (p. 165); and (3) "contextual v. rule based decision making" (p. 168).

Her results were far from definitive. Davis concluded that "sometimes, some women judges do [speak in a different voice]. But sometimes, some men judges also speak in that different voice." In the end she acknowledged that, contrary to the expectation that placing more women in judicial office would affect the legal system, her data did not "provide empirical support for the theory that the presence of women judges will transform the very nature of law" (Davis, 1992–1993, 171). Assessing the results of her research, Davis suggested that there were either no gender-based differences or that women had been socialized into the norms of the judicial profession and the differences had faded.

Finally, also reflecting the influence of Gilligan's different voice theory, Allen and Wall's (1993, 158–59) study of state supreme courts examined four possible role orientations of women judges: representatives (adopting "a pro-woman voting record on women's issues cases"); tokens ("characterized by voting records that lie within the central area of any continuum and do not exhibit behavior that differentiates them from other justices"); outsiders ("exhibit[ing] comparatively extreme voting behavior"); and the different voices role ("plac[ing] higher values on relational concerns, such as the community, as opposed to individual rights . . . and exhibit[ing] extremism and isolation in dissenting behavior"). Examining state high court decisions in cases involving criminal appeals, economic liberties (such as landlord–tenant disputes, negligence, and insurance claims), and women's issues (such as sex discrimination, sexual assault damages, and child support), they compared the liberal opinions of the women judges in twenty-one states with the liberal votes of the court as a whole in an attempt to place the women in an appropriate role category.

When they examined the women's rights cases, they found that most of the women judges in their analysis adopted a representative role. Focusing on the economic rights and criminal procedure cases only, they concluded that women were outsiders but that party identification affected their outsider status differentially. Women Democratic judges were much more liberal than male Democratic judges, while women Republican judges were more conservative than their party colleagues. The differences, however, were less pronounced among the Republicans.

Finally, there was some evidence that women judges also adopted a different voice in decision making in the criminal procedure and economic liberties cases. However, the authors explained that their measure of a different voice, unlike Gilligan's different morality approach or Sherry's preference for communitarian values, was limited solely to dissent behavior.

Appointments to the Federal Bench

Although a few women were serving on federal courts of limited jurisdiction as early as 1918, they were absent from the federal bench for most of the nation's history. The first woman was appointed to a federal court of general jurisdiction in 1934 when President Franklin Roosevelt nominated Ohio Supreme Court judge Florence Ellinwood Allen to the Sixth Circuit Court of Appeals. Allen, who served as chief judge of the Sixth Circuit before her retirement in 1959, began her judicial career on the Court of Common Pleas in Cuyahoga County, Ohio, in 1921; a year later, she was the first woman to be elected as a justice on a state supreme court. Despite the active lobbying by women's groups for Allen to fill one of the twelve Supreme Court vacancies during the Roosevelt and Truman administrations, she was never nominated.

It took more than a decade for the second Article III (life-tenured) woman judge to be named. In 1949 President Harry Truman appointed Burnita Shelton Matthews, who served as a full-time judge for eighteen years, to the District Court of the District of Columbia. A significant time again elapsed until John F. Kennedy appointed Sarah Hughes to the district court in 1961. Ironically, Hughes was the judge who swore in Kennedy's successor on an airfield in Dallas in November 1963. Then in a much briefer interval, Lyndon Johnson named Shirley Hufstedler of the California Court of Appeals to the Ninth Circuit Court of Appeals in 1968 (see Berkson 1982; Martin 1982; Perry 1991; Harrison 1996; Wilson 1996).

The modern era of women appointees to the federal bench began with the presidency of Jimmy Carter. In 1978 Congress had enacted the Omnibus Judgeship Act (OJA), creating 152 judgeships—117 at the district court level and 35 appellate seats. This allowed Carter to leave his imprint on the federal judiciary, and by the time his term ended, he had appointed a majority of the appellate judges on the Fifth, Sixth, Ninth, Eleventh, and the District of Columbia circuits (Gottschall 1983, 167). Although he was unable to appoint a justice to the Supreme Court, Carter took advantage of the opportunity offered by the OJA to appoint a record number of judges to the lower federal courts, including an unprecedented number of women and minorities.

The history of female appointments to the federal bench before Carter had been dismal. Until 1961, only Allen and Matthews, the Roosevelt and Truman appointees, served on federal courts of general jurisdiction. Between 1961 and 1981, a total of six new women judges were appointed: four during the Kennedy–Johnson administrations and two during the Nixon–Ford administrations (Goldman and Saronson 1994, 68 n.1). Table 9.1 summarizes lower federal court appointments from 1964 to 1994.

Carter took advantage of his opportunity to diversify the federal bench. When he assumed office, there were 6 women (and 22 nonwhite judges) out of approximately 500 federal court judges (Slotnick 1984, 374). Reflecting a highly visible affirmative action policy as well as an emphasis on merit selection, Carter appointed a record number of women and minorities to federal court judgeships: 93 women, African Americans, and Hispanics out of a total of 258 appointments (*Congressional Quarterly Weekly Report* 1997, 369). He was able to appoint

Table 9.1

Presidential Appointments to the Lower Federal Courts by Sex (1964–1994)

Judges appointed	Presidents						
	Johnson	Nixon	Ford	Carter	Reagan	Bush	Clinton*
Women							
percent	1.9	0.4	1.6	15.5	7.6	19.5	32.9
number	(3)	(1)	(1)	(40)	(28)	(36)	(29)
Men							
percent	98.1	99.6	98.4	84.5	92.4	80.5	67.0
number	(159)	(223)	(63)	(218)	(340)	(149)	(59)
Total							
number	162	224	64	258	368	185	88

Sources: (Carter, Reagan, Bush, Clinton): Goldman and Saronson (1994, table 3); (Johnson, Nixon, Ford): Percentages calculated by the author from Goldman (1989, Tables 2 and 4).

*Based on the authors' assumptions that nominees through June 1, 1994, would be confirmed.

56 judges to the U.S. Court of Appeals; of these, 11 (19.6 percent) were women (Goldman 1995, Table 4). On the district court level, Carter appointed a total of 202 judges, including 29 (14.4 percent) women. When his administration ended, he had increased the percentage of women on the federal bench from 1 percent to almost 7 percent (Goldman 1981, 349).

Despite his act of placing a woman on the Supreme Court, Reagan did not continue Carter's affirmative action policy, appointing only 45 women and members of racial minorities out of 368 appointments (*Congressional Quarterly Weekly Report* 1997, 369). While overall he appointed many more women to the bench than the presidents preceding Carter, and his record of naming women to the district courts did not veer very sharply from Carter's, Reagan's appointment of nonwhite judges was vastly different from Carter's. Additionally, there was a " 'dramatic' retreat from Carter's record" on appointments of women to the appellate level (Slotnick 1988, 319).

Some, like Goldman (1983), suggested Reagan was essentially indifferent to the idea of appointing women, but feminists argued that he was actually hostile to it. Martin (1987) believed that Reagan's record with respect to women appointments can be traced to a number

Table 9.2

Presidential Appointments to the U.S. Courts of Appeals by Sex (1976–1996)

Judges appointed	Presidents			
	Carter % (N)	Reagan % (N)	Bush % (N)	Clinton % (N)
Women	19.6	5.1	18.9	31.0
	(11)	(4)	(7)	(9)
Men	80.4	94.9	81.1	69.0
	(45)	(74)	(30)	(20)
Total	56	78	37	29

Source: Goldman and Slotnick (1997, Table 6).

of factors: a diminished pool of eligible candidates because of his abolition of the Carter-established circuit nominating panels; his reversion to the practice of "senatorial courtesy" for district court appointments (de-emphasized by Carter); and his insistence on the potential nominee's ideological commitment to traditional family values and opposition to reproductive rights.

Like Carter, President George Bush was aided in leaving his mark on the federal judiciary—although he had only four years to do so—by passage of the 1990 Federal Judgeship Act, creating eighty-five new judicial positions. Although committed to continuing the Reagan policy of appointing judges with conservative views, he also sought to expand the recruitment process to include "appropriately qualified women and minorities" (Goldman 1991, 297). Bush appointed 56 women and racial minorities out of a total of 185 (*Congressional Quarterly Weekly Report* 1997, 369). During his first two years in office, though he outdid Reagan in appointing women to the district and appellate courts, he did not surpass the Carter record despite the increasing number of eligible women in the recruitment pool (Goldman 1991, Tables 1 and 2). But during the last two years of his presidency, he exceeded Carter's record of appointing women to the district and appellate courts (Goldman 1993, Tables 2 and 4). Despite these achievements, Bush's judicial legacy will always be tainted by the nomination of Clarence Thomas to the Supreme Court, an appointment vigorously contested by women's groups and liberal organizations, only in part because of the

Table 9.3

Presidential Appointments to the U.S. District Courts by Sex (1976–1996)

Judges appointed	Presidents			
	Carter % (N)	Reagan % (N)	Bush % (N)	Clinton % (N)
Women	14.4	8.3	19.6	30.2
	(29)	(24)	(29)	(51)
Men	85.6	91.7	80.4	69.8
	(173)	(266)	(119)	(118)
Total	202	290	148	169

Source: Goldman and Slotnick (1997, Table 3).
Note: Courts of general jurisdiction.

accusations of sexual harassment against Thomas by University of Oklahoma law professor Anita Hill.

Clinton was even more committed than Carter to appointing non-traditional judges to the federal bench, and his nomination of women and minorities reflected the depth of his belief in producing a diversified court (Perry and Abraham 1998). By July 1, 1994, three-fifths of all his appointees were members of racial minority groups and women (Goldman and Saronson 1994, 68). More recent data show that of 198 federal judges he appointed by the end of 1996, 111 were women, African Americans, and Hispanics (*Congressional Quarterly Weekly* 1997, 369).

Table 9.2 shows the number and percentage of women and men appellate judges appointed during the twenty years of the Carter, Reagan, Bush, and Clinton administrations.

Table 9.3 presents the number and percentage of women and men appointed over a twenty-year period to the district courts. Here again, the data show Clinton's commitment to diversifying the federal court by appointing women judges.

Like Carter, Clinton followed an affirmative action policy in judicial appointments. Reacting to Clinton's efforts to carry out his pledge, his opponents leveled charges that to meet his self-imposed quota, he appointed less qualified women and members of racial minority groups. However, after assessing the background characteristics and experience of the Clinton appointees, Goldman and Saronson (1994, 73) concluded that:

> In accord with the concept of affirmative action as widening the recruitment net to bring in highly qualified women and minorities, greater diversity has not come at the expense of qualifications. Clinton's nontraditional appointees are as qualified, if not more so in terms of their ABA ratings and professional experience, as the appointees of Reagan and Bush. . . . The end result is a more diversified federal bench consistent with the principle of merit.

Does Gender Affect Judicial Decision Making?

Over the last two decades, as the number of women federal judges increased, judicial scholars have addressed the issue of whether women judges "act for" women or merely "stand for" them.

Research on federal court judges differs from research on legislators because the latter may be questioned about their policy preferences and political beliefs. Moreover, besides counting votes, there are manifestations of a legislator's policy concerns, including co-sponsoring legislation, proposing amendments, and speaking on the floor of the chamber. Such methods are generally unavailable to judicial scholars (but see Martin 1993). With judges trained to rely on and cite legal principles for their decisions and to suppress their personal beliefs, researchers are typically limited to counting their votes or analyzing their written opinions. Thus, with some exceptions, research on the courts typically imparts a snapshot view of judicial behavior that can only suggest a judge's beliefs.

Scholars such as Goldman (1981) and Martin (1982) predicted that as a result of Carter's commitment to diversity and his affirmative action policies, the federal bench would become more activist and liberal and that women judges would manifest a greater sensitivity to issues of race and sex discrimination on the bench. More specifically, they hypothesized that because women experienced societal discrimination, they would be more likely to take a liberal posture in rights and liberties cases. Alternatively, however, it has been argued that because women have been socialized into a common legal subculture, their decisions will closely resemble the decisions of the men with whom they serve (see, for example, Songer, Davis, and Haire 1994).

Martin's (1993) study of members of the National Association of Women Judges (NAWJ) showed that most of the NAWJ members they surveyed at their annual conference in 1989 believed their presence made a difference to women attorneys and that they encouraged other women to seek judgeships; they also thought they helped change the attitudes of men judges toward professional women. Martin's questions, however, related to women judges as role models and gender representatives, and her research, limited to women only, was unable to determine whether gender affected judicial voting behavior.

In his study of votes on federal courts of appeals from July 1, 1979, to June 30, 1981, Gottschall (1983) assessed how Carter's affirmative action policy affected judicial decision making by comparing the votes of appellate judges in cases involving gender and racial discrimination and criminal defendants' rights. Not surprisingly, he found that the Carter-, Johnson-, and Kennedy-appointed judges were more liberal than the Nixon- and Ford-appointed judges in all three issue areas. When he compared Carter's white female appointees with his white male appointees, Gottschall found they were alike in prisoners' rights cases but that women were slightly more liberal than men on issues related to gender and racial equality, although the differences were not significant.

Walker and Barrow's (1985) study of the diversification of the federal bench also examined the degree to which Carter's affirmative action policy led to greater substantive representation for women and minorities. Their matched sample included twelve pairs of male and female Carter-appointed judges in the same district and of the same race.

Their data cast doubt on the degree to which women judges "act for" other women. Although these differences were also insignificant, men were more supportive of women's rights claims in cases involving sexual harassment, gender discrimination, maternity rights, affirmative action, equal employment, and reproductive rights. Similarly, although the differences were also insignificant, men were slightly more pro-defendant in the criminal rights cases. They found significant differences between women and men in three areas of law: personal liberties (civil liberties and equality); minority policy issues (ethnic and racial discrimination, welfare rights, police brutality, fair housing, and the rights of the disabled and the elderly); and economic regulation. But contrary to gender stereotypes, their data showed that men were more liberal in the first two categories, with women more likely to favor the government in the economic regulation cases.

Their study showed that the women judges exhibited greater deference to the political branches of government and hardly evoked the image of activist liberal judges. After doing the same analysis on a matched set of white and black judges, they concluded that "the assumptions that female and black judges will be more receptive to the policy goals of women and minorities, and more liberal and activist in the use of judicial power find no support in the decision-making patterns of the judges studied" (Walker and Barrow 1985, 614).

Similarly, Davis (1986) examined the voting behavior of appellate judges from July 1, 1981, to June 30, 1983, in eight issue areas: individual rights—freedom of expression and privacy; individual rights—equality; prisoner petitions; criminal appeals; labor–management; income tax; employee injury; and other personal injury. She found that women were more liberal than men when all the case types were considered together, but they were only significantly more liberal in the areas of income tax and employee injury.

Seeking to reconcile conflicting reports of gender differences on the bench, Songer, Davis, and Haire (1994) examined three types of cases: obscenity, employment discrimination, and search and seizure. Basing their analysis on the decisions of judges in all twelve circuits, they classified the votes in each issue category as liberal or conservative—obscenity opinions against censorship were considered liberal. Using separate models for each set of cases, they also included ideology of appointing president, region, and selected case facts as independent variables. Their results showed that there were no significant gender differences in either the obscenity or search and seizure cases, but that gender had a strong significant effect on votes in employment discrimination cases. They concluded that "the effect of gender on judicial behavior varies with the context of the decision-making process" (Songer, Davis, and Haire 1994, 436). Overall, they believed it premature to reach firm conclusions about how gender affects judicial behavior, suggesting that more women must be appointed to the federal bench before more definitive results could emerge.

The Women "Brethren"

Writing about O'Connor, the only woman on the high court at the time, Behuniak-Long (1992, 417) asked: "What is expected of a justice who is appointed to a 'representational' seat on the Court? In particular, what contribution was O'Connor, as a female, expected to make?" Thus, this chapter concludes with a brief examination of O'Connor and her more recently appointed female colleague, Ruth Bader Ginsburg, focusing particularly on evidence of their contributions to gender equality.

Justice Sandra Day O'Connor

Naming O'Connor to the Supreme Court was one of Reagan's first presidential acts, fulfilling his campaign pledge to "name the most qualified women [he] could possibly find" (Salokar and Wilson 1996, 213). Sworn in on September 25, 1981, she became the first woman to sit among the brethren. Not surprisingly, her views were largely consistent with Reagan's conservative positions, but there was speculation that her experiences might make her more favorably disposed to women's concerns.

O'Connor was viewed as a woman justice as well as a woman's justice. There was much discussion of her inability to get a job in a private law firm, other than as a legal secretary, despite her graduating third from Stanford University's law school. It was duly noted that as a legislator she supported the Equal Rights Amendment, opposed laws discriminating against women in employment and child custody, and resisted limits on access to abortion. During questioning in her confirmation hearings, she refused to express an opinion on *Roe v. Wade* (1973) and, although she gave assurances that she was "opposed to abortion as a matter of birth control or otherwise," her nomination to the Supreme Court drew opposition from conservative groups such as the National Right to Life Committee. Conversely, she received support from major women's groups like the NAWJ, the National Organization for Women (NOW), and the National Women's Political Caucus (Salokar and Wilson 1996, 214–215; Maveety 1996, 17). Indeed, Eleanor Smeal, president of NOW, characterized her appointment as "a major victory for women's rights" (Wohl, 1989, 44).

Scholars who have examined her behavior on the Court in depth, however, have concluded that there is little about O'Connor to justify the fears of one side and the faith of the other that she would pursue an ideologically driven feminist agenda (but see Sullivan and Goldzwig 1992).

In her study of O'Connor, Behuniak-Long (1992, 427) accepted, in part, Sherry's conclusion that judges speak in different voices, but challenged her assumption that there was a revolutionary potential in the "feminine voice"; unlike a feminist perspective, the "feminine voice" does not strive to create egalitarian changes in society through law. Examining O'Connor's concurring opinions in selected privacy and due process cases, she described her jurisprudence as a "feminine" one, but concluded that she did not use her voice to "act for" women's interests.

Davis (1993, 134) also contended that O'Connor "has neither championed women's rights nor has she engaged in constructing feminist legal theory." Testing Sherry's thesis that O'Connor speaks in the "feminine" voice, Davis compared her votes with Rehnquist's in six issue areas (gender, civil rights, establishment clause, equal protection, race, and criminal procedure) in the 1981 to the 1991 terms. Some of her findings supported Sherry's analysis of O'Connor's "feminine" voice, showing O'Connor's special concern for the value of community membership. However, while recognizing that O'Connor cast more liberal votes than Rehnquist in civil rights and establishment clause cases, Davis also showed that O'Connor was more liberal in all issues areas (although not all differences were statistically significant) and that her gender appeared irrelevant to her behavior on the Court (see also Aliotta 1995).

Finally, Maveety (1996, 22) also rejected the idea of observing O'Connor through a "Gilliganesque 'feminine voice'" lens. In her view, this approach "conceals as much as it purportedly reveals about the nature of O'Connor's judicial accommodationism, because it fails to focus on the correct jurisprudential and behavioral factors and to identify them specifically as jurisprudential or behavioral and not gender-related factors" (Maveety 1996, 25–26). She found instead that O'Connor displayed a pragmatic, "accommodationist" fact-based approach to law that defied easy analysis and was not based on gender concerns.

Surprisingly, Maveety's examination of O'Connor's role on the Court did not mention her majority opinion in *University of Mississippi v. Hogan* (1982). For despite agreement among scholars that

O'Connor's decision making resisted a gender analysis, her opinion for a 5–4 majority in *Hogan* appeared to move the Court closer to a stricter review of gender discrimination cases by specifying that such classifications required "an extremely persuasive justification" (p. 724) to pass constitutional muster. Although it was surely an easy call to order the University of Mississippi to admit the male applicant to its all-female nursing school—and O'Connor remained well within the bounds of precedent in doing so—most would agree she furthered the feminist agenda by placing an additional obstacle in the path of those seeking to arrange society along traditional gender lines (see Mezey 1992, chap. 1).

Justice Ruth Bader Ginsburg

When Ruth Bader Ginsburg was sworn in to the nation's highest court on August 10, 1993, she also brought first-hand experience of gender discrimination in employment. Like O'Connor, she was refused a job by the private law firms to which she applied despite her position at the head of her class at both Harvard and Columbia law schools. However, unlike O'Connor, she came with a distinguished record of litigating gender discrimination issues, including six oral arguments before the Supreme Court, in which she won five, and nine appellate briefs. Also unlike O'Connor, who had no experience on the federal bench, Ginsburg spent thirteen years on the Court of Appeals for the District of Columbia before taking her seat on the high court.

Ginsburg was the first director of the American Civil Liberties Union Women's Rights Law Project (Salokar, 1996, 81). Thus, not surprisingly, in the days following her nomination she was characterized as "the Thurgood Marshall of gender equality law" (Lewis 1993a, quoting Janet Benshoof, president of the Center for Reproductive Law and Policy).

Although Ginsburg was an outspoken proponent of women's rights, feminists nevertheless criticized her for making charges—first made public in 1984—that *Roe* (1973) was too expansive, had gone too far in sweeping all abortion laws aside, and should have been grounded in principles of equality rather than privacy. A few months before Clinton announced her nomination, she delivered a lecture at New York University School of Law in which she maintained that *Roe* had created a backlash that led to political divisiveness, and the Court should have exhibited greater restraint in deciding it (see Garrow 1993; Greenhouse 1993). In her confirmation hearing, however, she strongly defended women's reproductive rights: "It is essential to a woman's equality with man that she be the decision maker, that her choice be controlling," adding, "[T]he state controlling a woman would mean denying her full autonomy and full equality" (Lewis 1993b).

Compared with O'Connor, there have been fewer studies of Ginsburg's judicial temperament and her voting record since her appointment to the high court. One exception is Smith et al. (1994; see also Baugh et al. 1994; Perry and Abraham 1998), who assessed her performance as a first term justice and found that she aligned herself at times with both liberal and conservative camps, most frequently voting with the latter in criminal procedure cases. Although they acknowledged that her views might change over time, they indicated that her "first term clearly did not place her in the mold of the Warren Court justices who consistently advanced broad interpretations of constitutional rights" (Smith et al. 1994, 78). Analyzing her votes in gender discrimination claims, they rejected the comparison with Marshall. Although they found she favored women's rights in the five cases involving women's rights claims, she had only interjected a brief concurring opinion in which she alluded to the level of scrutiny applied to gender-based classifications. They concluded that "she does not presently appear intent on advancing a broad women's rights agenda . . . [and] may not be inclined to seize available opportunities to present her views on women's rights generally" (p. 80).

Depicting Ginsburg as a women's rights advocate in the past, Smith (1995) assessed Ginsburg's likely posture in future sexual harassment cases. After surveying the state of sexual harassment law as well as Ginsburg's experiences and values, she concluded that Ginsburg would favor sexual harassment plaintiffs only in cases in which "Supreme Court precedent or her interpretation of legislative intent allows it" (Smith 1995, 1945). Nevertheless, she believed that this area of law "may be the best opportunity for Justice Ginsburg to advocate positive change in the women's rights arena" (p. 1945).

Despite some pessimism about her support for women's rights claims, two years later Ginsburg wrote the majority opinion in *United States v. Virginia* (1996), a case involving gender discrimination in education, specifically, the Virginia Military Institute's (VMI) policy of excluding women. In her days as a women's rights litigator, Ginsburg had favored applying the strictest scrutiny to gender-based laws (Baugh et al. 1994, 25). Twenty-five years later, in forcefully rejecting VMI's attempts to justify single-sex admissions, she appeared to move the Court closer to adopting a higher level of scrutiny for gender-based classifications (see Mezey 1992, chap. 1). Although the Court retained the middle level of scrutiny common in sex-based classifications, in affirming the "exceedingly persuasive justification" for a majority Court, Ginsburg's analysis prompted Rehnquist's concurring opinion complaining that she had gone too far in taking the Court in that direction.

Conclusion

Twenty-five years ago, there were only a handful of women judges on the federal courts. During the administrations of Presidents Carter, Bush, and Clinton, especially the latter, an increasing number of women were appointed to the federal bench. The rising tide of women jurists led to speculation that these women would represent the interests of their "sisters" in society, at a minimum, by serving as role models for professional women. Adopting the principles developed by legislative scholars on whether legislative women "act for" women by supporting women's (or feminist) issues, this study has explored the degree to which women judges represent the interests of women, that is, seek to accomplish goals that benefit women as a group.

Assessing the results of studies of gender differences on the courts, this analysis has shown that while some scholars believe that women judges may act differently from men judges, most judicial scholars remain skeptical about the extent to which judicial decision making is subject to gender influences. The majority of studies reported only slight evidence that women judges differ from their male colleagues; that is, for the most part, scholars found few systematic significant gender-based differences in judicial voting behavior.

Notwithstanding the findings in one study that women judges believed they exert a positive influence as role models for women attorneys, the findings of most scholars cast doubt on the transforming effect of women on the federal courts. The doubt, moreover, is heightened by the fact that the gender differences that were found were not always in a predictable direction. Contrary to popular belief, and in some cases their own expectations, employing a variety of methodologies, the studies showed that women did not always vote in a more liberal, more civil libertarian manner than men, nor were they always more sensitive to issues of sex or race discrimination. Indeed, in some studies, women judges were reported to be even less supportive of women's rights issues than men.

This analysis also showed that scholars found mixed results in applying Gilligan's "different voice" theory to the study of judges. While some believed that the voices of women judges consistently differed from those of men, none claimed that women judges always responded positively to voices with a higher pitch. They found, in other words, that the decision making of women judges was not necessarily consistent with feminist ideology nor was it always more liberal than that of their male colleagues. At most, some reported the existence of a "feminine" voice, but it was unclear what effect it had on a judge's voting behavior.

Finally, scholars who focused on the voting behavior of the women "brethren" produced little evidence to disturb the conclusions cited above. Although Justice Ginsburg's role in the VMI case suggests she has a greater inclination to champion women's egalitarian interests, Justice O'Connor's unwillingness to further a feminist agenda indicates that gender is not a safe predictor of support for women's issues.

Taken as a whole, this inquiry into the extant judicial scholarship of gender differences on the courts shows that there is little evidence to support the claim that women judges "act for" women. Rather, the scholarship indicates that gender has little effect on judicial voting, and it is unlikely that the appearance of more women on the bench will prod the federal courts into becoming more responsive to the voices of women in society.

References

Aliotta, Jilda M. 1995. "Justice O'Connor and the Equal Protection Clause: A Feminine Voice." *Judicature* 78(5): 232–235.

Allen, David, and Diane Wall. 1987. "The Behavior of Women State Supreme Court Justices: Are They Tokens or Outsiders?" *Justice System Journal* 12(2): 232–245.

———. 1993. "Role Orientations and Women State Supreme Court Justices." *Judicature* 77(3): 156–165.

Baer, Judith A. 1991. "Nasty Law or Nice Ladies? Jurisprudence, Feminism, and Gender Difference." *Women and Politics* 11(1): 1–31.

Baugh, Joyce Ann, Christopher E. Smith, Thomas R. Hensley, Scott Patrick Johnson. 1994. "Justice Ruth Bader Ginsburg: A Preliminary Assessment." *University of Toledo Law Review* 26(1): 1–34.

Behuniak-Long, Susan. 1992. "Justice Sandra Day O'Connor and the Power of Maternal Legal Thinking." *The Review of Politics* 54(Summer): 417–444.

Berkson, Larry. 1982. "Women on the Bench: A Brief History." *Judicature* 65(6): 286–293.

Carney, Dan. 1997. "Battle Looms Between Clinton, GOP Over Court Nominees." *Congressional Quarterly Weekly Report* 55(6): 367–370.

Carp, Robert A., and C.K. Rowland. 1983. *Policymaking and Politics in the Federal District Courts.* Knoxville: University of Tennessee Press.

Davis, Sue. 1986. "President Carter's Selection Reforms and Judicial Policymaking: A Voting Analysis of the United States Courts of Appeals." *American Politics Quarterly* 14: 328–344.

———. 1992–1993. "Do Women Judges Speak in a 'Different Voice'? Carol Gilligan, Feminist Legal Theory, and the Ninth Circuit." *Wisconsin Women's Law Journal* 8(1): 143–173.

———. 1993. "The Voice of Sandra Day O'Connor." *Judicature* 77(3): 134–139.

Dolan, Kathleen, and Lynne E. Ford. 1995. "Women in State Legislatures: Feminist Identity and Legislative Behaviors." *American Politics Quarterly* 23(January): 96–108.

Garrow, David. 1993. "What Clinton's Supreme Court Nominee Doesn't Know About Roe." *Washington Post* (20 June): C3.

Gilligan, Carol. 1982. *In a Different Voice: Psychological Theory and Women's Development.* Cambridge: Harvard University Press.

Goldman, Sheldon. 1975. "Voting Behavior on the U.S. Courts of Appeals Revisited." *American Political Science Review* 69(2): 352–362.

———. 1981. "Carter's Judicial Appointments: A Lasting Legacy." *Judicature* 64(8): 344–355.

———. 1983. "Reagan's Judicial Appointments: Shaping the Bench in His Own Image." *Judicature* 66(8): 335–347.

———. 1989. "Reagan's Judicial Legacy: Completing the Puzzle and Summing Up." *Judicature* 72(6): 318–330.

———. 1991. "The Bush Imprint on the Judiciary: Carrying on a Tradition." *Judicature* 74(6): 294–306.

———. 1993. "Bush's Judicial Legacy: The Final Imprint." *Judicature* 76(6): 282–297.

———. 1995. "Judicial Selection Under Clinton: A Midterm Examination." *Judicature* 78(6): 276–291.

Goldman, Sheldon, and Matthew D. Saronson. 1994. "Clinton's Nontraditional Judges: Creating a More Representative Bench." *Judicature* 78(2): 68–73.

Goldman, Sheldon, and Elliot Slotnick. 1997. "Clinton's First Term Judiciary: Many Bridges to Cross." *Judicature* 80: 254–273.

Gottschall, Jon. 1983. "Carter's Judicial Appointments: The Influence of Affirmative Action and Merit Selection in Voting on the United States Courts of Appeals." *Judicature* 67(4): 165–173.

Greenhouse, Linda. 1993. "On Privacy and Equality." *New York Times* (16 June): A1.

Gruhl, John, Cassia Spohn, and Susan Welch. 1981. "Women as Policymakers: The Case of Trial Judges." *American Journal of Political Science* 25(2): 308–22.

Gryski, Gerard S., and Eleanor C. Main. 1986. "Social Backgrounds as Predictors of Votes on State Courts of Last Resort." *Western Political Quarterly* 39(3): 528–537.

Gryski, Gerard S., Eleanor C. Main, and William J. Dixon. 1986. "Models of State High Court Decision Making in Sex Discrimination Cases." *Journal of Politics* 48(1): 143–152.

Harrison, Cynthia. 1996. "Burnita Shelton Matthews." In *Women in Law*, ed. Rebecca Mae Salokar and Mary Volcansek, pp. 150–158. Westport, CT: Greenwood Press.

Kritzer, Herbert M., and Thomas M. Uhlman. 1977. "Sisterhood in the Courtroom: Sex of Judge and Defendant in Criminal Case Disposition." *Social Science Quarterly* 58(1): 77–88.

Lewis, Neil, A. 1993a. "Rejected as a Clerk, Chosen as a Justice."*New York Times* (15 June): A1.

———. 1993b. "Ginsburg Affirms Right of a Woman to Have Abortion." *New York Times* (22 July): A1.

Martin, Elaine. 1982 "Women on the Federal Bench: A Comparative Profile." *Judicature* 65(6): 306–313.

———. 1987. "Gender and Judicial Selection: A Comparison of the Reagan and Carter Administrations." *Judicature* 71(3): 136–142.

———. 1993. "The Representative Role of Women Judges." *Judicature* 77: 166–173.

Maveety, Nancy. 1996. *Justice Sandra Day O'Connor: Strategist on the Supreme Court*. Boston: Rowman & Littlefield.

Mezey, Susan Gluck. 1978. "Women and Representation: The Case of Hawaii." *Journal of Politics* 40(2): 369–385.

———. 1992. *In Pursuit of Equality: Women, Public Policy and the Federal Courts*. New York: St. Martin's Press.

———. 1994. "Increasing the Number of Women in Office: Does It Matter?" In *The Year of the Woman: Myths and Realities*, ed. Elizabeth Adell Cook, Sue Thomas, and Clyde Wilcox pp. 255–270. Boulder, CO: Westview Press.

Minow, Martha. 1990. *Making All the Difference: Inclusion, Exclusion, and American Law*. Ithaca: Cornell University Press.

Perry, Barbara A. 1991. *A "Representative" Supreme Court?* New York: Greenwood Press.

Perry, Barbara A., and Henry J. Abraham. 1998. "A Representative Supreme Court: The Thomas, Ginsburg, and Breyer Appointments." *Judicature* 81(4): 158–165.

Pitkin, Hannah. 1967. *The Concept of Representation*. Berkeley: University of California Press.

Reingold, Beth. 1992. "Concepts and Representation Among Female and Male State Legislators." *Legislative Studies Quarterly* 17(4): 509–538.

Roe v. Wade, 410 U.S. 113 (1973).

Rowland, C.K., and Robert A. Carp. 1980. "A Longitudinal Study of Party Effects on Federal District Court Policy Propensities." *American Journal of Political Science* 24(2): 291–305.

Saint-Germain, Michelle A. 1989. "Does Their Difference Make a Difference? The Impact of Women on Public Policy in the Arizona Legislature." *Social Science Quarterly* 70(4): 956–968.

Salokar, Rebecca Mae. 1996. "Ruth Bader Ginsburg." In *Women in Law*, ed. Rebecca Mae Salokar and Mary Volcansek, pp. 78–87. Westport, CT: Greenwood Press.

Salokar, Rebecca Mae, and Michael Wilson. 1996. "Sandra Day O'Connor." In *Women in Law*, ed. Rebecca Mae Salokar and Mary Volcansek, pp. 210–218. Westport, CT: Greenwood Press.

Sherry, Suzanna. 1986. "Civic Virtue and the Feminine Voice in Constitutional Adjudication." *Virginia Law Review* 72(3): 543–615.

Slotnick, Elliot E. 1984. "The Paths to the Federal Bench: Gender, Race and Judicial Recruitment Variation." *Judicature* 67(8): 371–388.

———. 1988. "Federal Judicial Recruitment and Selection Research: A Review Essay." *Judicature* 71(6): 317–324.

Smith, Christopher E., Joyce Ann Baugh, Thomas R. Hensley, and Scott Patrick Johnson. 1994. "The First-Term Performance of Justice Ruth Bader Ginsburg." *Judicature* 78(2): 74–80.

Smith, Sheila. 1995. "Justice Ruth Bader Ginsburg and Sexual Harassment Law: Will the Second Female Supreme Court Justice Become the Court's Women's Rights Champion?" *University of Cincinnati Law Review* 63(4): 1893–1945.

Songer, Donald R., and Sue Davis. 1990. "The Impact of Party and Region on Voting Decisions in the United States Courts of Appeals, 1955–1986." *Western Political Quarterly* 43(2): 317–334.

Songer, Donald R., Sue Davis, and Susan Haire. 1994. "A Reappraisal of Diversification in the Federal Courts: Gender Effects in the Courts of Appeal." *Journal of Politics* 56(2): 425–439.

Sullivan, Patricia A., and Stephen R. Goldzwig. 1992. "Abortion and Undue Burdens: Justice Sandra Day O'Connor and Judicial Decision-Making." *Women and Politics* 16(3): 27–54.

Tate, C. Neal. 1981. "Personal Attribute Models of the Voting Behavior of U.S. Supreme Court Justices." *American Political Science Review* 75(2): 355–367.

Thomas, Sue, and Susan Welch. 1991. "The Impact of Gender on Activities and Priorities of State Legislators." *Western Political Quarterly* 44(2): 445–456.

United States v. Virginia, 518 U.S. 515 (1996).

University of Mississippi v. Hogan, 458 U.S. 718 (1982).

Walker, Thomas G., and Deborah J. Barrow. 1985. "The Diversification of the Federal Bench: Policy and Process Ramifications." *Journal of Politics* 47(2): 596–617.

Welch, Susan. 1985. "Are Women More Liberal Than Men in the U.S. Congress?" *Legislative Studies Quarterly* 10(1): 125–134.

Wilson, Sarah. 1996. "Florence Ellinwood Allen." In *Women in Law*, ed. Rebecca Mae Salokar and Mary Volcansek, pp. 17–24. Westport, CT: Greenwood Press.

Wohl, Alexander. 1989. "O'Connor, J., Concurring." *ABA Journal* (December): 42–48.

10

Gender and Congressional Elections

Richard L. Fox

Introduction

During the 1990s women have achieved greater and greater levels of success in winning elections to the U.S. Congress. Across this decade, more women have sought the nomination of their party and more women have won entrance into the U.S. House of Representatives. Although this progress has been encouraging to many social commentators and gender politics scholars who feel it is essential for the United States to move toward some semblance of gender balance in government, the undeniable truth remains, as we stand on the verge of the twenty-first century, that the legislative branch of the federal government remains a decidedly male bastion. What does it mean to say that it is a "male bastion?" It means that still almost 90 percent of House members and Senators are men. It means that there are no women serving in top leadership positions in Congress. It means that Congress is still dominated by "masculine values" and ways of doing things. This chapter focuses on the gender dynamics of the congressional election process.

There is a traditional manner in which one chooses to run for Congress in the United States. To begin with, the traditional candidate is a man. In the history of House of Representatives there have been roughly 11,500 male representatives and fewer than 200 female representatives (Center for the American Woman and Politics [CAWP] Fact Sheets, 1998). Next, the prospective candidate is a member of the political or economic elite in the district where he would like to serve. He is typically a lower level elected official or a successful lawyer or businessman in the community. He is often encouraged to run for office by other elites in the community, most likely by party officials or business leaders, or he may even be anointed by the outgoing incumbent congressman. The same elites who are encouraging him to run for office also contribute money to his campaign and hold fundraisers for him. He is their candidate and he will be their man in Washington. This model has been in place for most of the recent history of congressional candidacies. While the types of candidacies have diversified, this model is still prevalent (Thomas and Lamb 1965; Hibbing 1991; Loomis 1998).

For obvious reasons this model has served men well and has served women very poorly. Women have been largely excluded from the economic and political elite of their communities throughout much of the twentieth century. Thus, women who have sought to enter Congress have often had to resort to other means. The first wave of successful women candidates was dominated by widows of congressmen (who died while they were in office). Between 1916 and 1964, thirty-two widows were nominated to fill the vacancies of their husbands and twenty-eight of them were elected, an astounding victory rate of 88 percent. Across the same time period, 199 nonwidows were nominated and only thirty-two were elected for a victory rate of only 14 percent (Gertzog 1984, 18).

The second wave of women candidates was the group of women who turned their attention from civic volunteerism to politics in the 1960s and 1970s (Burrell 1994, 58). During this tumultuous period women were involved in grassroots politics in their communities, and some small numbers of women rode this activism to Washington. Notable figures who succeeded were such women as Pat Schroeder, elected in 1972, and Shirley Chisholm, elected in 1968.

Now we are in the midst of the third wave of women candidates. In the third wave it appears that two dynamics have converged. For one, the prevailing model for running for Congress, described above, has become far less rigid. Women and men with more diverse backgrounds are now able to compete successfully for their party's nomination. As the political parties have become less powerful and the media have become more central in campaigns, there are now a number of different paths that lead to election to Congress. The second factor is that the number of women who now fit the profile of a traditional candidate has increased. The number of women serving in state legislatures, a springboard to Congress, has increased by almost six times since 1970 (Norrander and Wilcox 1998, 106). Further, the numbers of women in the professions of business and law have dramatically increased. Both of these developments indicate that the eligibility pool of prospective women candidates was much larger in the 1990s (Darcy, Welch, and Clark 1994).

Nevertheless, the fluctuating fortunes for women candidates reveal two things that will be the focus of this chapter. First, that we are currently in a time when women have excellent opportunities to run successfully for Congress. The electoral playing field in House races largely has leveled out in many districts (but not all) in the United States. Second is the contention that men and women congressional candidates still enter an electoral environment that is characterized by gender stereotypes and gender expectations. Ultimately this means that men and women often have different experiences in the electoral process, and these different experiences are highly instructive of the gendered political dynamics that are still present in American politics.

In examining the role of gender in congressional elections, this chapter is divided into three sections. Section one examines some of the general indicators of electoral success by comparing the performances of men and women candidates. This includes analysis of sex differences in winning percentages, vote totals, and fundraising totals. The second section examines the performance of men and women candidates by region and state. This section reveals that success rates of men and women candidates differ dramatically in different parts of the country. The final section relies on interview data and anecdotal evidence from the campaign trail to highlight many of the gendered dynamics that still persist in congressional elections. The findings in this section of the chapter are based on a survey of roughly 100 campaign managers for men and women House candidates in California in 1992 and 1994.[1] In keeping with the central theme of this book, we will consider the experiences of both men and women congressional candidates.

Gender and the Study of Congressional Elections

When political scientists began to seriously examine women candidates, beginning in the 1980s, most researchers undoubtedly turned to the subject expecting to find some gross injustices in the political system. After all, it seemed that only discrimination or subversive oppression could lead to a system that elected so few women to high level political offices. However, most recent work on the subject of gender and political candidacies has failed to turn up systemic and widespread evidence of gender bias and discrimination in the electoral process. One group of investigators has even concluded that women who enter the electoral process are on equal footing with male candidates. This group of researchers generally has focused on the central indicators of electoral success in congressional elections: winning percentages (in primary and general elections), vote totals, and fundraising receipts (Burrell 1998; Seltzer, Newman, and Leighton 1997; Chaney and Sinclair 1994). These researchers conclude that the single greatest barrier to electing more women to Congress is the lack of women candidates.

However, another group of researchers has asserted that the political and electoral system is laden with gender stereotypes and gender expectations. These assumptions about gender roles presume certain traits and behaviors for men and women. For instance, Conover and Gray (1983), have defined traditional assumptions about the role of men and women this way: "[If] the role of a woman is defined by her reproductive, sexual, and child-rearing functions within the family, then there is a . . . division of activities into the public extrafamilial jobs done by the male and the private intrafamilial ones performed by the female" (pp. 2–3). Substantial vestiges of these antiquated notions of the "proper" gender roles still exist and are present in the electoral environment. In congressional elections, men and women candidates face an electorate, a press corps, and a political establishment that often rely on masculine and feminine stereotypes to assess candidates. The conclusion of this research is that gender stereotyping and assumptions about gender roles usually disadvantage women (Fox 1997; Kahn 1996; Huddy and Terkildsen 1993a and 1993b).

Before moving on, however, it is important to think about congressional elections as a venue for study. Social scientists have focused on fundraising totals, vote totals, and winning percentages, because that type of data is reliable and available. Researchers have also been able to look at Senate campaign commercials that have been meticulously archived (Williams 1998; Kahn 1996). However, beyond these election indicators, it is difficult to systematically measure what goes on in an election for the House of Representatives. A great deal of the information about House campaigns is elusive because of the ephemeral quality of elections. The decisions and events of campaigns are usually not chronicled, and within days or sometimes hours after an election, campaign offices are disassembled and campaign workers have left the area. Important campaign components such as internal campaign polls, meetings with party leaders, and the campaign media, such as television and radio commercials and direct mail advertising, are not recorded or archived. Thus, researchers are left only with anecdotal information when examining such things as campaign decision making, interactions with the local media, and candidate interaction with the voters. However, it is in these less chronicled aspects of the campaign where gender, gender stereotyping, and the effects of candidate sex are most likely to be apparent.

Men and Women Running for Congress: The General Indicators

As mentioned, the decade of the 1990s has demonstrated that the gender dynamics of the congressional election process are definitely changing as the numbers of women in Congress have increased significantly. Prior to the 1998 elections, there were 55 women and 380 men in the House of Representatives. There were 9 women and 91 men in the U.S. Senate. Both of these numbers are highs for women and lows for men. The increase in the number of women winning congressional elections in the last few election cycles has jumped tremendously in comparison to previous decades. Before the 1992 election, there were only 2 women senators and 27 women House members.[2] For the purpose of this analysis we will focus more specifically on the House elections. If we turn to Table 10.1, we can see the evolution of women running for the House over the last thirty years.

Table 10.1 reveals tremendous growth in the number of women seeking and winning congressional elections. The 1998 election set the record with 121 women candidates winning their party's nomination for a House seat. To put that in perspective there were roughly 700 major party male candidates nominated in 1998. Beyond the increasing numbers of women running for Congress, the clear difference between the parties is important. Since 1992 the Democrats have nominated almost twice as many women House candidates as Republicans. The disparity between the two parties is particularly noteworthy in open seat elections, which generally offer the best opportunity for non-incumbents, whether male or female, to win entrance to Congress.

Overall, these numbers reveal that women are making important strides and progress in moving into the U.S. Congress. These figures

Table 10.1

Growth in the Number of Women Candidates Running for the U.S. House of Representatives

	1970	1980	1990	1992	1994	1996*	1998
Democratic candidates							
General election	15	27	39	70	72	77	76
Incumbents	7	10	15	17	34	27	34
Challengers	4	13	17	27	28	41	29
Open seats	4	4	8	26	10	9	12
General election winners	10	11	19	35	30	35	39
Republican candidates							
General election	11	25	30	36	40	43	46
Incumbents	2	5	9	9	10	14	16
Challengers	6	18	20	14	24	24	25
Open seats	3	2	1	13	6	5	5
General election winners	3	10	9	12	17	16	17

Source: Compiled from Center for the American Woman and Politics (CAWP) Fact Sheets, 1998. Entries are raw number of women candidates in each category who ran the year of that election.
Note: *Four women won special elections between the 1996 and 1998 elections.

also lend a lot of credence to the argument that incumbency is a leading reason why the great disparity between the number of men and women in Congress persists. A number of gender politics scholars have argued that the incumbency factor provides a primary explanation for why women have been slow to move toward gender parity with men in the U.S. Congress (see Burrell 1994; Darcy, Welch, and Clark 1994). Because the vast majority of incumbents are men, and because incumbents are so difficult to displace, this dynamic has served to limit the rate at which women have been able to move into Congress.

Vote Totals

A wide range of recent work on how candidates' sex impacts the vote choice has produced mixed results.[3] However, a great deal of research focusing on actual vote totals has found that differences in the performance of men and women candidates has been negligible. Burrell, who has studied vote totals for House candidates from 1968 to 1992, concludes that candidate's sex accounts for less that one percent of variation in the vote for men and women candidates (1994, 141). If we

Table 10.2

Comparison of General Election Vote Totals for Men and Women House Candidates, 1994 and 1996 (percent)

	1994		1996	
	Women	Men	Women	Men
Democrats				
Incumbents	61	60	69	66
	(30)	(181)	(25)	(132)
Challengers	31	30	39*	37
	(26)	(101)	(40)	(160)
Open seats	50*	44	47	50
	(10)	(43)	(9)	(43)
Republicans				
Incumbents	68	68	57	61
	(8)	(118)	(12)	(189)
Challengers	36	38	33	31
	(28)	(184)	(21)	(131)
Open seats	53	54	49	48
	(4)	(49)	(4)	(48)

Source: Vote totals reported in *Congressional Quarterly Almanac*, 1994 and 1996.
Notes: Candidates running unopposed were not included in these results. Parentheses indicate the number for each category. Difference of means test, * $p < .10$, borderline significance.

turn to the performance of men and women in House elections in 1994 and 1996, we can see that in terms of vote totals, there is little or no difference in the performance of women and men candidates.

Table 10.2 reveals that in two of the most recent House elections, women and men have fared similarly in terms of raw vote totals. For the most part differences between men and women candidates are entirely negligible. In two categories where the difference of means test was of at least borderline statistical significance ($p < .10$), women actually had an advantage over men. Thus what can we conclude about gender and voting? At the very least we can conclude there is not widespread voter bias for or against men and women candidates.

Fundraising

Throughout much of the 1970s and 1980s there was a general assumption in electoral politics that women had trouble raising money.

In fact, several studies indeed found that women ran campaigns with lower levels of funding than men (Mandel 1981; Baxter and Lansing 1980). However, these hypotheses and findings about differences in campaign financing are not supported by more recent systematic examinations of campaign receipts. Two early studies of campaign contributions in congressional elections found little evidence of sex differences in fundraising. Burrell (1985), in a study of congressional candidates from 1972 to 1982, found a "very weak" relationship between gender and the ability to raise campaign funds. Similarly, Uhlaner and Schlozman (1986) determined that women incumbents in the U.S. House, on average, raised about twenty-five thousand dollars less per race than men incumbents. However, they explain the difference by noting that men incumbents generally held positions of greater political power, and were thus likely to attract more large contributions. More recently, Burrell (1994), in analyzing gender and campaign funds since the early 1970s, found that by the time of the 1988 House elections, the disparity between men and women in campaign fundraising had completely disappeared (p. 105) (see also Burrell 1998).

Table 10.3 shows the fundraising totals of men and women general election candidates in 1994 and 1996. Table 10.3 confirms other recent studies that have shown that women do as well as, and in some cases better than, their male counterparts in raising money. While Table 10.3 appears to show large differences between men and women in some of the categories, these results are often inconclusive because of the small sample size in some categories. The only statistically significant differences were with challengers in 1996. Women challengers from both the Republican and Democratic parties raised more than their male counterparts.

Based on the general indicators discussed above, we are presented with the appearance of a gender-neutral electoral environment. Women are steadily increasing their numbers in Congress (Table 10.1), and men and women perform similarly in terms of average vote totals (Table 10.2), and fundraising (Table 10.3). These indicators certainly suggest that men have lost their stranglehold over the congressional election process and that there are excellent opportunities for women candidates running for the House of Representatives. However, these indicators only tell part of the story.

Table 10.3

Comparison of Campaign Receipts for Men and Women General Election House Candidates, 1994 and 1996

	1994		1996	
	Women	Men	Women	Men
Democrats				
Incumbents	$687,843	616,010	601,260	656,240
	(30)	(181)	(26)	(134)
Challengers	200,363	171,906	425,549*	280,081
	(26)	(101)	(40)	(161)
Open seats	605,812	541,717	486,818	692,422
	(10)	(43)	(9)	(43)
Republicans				
Incumbents	533,291	578,240	846,440	811,006
	(8)	(118)	(12)	(190)
Challengers	251,500	247,735	336,786**	196,536
	(28)	(184)	(22)	(140)
Open seats	613,457	618,330	840,159	654,009
	(4)	(49)	(4)	(48)

Source: Campaign receipts compiled from Federal Election Commission reports.
Notes: Candidates running unopposed were not included in these results. Parentheses indicate the N for each category. Difference of means test, $* p < .10$, $** p < .05$, borderline significance.

State and Regional Differences

If we examine the performance of men and women House candidates by region and by state, we get our first glimpse of the gendered culture in some locations in the United States. Hill (1981) has argued that state political culture is an important determinant of women's ability to win elective office. Norrander and Wilcox (1998) in a study of state legislatures found considerable disparities in the progress of women across various states and regions. They explain the disparities by pointing to state differences in political culture, namely state ideology, state culture, and region (p. 116). States with a conservative ideology, "traditionalist or moralist" cultures, as defined by Elazar (1984), were less likely to elect women.

Disparities among the states also exist in congressional elections. Consider for instance, that heading into the 1998 elections, twenty-

Table 10.4

States with a Poor Record of Electing Women to the House of Representatives, 1970–1996

States electing one women representative once	Medium-sized states with no women representatives	Small states with no women representatives
Arkansas (4)	Alabama (7)	Alaska (1)
Arizona (6)	Iowa (5)	Delaware (1)
Kentucky (6)	Minnesota (8)	Montana (1)
Pennsylvania (21)	Mississippi (5)	New Hampshire (2)
Virginia (11)	Oklahoma (6)	North Dakota (1)
	Wisconsin (9)	South Dakota (1)
	West Virginia (3)	Vermont (1)

Source: Center for the American Woman and Politics (CAWP) Fact Sheets.
Note: Number in parentheses is the size of the House delegation, after 1990 redistricting.

seven of the fifty states had no women senators or representatives in Washington. Several states with relatively large House delegations, such as Pennsylvania (20), Illinois (19), Virginia (13), and Massachusetts (12), have no women representatives. Further, thirty-three states have never been represented by a woman in the U.S. Senate and only nine states have ever elected a woman to a full term in the Senate (CAWP Fact Sheet, 1998). Table 10.4 shows the states with the worst records in terms of sending women to serve in the House of Representatives since 1970.

Table 10.4 reveals that certain states and perhaps even geographic regions have been much less likely to send women to Washington. While we would assume a strong correlation between a state having women in the state legislature and the number of women in Congress, this is not always the case. For instance, Wisconsin, Minnesota, and Massachusetts are above average in terms of the number of women serving in the state legislature, yet none of these states have any women serving in the 105th Congress (1997–1999).

There are also a number of states where women congressional candidates have been very successful. For instance, heading into the 1998 elections, Connecticut (3/6, 50 percent), Missouri (3/9, 33 percent), California (13/52, 25 percent), New York (7/31, 23 percent), and Florida (5/23, 22 percent), are all states where women have done very well. Women

Table 10.5

Regional Differences in Electing Men and Women House Candidates, 1970–1998 (percent)

	West		South		Midwest		Northeast	
	Women	Men	Women	Men	Women	Men	Women	Men
1970	3.9	96.1	0	100	2.5	97.5	4.9	95.1
1980	2.6	97.4	1.6	98.4	3.3	96.7	8.1	91.9
1990	8.2	91.8	2.3	97.7	6.2	93.8	9.6	90.4
1992	17.2	82.8	7.9	92.1	6.7	93.3	12.4	87.6
1994	18.3	81.7	7.9	92.1	7.6	92.4	11.3	88.7
1996	23.7	76.3	8.6	91.4	8.6	91.4	12.4	87.6
1998	21.5	78.5	8.6	91.4	12.3	87.6	10.3	89.7
Net change	+17.6	−17.6	+8.6	−8.6	+9.8	−9.8	+5.4	−5.4

Source: Compiled from Center for the American Woman and Politics (CAWP) Fact Sheets. Percentages are based on the size of each region's House delegation. The size of the delegation is different for 1970, 1980, 1990, and 1992–1998 as a result of redistricting.

have also done well historically in Maryland: in 1984 four of the eight members of the House delegation were women. Why have women done well in these states and not in others? Three of these states, California, New York, and Florida, are among the largest states with the biggest delegations; thus we might be able to assume that many more opportunities ultimately will exist. However, what explains success in states like Missouri? Missouri borders Iowa, which has never elected a woman House candidate, and Oklahoma, which elected their only woman House member to one term in 1921. By the same token why has Connecticut elected so many more women than neighboring Massachusetts?

Turning more specifically to the broad regional patterns we can see some distinct differences in how women and men House candidates have fared throughout the United States. Table 10.5 tracks the performance of women and men in House races since 1970 by the four major geographic regions.

Some striking regional differences occur over the percentages of men and women elected to Congress. Before 1990, the Northeast had two and three times as many women candidates as any other region in the country. However, things changed dramatically with the "year of the woman" elections in 1992. In the West the numbers of women winning elections to Congress more than doubled, and in the South the numbers more than tripled. The numbers were stagnant in the Midwest until 1998, and there were only modest gains in the Northeast. This puts the year of the woman elections in 1992 into a little perspective, suggesting that the phenomenon was clearly situated in the Western and Southern regions of the country. Based on Tables 10.4 and 10.5, we can see that there are some severe state and regional variations in the number of women and men who win congressional elections. Diagnosing the specific causes of regional and state differences in electing women House members is beyond the scope of this chapter; however, the findings suggest certainly that interaction of gender with state culture requires more extensive exploration.

Gender Dynamics in Congressional Elections

While the general indicators discussed above provide important overviews of how women and men are faring in congressional elections, they do not provide any in-depth assessments of what is going on behind the numbers. In this section we will focus on the experiences of men and women in the electoral process and how they have perceived the process. Here we will rely on interview data. In examining perceptions, we will focus on four areas: fundraising, party support, media coverage, and men who run against women. In assessing these areas, and listening to the voices of the candidates and campaign officials, we see that important gender dynamics are still at work in the electoral process, and that those who work with women candidates still perceive the electoral system as unfair toward women.

Fundraising

While the data presented in Table 10.3 show that women do not suffer any disadvantage and may even have greater success than men in raising money, evidence from interviews with women and men candidates and political consultants suggests otherwise. Many campaign managers and consultants familiar with women candidates across the country reveal that they often have the perception that certain channels of fundraising are shut down to women. Perceptions about the system ultimately are very important if women and men are going to compete on a fair playing field. Further, if the environment is perceived to be unfair, then women may be less likely to get involved or stay involved (Naff

1995). If we turn to the words of campaign advisers for women candidates we can see that even in recent elections the system is perceived as unfair. For instance, one manager who has worked for many women candidates across the country believes that women do not have the same access as men to traditional fundraising networks:

> Women do not have the ties with the business community and they are in many ways still excluded from the serious power networks. . . . When I take over a campaign I want my candidate doing two things, either out meeting voters or on the phone asking people for money. In the early days of a campaign a candidate needs to spend six or seven hours a day on the phone asking for money. . . . The women I have worked for did not have the comfort level or list of contacts to do this well.

Another manager for a Democratic woman challenger in a congressional election in California in 1994 sounded a similar sentiment:

> Our candidate was the natural labor candidate [favored worker rights and opposed NAFTA and GATT], but for no clear reason they were lukewarm toward us. I called them and went to meet with them and they promised money and volunteers, but after that it was like pulling teeth getting any kind of support from them. . . . I just think certain sources, particularly labor unions, are hesitant to support women candidates. . . . Union leadership is still a male enclave.

Another campaign manager, who had worked for both men and women House candidates, summed up the fundraising dilemma for women:

> Men have much better access to the individual contributions of executives and businessmen. I don't want to be so trite as to say that this is sexism pure and simple—it is just that business people, mostly men, are accustomed to dealing with the congressman, a man.

A final example from the 1994 congressional elections illustrates the clearest display of direct discrimination found in any of the interviews: a woman running in northern California was denied financial assistance from her national party headquarters. The national party determines whether to financially support a candidate based on the candidate's viability in the election. The campaign manager described what happened when he contacted the party seeking financial support:

> I talked to the party leaders and I tried to sell them on the idea that our candidate was viable. I gave them the results of a poll we conducted that showed we were in striking distance of our opponent, but ultimately they decided that we did not have a good chance to win. . . . Then I heard that they funded . . . [a male] candidate running in the neighboring district. I thought this was odd considering we had almost identical poll numbers. I called up the party and asked why they funded our neighbor and not us. The director of finance stated that this was the old-boy network in action. They gave him party money because he has contacts in the leadership and we don't.

The manager for this woman candidate was told bluntly that his candidate was being subjected to gender discrimination.

The experiences of female candidates who felt cut off from male-dominated fundraising networks was similar to some of the perceptions of exclusion felt by women state legislators in Texas and Arkansas. Blair and Stanley (1991), in a survey of state legislators, found that women legislators often believed that they were removed from the typical socializing (this refers to drinks and golf, not socialization) that would take place with other legislators and lobbyists. Thus there is certainly evidence that the "old-boy network" can still exclude women. The alternative assessment is that for the most part women only perceive greater difficulty in fundraising, and that their success (as illustrated by Table 10.3) indicates no substantial bias.

If this is the case, this also presents an important impediment to the full inclusion of women candidates. If the process continues to seem unfair to women, then this will have the affect of turning away women candidates who do not want to take on the challenge of overcoming a sexist environment.

Media Coverage

Every election year in the 1990s seems to present something new for women candidates. Most of this newness can be attributed to a media establishment that attempts to apply a different label to what each election has meant for women. The media have rarely analyzed what an election means for men. In 1990, women candidates were labeled a "novelty." The 1990 elections resulted in only minor gains for women in terms of congressional representation but it has been argued that this election paved the way for the 1992 elections. The 1992 election year was the much ballyhooed and analyzed "year of the woman." Women, in part spurred on by the Supreme Court confirmation hearings of Clarence Thomas and the accusations of Anita Hill, set a record for the number of major party candidates nominated and elected to Congress (Cook, Thomas, and Wilcox 1994). It was apparently a good year to be a woman candidate, as the press ran numerous features on women candidates and many voters supported the idea that more women needed to be sent to Congress. In the end, women almost doubled their numbers in Congress in 1992. However, things turn quickly, and 1994 was apparently a bad year to be a woman candidate. The excitement over women candidates from 1992 was completely gone and some commentators and a number of women candidates even posited that there was a backlash against women candidates (Berke 1994). Consequently, women made almost no additional gains in the 1994 election.

The elections of 1996 and 1998 appear to provide a mixed bag of characterizations for women candidates. In Illinois 1996 was reported to be a bad year to be a woman congressional candidate (Sweet 1996). However, only two years later pundits were anticipating a big year for women in Illinois (Neal 1998). In Missouri in 1996, the "year of the woman" was said to have become an annual event, with many women on the ballot (Mannies 1996). Prospects were also good for women congressional candidates in Michigan in 1996, with one newspaper reporter even referring to the primary election as "ladies day" (Waldmeir 1996). One commentator, who pointed out that the year of the woman really never hit Massachusetts, was predicting that 1998 was shaping up as the year for women to roar to power (Aucoin 1997). Even in California, where women had done so well in 1992, electing two U.S. Senators and a record number of House members, things had apparently turned sour for women candidates by 1998.

What about the candidacies of men during all of these various media incarnations of the good and bad years for women? The analysis of women as candidates has been dissected and analyzed, while the candidacies of men have almost never been discussed in these terms in media analysis. Male candidates for Congress are the norm and the baseline from which all comparisons are made; women candidates are still often viewed by the mass media as women first, and candidates second.

The role of gender and campaign coverage has been explored in the scholarly literature only recently, most notably by Kahn (1993, 1992). Kahn and Goldenberg (1991) in a study of men and women U.S. Senate candidates concluded that there were important gender differences in press coverage. They found that female candidates received less coverage than male candidates and that the coverage they did receive tended to focus on their viability as candidates. Kahn (1993) also found that the media tend to cover women in stereotypical ways, often downplaying the personal qualities of leadership and effectiveness.

To further assess how the media has covered women candidates in House races, we again turn to the experiences from the campaign trail. In the survey of women candidates running for Congress in 1992, the campaign managers for five of the nineteen women candidates surveyed believed that the news media were uncertain about how to "deal with" women candidates. Three of these candidates' managers believed that women candidates were not taken as seriously as men at the beginning of a campaign. One of these women candidates was constantly referred to in the local papers by her first name while her opponent was always addressed as "Mr." or by his last name. In another example, the campaign manager for a woman candidate running in southern California noted:

> At the start of the campaign we really had to prove ourselves. We had to prove that we were a credible alternative to the incumbent. At first the local papers were not very interested in this race, then when a poll showed we were close, they suddenly began to take us seriously. . . . Also the fact that women were a big story this year encouraged them to cover our campaign. Without the poll and the "year of the woman" going on, I don't really think the media would have given us a second look.

This manager believed that the media were predisposed to disregard his candidate and to not take her seriously. Another campaign manager for a woman candidate described what he saw going on in the election:

> The local press did not know what to make of us in the beginning, it was as if they did not know how to cover the campaign merely because she

was a woman. You could really see it at the candidate forum we had with our opponent. . . . [The journalist] got up and asked him a tough question about immigration. . . . Then the same guy meekly asked [our woman candidate] a question about her experiences on the school board.

This treatment of women candidates largely could be attributed to the newness of women candidacies in 1992. Women in 1992 were in large part breaking down the stereotype of the male politician.

Since 1992 women candidates and their consultants have been less likely to report instances of gender discrimination. The burst of women candidates in 1992 may have prepared journalists to treat women as ordinary candidates in future races. Nonetheless, several campaign managers for women candidates reported specific instances in which they felt the media demonstrated gender bias in reporting. One female candidate spoke of her problems with the press:

> I got little press, but when I was mentioned, it was often in reference to my family, particularly the amount of money my husband and I have. . . . My identity was always associated with my husband.

Another manager, working for a woman candidate who had gone through a "nasty divorce," thought the press focus on the divorce was gender-driven:

> I'll give you an example of gender bias. The press totally over-emphasized her divorce. She had a nasty divorce with child custody battles and the whole thing. The press was always bringing it up. I really don't believe a male divorcee candidate would have been subjected to as much focus on this personal issue. . . . Our [male] opponent had a host of personal and family scandals and the press stayed away from them.

This example illustrates the dual expectations society has of women in professional positions. If the traditional family unit breaks apart, this reflects much more poorly on the mother than on the father. As the manager for one women candidate quipped:

> Nobody cares if a man does not stay home to fix the kids' school lunch, but if a woman appears to be neglecting her children by not making them their lunch, than the woman has a big appearance problem.

The problems women candidates have in fulfilling the many roles today's women are typically expected to fulfill—mother, wife, and career woman—are colorfully chronicled by Witt, Paget, and Matthews (1994, chap. 4).

In a survey of women state legislature candidates in Illinois in 1992, Poole (1993), found numerous examples of media bias against women candidates. One female candidate in Poole's study stated:

> [The media covering the race] concentrate[d] on stupid, little things such as clothes, hair, etc., which never comes up with men. They also use loaded adjectives to describe us such as feisty, perky, small, and lively.

Another woman candidate from Poole's study noted:

> Women candidates need to be aware of where they are campaigning and of the need to dress appropriately. A more presentable appearance seems to be expected. There seems to be a feeling among the media that most female candidates are bored housewives who "dabble in politics" after their families are raised.

The general conclusions drawn by Poole were that women feel they must work much harder to gain credibility with the press. Many of the women House candidates interviewed for this examination had similar feelings. In conducting these interviews, not one manager for a male candidate reported any of the credibility problems mentioned by the staffs of women candidates.

The recent experiences of women candidates suggest that they are often held to different standards. Most of the gender differences in media coverage could be attributed to gender stereotyping by reporters. The effect is that many of the women candidates believed they had to fulfill two roles to compete successfully under the media eye of a campaign. They had to meet the standards of someone with high political qualifications and they also had to fulfill their stereotypical traditional roles as women. These experiences with the media are consistent with Jamieson's (1995) analysis of the "double bind" faced by women in the public eye. Women have to appear extra professional, while maintaining their traditionally feminine personas. The media coverage women candidates receive places additional burdens on women in two ways. First is simply that there seems to be evidence of considerable gender bias in the coverage. This makes the system unfair and discourages women's participation. Second, many women expect and perceive a higher level of scrutiny and criticism from the media. Both of these phenomena place a greater burden on women candidates in how they must strategize about a campaign and the care with which they must present themselves as candidates.

Party Support

Another important aspect of the electoral environment is the interaction between a candidate and his/her political party. In a study on the role of political parties in the "year of the woman," Biersack and Herrnson found almost no relationship between the level of party support and gender (1994). The viability of the candidate in the election was the sole criterion used by the parties in determining the level of candidate support. In 1992, the parties provided money and other services to men and women candidates in roughly equal proportions (Biersack and Herrnson 1994). Earlier studies have found discrimination by the political parties, yet these trends did not seem to persist into the 1990s (Kendrigan 1984; Boneparth 1977). The most current assessments indicate that women are not discriminated against by the party organizations.

Among the women and men candidates surveyed for this analysis, almost 25 percent of women and men challengers believed their party showed some bias toward them. Most of these instances of bias were perpetrated at the local levels and centered on petty personality clashes. Again, if we turn to the comments of the candidates and their campaign staff we see some evidence of party and gender interacting. For instance, some women congressional candidates running in 1992 and 1994 did not believe that their party took them seriously as candidates. One of the managers, running the campaign of a Democratic woman challenger in a tight race, described her campaign's experience with the local party:

> Here we were in the midst of a tight race, our race was written-up as one of the top 100 races in the country . . . and the old boys running the local party office had no interest in helping us. . . . This is a district filled with Reagan Democrats and they thought . . . [our candidate] must be an old time liberal because she was a woman . . . they hardly did anything.

When this manager was pressed to cite specific evidence of gender bias, she could only identify the local party's seemingly inexplicable lack of interest in her campaign. Another manager for a woman candidate described her experience with the party:

> I called the state offices, I tried to work with the local party, but we got no help. You know when you are not being taken seriously, and that was the feeling I always got when I tried to work with the party here. . . . I can only think that it was because my candidate was a woman.

These perceptions are uncorroborated. Nonetheless, the perception of party discrimination, whether confirmed or not, is potentially as harmful as actual discrimination.

In sum, there is evidence of sporadic gender bias by the parties. The 1992 elections demonstrated a broad effort by the Democratic Party to recruit and support women candidates. Yet, the willingness to support women candidates will be undertaken only if the parties believe that women are credible candidates in the election process. Thus, if women candidates are vulnerable in a given election, the political parties may be less likely to promote the candidacies of women. The fluctuating fortunes of women candidates and the parties' responses to them were evident in the Democratic Party across the elections of the 1990s. In 1992, the Democrats recruited and promoted women congressional candidates across the country. In 1994, all specific efforts to promote women candidates disappeared. The evidence for 1996 and 1998 is less clear. Thus, how parties address men and women candidates will need to be monitored carefully in upcoming election cycles.

When Men Run Against Women

This section of this chapter hopes to broaden the ways in which the impact of gender on the electoral arena is examined. Studying the reactions of men candidates to women candidates demonstrates that the presence of women is transforming the political arena in important ways. The question of how the presence of a woman candidate affects the behavior of her male opponent has received little attention in the gender politics literature. In order to have a broad understanding of the role of women candidates and their overall influence in an electoral campaign, the behavior of the candidates running opposite them must be understood. While there are currently no systematic examinations of the behavior of women's opponents, there are some indicators and studies of individual races that suggest women candidates affect the behavior of their electoral opponents in significant ways. For instance, Renner (1993), in a study of the 1992 Pennsylvania Senate race between Arlen Specter and Lynn Yeakel, shows how Yeakel's gender and the gender-related issue of the Thomas/Hill hearings caused Specter to change his strategy. Renner found that Specter consciously avoided making direct public attacks against Yeakel. This was especially apparent in a series of television advertisements that raised questions about Yeakel, but never directly attacked her. Also, Renner argues that Specter made additional efforts to demonstrate support for "women's issues" such as breast cancer and day care. Specter's altered strategy was an attempt to offset Yeakel's appeal to women voters.

In studying congressional races, there is evidence that men candidates change their campaign strategy in two ways when confronted with a woman candidate. First, they are more hesitant to engage in negative campaigning, and second, they go to extra lengths to demonstrate that they are in touch with the desires of women voters. These patterns help to establish a framework for understanding how the presence of women candidates alters the behavior of men candidates in the electoral process. If we look to the specific responses of the managers for men candidates running against women, it clearly demonstrates that these men candidates are carefully weighing what it means to run against a woman.

Most of the candidates and campaign managers for male candidates interviewed for this study believe that it was more difficult to attack a woman because of the way this could be perceived by voters. The fear of a negative reaction by the electorate stemmed from the traditional notion that it is not "gentlemanly" to attack a woman. Tolleson-Rinehart found this traditional reluctance to attack present in studies of California (1994) and Texas (with Stanley, 1994). For instance, one campaign manager of a male candidate running against a woman noted:

> Oh, he would never attack a lady, he just does not believe in that. He will treat the opponent graciously and with respect in the campaign.

Another campaign manager of a male candidate, who was running against the daughter of a popular incumbent, stated:

You can't go around bashing his little girl. The appearance of being mean to the congressman's daughter would be devastating.

One male candidate was even more open in his chivalry (or sexism):

I don't think it is proper to attack a woman. I was completely constrained in how I went about campaigning. It was a constant struggle to show the proper politeness towards my opponent. Women cannot handle criticism or high stress so I had to watch what I said closely so that I would not appear to be causing my opponent any grief.

The fear of attacking a woman opponent will undoubtedly be a time-bound phenomenon, as women become less of a novelty as candidates. Men candidates will realize that in order to win elections they will have to attack their opponents, and voters will likely become more accustomed to women running for high elective office. There have already been several instances of men and women engaging in extremely nasty races, such as the Senate race between Huffington and Feinstein in California in 1994. In this race it did not appear Huffington was stigmatized for harshly attacking Feinstein. However, this was a large-scale, statewide race. Most of the campaign managers for House candidates in this study believed that attacking a woman was not appropriate for district level elections because the candidates are much closer to the voters and need to create an amiable district persona (see Fenno 1978).

Men candidates' reluctance to attack their women opponents was exhibited in candidate debates and public forums. A number of campaign managers for men candidates stated that when the opponent was a woman, their candidate was less aggressive during a debate or public forum than they would be against a male opponent. One candidate went so far as to send a representative of his campaign to debate his female opponent. The aide commented on why he was sent to debate the opponent:

She was a nice elderly woman, having the candidate hammer away on her record and issue positions would not look good. Instead I went to debate her. I am much older than the congressman and could get away with a lot more.

By and large, men candidates have been careful not to present the image of a man "bullying" a woman in public. Several men candidates running for Congress in 1992 and 1994 demonstrated that they were "gentlemen" by treating their women opponents in traditional ways. As one manager noted:

> We feared we had been a little too harsh in some of our T.V. ads, so in the upcoming debate we wanted [our candidate] to appear kind and gentlemanly. We had him pull out her chair for her at the debate and made sure he referred to her very respectfully over the course of the debate. We were always a little concerned about how our interactions appeared.

The attempt to appear "gentlemanly" at various points in a campaign does not mean that men candidates do not attack their women opponents on issues or past indiscretions, rather that they tended to present these issues more carefully. These gentlemanly acts also reinforce the idea that women are weak and in need of special treatment and thus might present a subtle way for the men candidates to discredit their woman opponent. Significantly, in comparing the responses of men running against men with those of men running against women, none of the men candidates who ran against men mentioned any fear of a negative public reaction if they chose to attack their opponent.

While many campaign managers of men candidates felt that it was more difficult to attack women opponents, others felt that they could attack through alternative strategies. For example, one manager insisted that they wait for their female opponent to attack first:

> [Waiting for the woman to attack first] averted the problems associated with attacking a woman because you were only responding to attacks. . . . Also, when a woman attacks first she demonstrates that she is not above the typical fray of electoral politics.

A political consultant working for a House candidate in northern California explained why he believed it was bad strategy to attack a woman first:

> If you attack her first you look like you are brow-beating a woman. You have to let her cast the first blow, and once she has done that, the perception of unfairly beating up a helpless woman is minimized.

Does the reluctance to attack a woman opponent directly change the dynamics of the electoral process? Considering that negative campaigning has become such an important tool in the modern campaign, this is an especially important question to address (Kern 1989). Men candidates reluctant to attack their female opponents may have a more difficult time highlighting the defining issues in the campaign or raising issues of personal character. If men candidates are not at ease confronting women candidates on issues they would raise against a man, this may have a number of consequences. The tone of the campaign may become less harsh as the candidates are less likely to exchange negative accusations. Also, the issue agenda of the campaign may be slightly altered if men candidates are not raising issues as vociferously as they otherwise would have. The presence of a woman candidate in an election may change the nature of political discourse in that election. Perhaps more important though, the prevalence of men candidates who changed their campaign strategies shows that a number of these men candidates are demonstrating stereotypical attitudes about the political involvement of women. With so many of the male candidates ready to adopt different strategies in reaction to a woman opponent, it shows that some male candidates do not treat women as equals in the electoral arena, and that they are employing strategies that they believe will help them win.

The second prominent reaction of men candidates running against women was to engage in some affirmative campaign activity designed to appeal to women voters. A perception within the media is that women candidates have greater appeal to women voters than do men candidates (see Rosenthal 1995). Many of the men candidates running against women were operating under this principle. The men candidates in this study usually sought to offset this perceived advantage by attempting to reach out to women voters. Typically, the goal of men's efforts to reach out to women voters was to convey the impression that the candidate was sensitive to women's needs. More than half of the male candidates who were contacted for this study engaged in campaign behavior designed to illustrate the candidate's connection with the concerns of women. Male candidates tried to reach out to female voters in a variety of ways, including trying to demonstrate that the candidate cared about the needs and interests of women just as much as those of men. For instance, one campaign manager noted that in his candidate's television commercials about constituent service, the incumbent was seen helping women constituents. The manager continued:

> We had never really thought about women and the constituent service ads before, but this year with all the year of the woman stuff going on, we wanted voters to see that the congressman was there for women too.

Similarly, another candidate's campaign commercials and literature always showed the congressman engaged in conversations with women, so the candidate would appear concerned about the interests of women. Another male candidate attempted to recruit more women into his campaign organization:

> The congressman decided that this year we would have a separate group of women supporters. This way, if his woman opponent ran around claiming she was the candidate for women, we could combat this by demonstrating our support from women.

In another example, a longtime incumbent running for reelection in 1992 visibly endorsed other women candidates, intending to show his support for women:

> We endorsed a woman in a neighboring district. We would have endorsed her even if it wasn't the "year of the woman," but this time we released the endorsement to the press and talked it up a bit. . . . We just wanted a little positive "year of the woman" coverage.

It is important to note that in all three of these situations, the men candidates were long-term incumbents who had never run against a woman candidate before. Thus, it is possible that the incumbent's involvement with women could change their political behavior in future legislative and electoral action. These congressmen's increased interaction with women in the political arena could have made them more aware and more sensitive to women's concerns. This was the case with one male incumbent whose manager admitted that the formation of a women's support group helped his candidate become more involved with certain woman-specific issues, such as sexual harassment and abortion. The candidate formed the group only because he was running against a woman. While there appeared to be an important substantive outcome in this instance, it is quite possible that any alterations in campaign behavior may only be campaign tactics used by men candidates having no lasting impact beyond the election.

The techniques male candidates employ to reach out to women voters focused on altering the substantive message put forth by the campaigns. This was potentially the most important change of behavior seen in the men candidates, as it goes straight to the question of representation. If men candidates running against women, and even men candidates running against men, raise more "women's issues" because of the increased number of women in the electoral process, the interests of women may be more fully represented in the electoral and legislative process.

Conclusion

To summarize briefly, three findings are presented in this analysis. First, women are more successfully competing in House races than at any time in history. There are few differences between men and women candidates in terms of the major indicators of electoral success. Second, there are sharp state and geographical differences in electing men and women to Congress. This finding cries out for further investigation to explain these differences. Third, an examination of the more nuanced experiences of men and women candidates suggests that the electoral environment still treats women and men differently. These differences in most instances tend to work against the interests of women candidates.

The central conclusion drawn from this analysis is that the electoral environment for congressional candidates still is laden with gender stereotypes and expectations. Men and women running for Congress still face an electoral system that employs traditional notions of male and female behavior. The acceptance of male candidates in the electoral arena remains unquestioned, whereas women are often measured against the norm of a male candidate. Further, women candidates and their staffs often perceive an electoral environment that is not entirely fair to women candidates. In the areas of fundraising, party support, and media coverage, many women candidates report a credibility problem. None of the male candidates contacted for this analysis mentioned credibility as an issue in any of these election areas. Credibility becomes a problem because women who become congressional candidates have broken the traditional expectations about gender roles. Only recently are women seen regularly as congressional candidates. In addition, the reaction of some male candidates to female opponents offers further evidence to the argument that women are treated differently from men.

These conclusions are not to argue that women do not have excellent opportunities in congressional elections. The increasing numbers of women successfully competing in elections clearly indicates that women who enter House races are able to compete on equal terms with men. However, the general indicators of electoral success often overlook the subtle gendered experiences of men and women candidates. These experiences show that our political system is still fraught with significant gender dynamics based upon expectations about traditional gender roles.

Notes

1. The interview responses reported in this article are not attributed to the specific campaign officials. Most of the campaign officials interviewed were assured anonymity. For a more detailed discussion of the interview procedures in 1992 and 1994, see Fox (1997, Appendix A & B).

2. This does not include Eleanor Holmes Norton, who was the nonvoting representative from the District of Columbia.

3. The question of how men and women candidates are viewed by voters remains unresolved. A growing body of literature has found that voters have little or no bias against women candidates (Cook 1998; Burrell 1994; Darcy, Welch, and Clark 1994). One group of researchers has gone so far as to state emphatically: "A candidate's sex does not affect his or her chances of winning an election . . . Winning elections has *nothing* to do with the sex of the candidate" (emphasis added) (Seltzer, Newman, and Leighton 1997, 79). In fact, some analyses show that women candidates actually seem to have an advantage over men with the voters (Chaney and Sinclair 1994). Other researchers have found that voters employ gender stereotypes which may work to the detriment of women candidates (Huddy and Terkildsen 1993a). Further, one recent study has found that bias against women congressional candidates does exist in certain regions of the country (Fox and Smith 1998). There are contexts in which candidate gender can have a serious impact on the outcome of an election. Moreover, biases that are statistically small and hard to measure (say, a 3 percent difference in the vote) can have substantial political impacts.

References

Aucoin, Don. 1997. "Beacon Hill's Glass Dome: Massachusetts Has One of the Nation's Worst Records in Electing Women to Statewide Office: An Ambitious Group of Candidates Hopes to Change That in 1998." *The Boston Globe* (2 November): 20.

Baxter, Sandra, and Majorie Lansing. 1980. *Women and Politics: The Invisible Majority*. Ann Arbor: University of Michigan Press.

Berke, Richard. 1994. "In '94, 'Vote for Woman' Does Not Play So Well." *New York Times* (3 October): A1, B10.

Biersack, Robert, and Paul S. Herrnson. 1994. "Political Parties and the Year of the Woman." In *The Year of the Woman*, ed. Elizabeth Adell Cook, Sue Thomas, and Clyde Wilcox, pp. 161–180. Boulder, CO: Westview.

Blair, Diane D., and Jeannie R. Stanley. 1991. "Personal Relationships and Legislative Power: Male and Female Perceptions." *Legislative Studies Quarterly* 16(4): 495–507.

Boneparth, Ellen. 1977. "Women in Campaigns." *American Politics Quarterly* 5(3): 289–300.

Burrell, Barbara. 1985. "Women and Men's Campaigns for the U.S. House of Representatives, 1972–1982: A Finance Gap?" *American Politics Quarterly* 13(3): 251–272.

―――. 1994. *A Woman's Place Is in the House*. Ann Arbor: The University of Michigan Press.

―――. 1998. "Campaign Finance: Women's Experience in the Modern Era." In *Women and Elective Office*, ed. Sue Thomas and Clyde Wilcox, pp. 26–37. New York: Oxford University Press.

Center for the American Woman and Politics (CAWP) Fact Sheets. 1998. "Women in Elective Office 1998." New Brunswick, NJ: Center for the American Woman and Politics.

Chaney, Carole. and Barbara Sinclair. 1994. "Women and the 1992 House Elections." In *The Year of the Woman*, ed. Elizabeth Adell Cook, Sue Thomas, and Clyde Wilcox. Boulder, CO: Westview.

Conover, Pamela Johnston, and Virginia Gray. 1983. *Feminism and the New Right: Conflict over the American Family*. New York: Praeger.

Cook, Elizabeth Adell. 1998. "Voter Reaction to Women Candidates." In *Women and Elective Office*, ed. Sue Thomas and C. Wilcox. New York: Oxford University Press.

Cook, Elizabeth Adell, Sue Thomas, and Clyde Wilcox, ed. 1994. *The Year of the Woman*. Boulder, CO: Westview.

Darcy, Robert, Susan Welch, and Janet Clark. 1994. *Women, Elections, and Representation*. Lincoln: University of Nebraska Press.

Elazar, Daniel. 1984. *American Federalism: A View from the States*. 3rd ed. New York: Harper and Row.

Fenno, Richard F., Jr. 1978. *Home Style: House Members in Their Districts*. Boston: Little, Brown.

Fox, Richard L. 1997. *Gender Dynamics in Congressional Elections*. Thousand Oaks, CA: Sage.

Fox, Richard L., and Eric R.A.N. Smith. 1998. "The Role of Candidate Sex in Voter Decision-Making." *Political Psychology* 19(2): 405–419.

Gertzog, Irwin. 1984. *Congressional Women*. New York: Praeger.

Hibbing, John. 1991. *Congressional Careers*. Chapel Hill: University of North Carolina Press.

Hill, D. 1981. "Political Culture and Female Political Representation." *Journal of Politics* 43(1): 159–168.

Huddy, L. and N. Terkildsen. 1993a. "Gender Stereotypes and the Perception of Male Female Candidates." *American Journal of Political Science* 37(1): 119–147.

―――. 1993b. "The Consequences of Gender Stereotypes for Women Candidates at Different Levels and Types of Office." *Political Research Quarterly* 46(3): 503–525.

Jamieson, Kathleen Hall. 1995. *Beyond the Double Bind*. New York: Oxford University Press.

Kahn, Kim Freidkin. 1992. "Does Being Male Help: An Investigation of Gender and Media Effects in U.S. Senate Races." *Journal of Politics* 54(2): 497–517.

———. 1993. "Gender Differences in Campaign Messages: The Political Advertisements of Men and Women Candidates for U.S. Senate." *Political Research Quarterly* 46(2): 418–502.

———. 1996. *The Political Consequences of Being a Woman*. New York: Columbia University Press.

Kahn, Kim Freidkin, and E.N. Goldenberg. 1991. "Women Candidates in the News: An Examination of Gender Differences in U.S. Senate Campaign Coverage." *Public Opinion Quarterly* 55(2): 180–199.

Kendrigan, Mary Lou. 1984. *Political Equality in a Democratic Society: Women in the U.S.* Westport, CT: Greenwood.

Kern, Montague. 1989. *30-Second Politics: Political Advertising in the Eighties*. New York: Praeger.

Loomis, Burdett A. 1998. *The Contemporary Congress*. 2nd ed. New York: St. Martin's.

Mandel, Ruth B. 1981. *In the Running: The New Woman Candidate*. New York: Ticknor and Fields.

Mannies, Jo. 1996. "This Election Year 'Politics as Usual' Means that Women Are Everywhere." *St. Louis Post-Dispatch* (23 October): 5B.

Naff, Katherine C. 1995. "Subjective vs. Objective Discrimination in Government: Adding to the Picture of Barriers to the Advancement of Women." *Political Research Quarterly* 48(3): 535–558.

Neal, Steve. 1998. "Women Make Inroads in Statewide Contests." *Chicago Sun-Times* (24 July): 9.

Norrander, Barbara, and Clyde Wilcox. 1998. "The Geography of Gender Power: Women in State Legislatures." In *Women and Elective Office*, ed. Sue Thomas and Clyde Wilcox. New York: Oxford University Press.

Poole, Barbara. 1993. "Should Women Identify Themselves as Feminists When Running for Political Office?" Paper presented at the annual meeting of the American Political Science Association, Washington, DC, 2–5 September.

Renner, Tari. 1993. "Lynn Yeakel Versus Arlen Specter: The Year of the Woman in Pennsylvania." Paper presented at annual meeting of the American Political Science Association, Washington, DC, 2–5 September.

Rosenthal, Cindy S. 1995. "The Role of Gender in Descriptive Representation." *Political Research Quarterly* 48(3): 599–612.

Seltzer, Richard A., Jody Newman, and M. Voorhees Leighton. 1997. *Sex as a Political Variable*. Boulder, CO: Lynne Reiner.

Sweet, Lynn. 1996. "Just Four Women Seek Illinois Seats in Congress." *Chicago Sun-Times* (22 May): 4.

Thomas, Norman C., and Karl A. Lamb. 1965. *Congress: Politics and Practice*. New York: Random House.

Tolleson-Rinehart, Sue. 1994. "The California Senate Races: A Case Study in the Gendered Paradoxes of Politics." In *The Year of the Woman*, ed. Elizabeth Adell Cook, Sue Thomas, and Clyde Wilcox. Boulder, CO: Westview.

Tolleson-Rinehart, Sue, and Jeanie Stanley. 1994. *Claytie and the Lady: Ann Richards, Gender, and Politics in Texas*. Austin: Texas University Press.

Uhlaner, Carole Jean, and Kay Lehman Schlozman. 1986. "Candidate Gender and Congressional Campaign Receipts." *Journal of Politics* 52(1): 391–409.

Waldmeir, Pete. 1996. "Tuesday Looks Like a Big Day for Women at the Polls." *The Detroit News* (5 August): C3.

Williams, Leonard. 1998. "Gender, Political Advertising, and the 'Air Wars.' " In *Women and Elective Office*, ed. Sue Thomas and Clyde Wilcox. New York: Oxford University Press.

Witt, Linda, Karen M. Paget, and Glenna Matthews. 1994. *Running as a Woman*. New York: Free Press.

Index